TECHNIQUES

OF

GOOD WRITING

*In memory of my father, Robie Washington Ford,
Principal of Wolfville High School, a teacher
who inspired in many young people
a love of learning*

TECHNIQUES
of
GOOD WRITING

MARGARET L. FORD, M.A.

True ease in writing comes from art, not chance.
Alexander Pope

A Publication of

THE BOOK SOCIETY OF CANADA
LIMITED

ISBN 0-7725-5001-8

PREFACE

This text is designed to give senior students advanced training in the techniques of good writing.

The course, as it develops, becomes increasingly demanding, progressing from clearly functional writing to writing that requires imagination and a grasp of difficult techniques in order to secure effects of atmosphere and mood, and to reveal nuances of character.

Throughout, I have emphasized the techniques used in writing specific literary forms. The study of each of these forms follows a similar pattern. First the particular form is clearly defined; then the class considers an example taken from the work of a professional writer or from that of a student. By means of an analysis carried out through discussion, the class determines how the writer has gained his effect. Next, students learn how to plan a composition in which they will put into practice what they have studied. Early in the year, then, each student should be conscious of improvement in his own writing, and should have a feeling of satisfaction — often of excitement — at the realization that writing has techniques that can be learned.

It has been my experience that a student becomes concerned about writing well only when he tries to put into words some ideas that he considers important. This experience has influenced the organization of the text. The lessons on style begin only after a student has written on a subject that interests him and of which he has considerable knowledge. From then on, the study of a specific literary form and the study of style alternate until the work on diction and on sentence structure has been completed. Thus the techniques for improving style are treated as a means to an end: tools a student uses to achieve his desired aims.

Not the least important part of this book is that requiring each student to examine critically some of the work written by his class-mates. This training in criticism should help him improve his own writing as well as enable him to write intelligent literary criticism.

Since a senior student is usually required to write essays on literary subjects, I have included a section on this kind of exposition, based on Shakespearean tragedy. This assignment should be undertaken only after the class has completed an intensive reading of one of Shakespeare's tragedies.

I should like to thank those of my students who have given me permission to use their work as models. I have included these compositions not because I consider them perfect essays, but because in them the students have sought to apply the particular techniques I am teaching.

Because writing is a skill developed only by practice, a student, if he is to learn to compose effective exposition, argument, narrative, description and literary criticism, should attempt several compositions of each type. With this amount of practice, the average student will learn to write creditably, and the gifted student often with astonishing skill.

MARGARET L. FORD

Wolfville, Nova Scotia
July 5th, 1960

Table of Contents

7

WRITING ESSAYS ON DRAMA

ANALYZING A REPORT

Since almost everyone, at some time in his life, is required to present a report, either oral or written, every senior student should master the techniques of making a satisfactory one. Your first written assignments in this course, therefore, will be to plan and write a report on some topic about which you know a great deal and in which you are keenly interested.

DEFINITION OF A REPORT

A report is a concise record of facts. It is always addressed to a particular person or group, and prepared for a specific purpose. For example, a dramatic club might set up a committee to organize a drama festival, and, at its completion, ask for an evaluation of the project. The chairman or an appointee of the committee would then gather the relevant facts, interpret the information collected, and embody his findings and his conclusions in a report. After having studied this report carefully, the drama club would probably discuss the feasibility of repeating the festival another year.

Types of Reports	Purposes
Annual	To make a survey of the year's activities or achievements for the benefit of those interested
Committee	To enumerate the findings, conclusions or recommendations of a committee set up to handle some specific business
Evaluation	To evaluate the success of some undertaking
Fact Finding	To present facts on a given subject
Financial	To summarize the financial position of a company, club or organization
Progress	To explain details of progress made on some unfinished business or project in hand
Scientific	To give, as concisely as possible, an account of a research project—the problem, the methods used to solve it or to investigate it, the experimentations undertaken, and the results

Pooling Information on Reports

1. Name a business or a profession that requires reports, either occasionally or frequently, and mention the possible purposes of some of them.
2. Name an organization that requires an annual report, and mention the purpose of such a report.
3. What would be some of the features of a good report made to the Student Council by the chairman of the committee that had organized an unsuccessful school party?

ANALYZING A REPORT WRITTEN BY A STUDENT

The student who wrote the following evaluation report was the chairman of a welfare committee. She collected her information from the members of the committee and from her own notes.

Study the preliminary decisions and the report. Then use the questions that follow the report to discuss its effectiveness.

List of Preliminary Decisions

Type of Report: evaluation report of a Christmas project undertaken by our club

To Whom: all members of the club

By Whom: the chairman of the committee that organized the project

Purpose: to evaluate the success of the project and to make recommendations for next year's Christmas project

Thesis: On the whole, the project was successful. However, some aspects should have been organized more carefully, and more of our members should have participated.

The Report

(The paragraphs are numbered for convenient reference.)

1. As chairman of the Welfare Committee, I should like to present to you, the members of the XYZ Club, an evaluation report of our Christmas project.

2. This year's project was one of the most successful ever carried out by our club. The committee feels, however, that the organization of future projects could be improved, and that there should be greater participation by all members.

3. As in the past three years, we "adopted" a needy family for Christmas. A suitable family was found by one of our members, who is in close contact with several welfare organizations. There were three small children—two girls, aged five and three, respectively, and a boy, aged two. The father being unable to work because of illness, the mother had taken on a part-time job, and her low wages constituted the family's sole income. They were living in a very poor section, in two sparsely furnished rooms, for which the rent was several months in arrears.

12

4. The organization was planned very efficiently, but, in spite of this, it fell down slightly on a few small details. To head up the project, we elected a committee of three: one to be responsible for food, one for gifts and one for the collection of money. Each club member brought:

a) 3 tins of food (total of 90 tins);
b) toys, games and clothing;
c) 75c (total of $22.50).

The money was used as follows:

a) $5.00 for Christmas tree and decorations;
b) $10.00 for Christmas dinner, including a large turkey and a 100-pound bag of potatoes;
c) $7.50, the balance, given to the family to help pay the rent.

Not enough staple foods, however, were included in the canned goods. Too many games and toys were collected, and relatively little in the way of clothing was brought. Because we put off the purchase of the food too long, we lost an opportunity to buy a turkey at half price.

5. On December 21, a meeting was called to wrap gifts and pack the canned goods. Only seven out of thirty girls were present—an indication of the lack of interest on the part of most of the members. We made an error in not addressing each gift to a particular member of the family. This omission caused some confusion among the three children.

6. Unfortunately, only four girls could visit the family on December 23 and see the happiness brought about by the efforts of our club. The whole family was extremely grateful, and they scarcely knew how to express their thanks. Wishing to let them decorate the tree and enjoy the gifts among themselves, we left soon after the presents were unpacked. All four girls felt that this visit was an experience they would not want to have missed.

7. Although the project was, on the whole, a success, we can learn a great deal from our mistakes, and make several improvements next year. The donations should be regulated so as to include more staple foods among the canned goods, and more clothing, rather than too many toys. We should plan important details, such as the purchase of a turkey, further in advance. The division of the work was unfair, in that all the work was done by the committee instead of being shared by the entire club. Those who visited the family felt that they learned a great deal. However, as not all thirty girls can deliver the gifts at Christmas, the club might take an interest in the family during the rest of the year, as well. This plan would give all members an opportunity for active participation. For example, as there are young children, the members, in pairs, could take turns baby-sitting throughout the year.

8. We believe that, if we act on these suggestions, our next undertaking will be equally successful, if not more so.

Discussion Questions

1. For what purpose has the student used her introduction?
2. What is the purpose of paragraph 2?
3. What is the purpose of paragraph 3? Of paragraph 4? Has each of these

paragraphs a topic sentence? Is each paragraph unified? Give reasons for your opinion.
4. Paragraph 5 has no topic sentence. Compose one that will prepare the reader for all of the facts included in this paragraph.
5. What purpose does the chairman who made the report intend paragraph 7 to serve? Is her topic sentence the correct one for this paragraph? Give reasons for your opinion.
6. A report is unified when every paragraph in it contributes to a discussion of the thesis. Has this report the quality of unity? Justify your opinion.
7. A report is emphatic, structurally, when it closes with an *effective* restatement of the thesis. Evaluate the conclusion of this report.

HOME WORK ASSIGNMENT

Bring to your next composition class the preliminary decisions for each of the following reports:
1. *an evaluation report of some project* about which you know a great deal and in which you are very much interested;
2. *an annual report of some organization* about which you know a great deal and in which you are very much interested.

Use the following outline for your preliminary decisions:

Type of Report:
To Whom Addressed:
By Whom Given:
Purpose of the Report:
Thesis of the Report:

Examples of Preliminary Decisions

a) *Type of Report*: annual report of a club
To Whom Addressed: the student body
By Whom Given: the president of the club
Purpose of the Report: to inform the students of the Rifle Club's activities and to engender enthusiasm so that the organization will have an increased membership next year
Thesis of the Report: The Rifle Club has just completed a most successful and interesting year.

b) *Type of Report*: evaluation report on a basketball tournament held at camp
To Whom Addressed: the athletic directors of the camp
By Whom Given: organizer of the tournament and his committee
Purpose of the Report: to evaluate the success of the tournament and to recommend improvements
Thesis: In some respects, the tournament was a success.

c) *Type of Report*: evaluation report on a project that involved many separate activities, such as the school's sports programme or the whole extra-curricular programme
To Whom: the whole student body
By Whom: the president of the Student Council

14

Purpose:	to evaluate the scope and the appeal of the sports (or the extra-curricular) programme
Thesis:	From reports handed in to us by the presidents of the various school organizations, we conclude that this year's extra-curricular programme (or sports programme) has been both varied and interesting.

d) *Type of Report*: weekly progress report

To Whom:	class 12T, the members of which elected the representative
By Whom:	a representative to the Student Council
Purpose:	to give all members of 12T a clear, accurate and thorough account of the Student Council's meeting held on December 2, so that they can vote on three important questions
Thesis:	The Council this week discussed three important matters, on each of which it would like an expression of opinion from the class.

REPORTS

LESSON TWO

PLANNING AND WRITING A REPORT

A report, because its purpose is to inform, is an exposition. A report is considered good when it has been well planned, when it gives accurate information and when it has a pleasing style.

THE OVERALL STRUCTURE OF A REPORT

Once you have made the preliminary decisions and collected your facts, you are ready to plan the overall structure (organization) of your report. A report has three parts:
1. introduction,
2. body,
3. conclusion.

1. The *introduction* should be used to acquaint the reader or audience with the purpose of the report, and its thesis, if the report is to have one.

The *purpose* of a report is the reason that this particular person is making this particular report to this particular person or group. The *thesis* is the central idea of the report. Some reports have no thesis.

2. The *body* should be used to give, in an organized way, the information that supports the thesis. In order to write a unified report, you must use for the paragraphs that comprise the body of

15

the report, topic sentences that develop your thesis. Here is an example:

Thesis: This year, the Community Tennis Club has held an unusually successful programme of activities.

Topic Sentences:

1. The tournament that our club organized this year was the most successful one we have ever undertaken.
2. In addition, we started a junior club that attracted a large group of enthusiastic and promising young tennis players.
3. The social committee's programme of Saturday evening parties was a popular innovation.
4. Finally, because of these various projects undertaken during the summer, the club paid its outstanding debts and established a reserve fund.

3. The *conclusion* should be used to emphasize the thesis, and, if recommendations are to be a part of the report, to give them.

The thesis may be emphasized in three ways:

    a) by repeating it;
    b) by summarizing the main points presented in the body of the report;
    c) by a combination of (a) and (b).

If a report has no thesis, the conclusion should summarize the facts that have been given.

CLASS DISCUSSION
Composing Topic Sentences for the Body of a Report

The president of the Drama Guild, after having examined the minutes of the club in order to evaluate the success of the year's activities, drew the following conclusion, which served as the thesis of his report: *The Drama Guild has completed the most successful year in its history.*

For each of the five sections in the following summary, compose and give orally a topic sentence that the president might use in the body of his report to develop the above thesis:

1. *Membership*:

    a) five years ago—   30
    b) four years ago—   25
    c) three years ago—   35
    d) two years ago—   20
    e) last year—   35
    f) this year—   85

2. *Enthusiasm*:

    a) Average attendance at meetings increased from 15 to 60.
    b) Two new ideas were suggested and tried:
        (i) presentation after school (and free of charge) of one-act plays produced by student directors
        (ii) organization of classes in theatrical make-up

3. *After-School Productions*:
   a) Competent judges were chosen to select the best plays from the six presented at the after-school performances.
   b) In February, a formal Drama Festival was held. Lorne Green, a well-known actor and producer, was the adjudicator.
   c) A large and appreciative student audience attended the after-school productions as well as the festival itself.
4. *Participation*:
   a) 45 acted in plays
   b) 15 worked on stage sets
   c) 15 worked on make-up
   d) 20 worked on costumes
   e) 6 worked as directors
5. *Plans*:
   a) The winning play will be entered in a regional drama festival.
   b) Theatre parties will be organized to give students the opportunity to see four good plays.
   c) Reading groups are being planned for those interested in studying drama.

WRITTEN EXERCISE

1. Compose topic sentences that will develop in the body of a report one of the following theses:
a) In some respects, the Current Affairs Club has had a disappointing year.
b) Our programme in sports this year proved to be very successful.
c) In spite of the success of three projects, the Photography Club has had a poor year.

2. Selecting a subject of your own, write a thesis for a report and compose topic sentences that will develop your thesis.

THE LENGTH OF A REPORT

The length of a report varies according to its purpose. If a committee is one of half a dozen groups asked to report at a one-hour meeting of the Student Council, it should make a brief report. If, on the other hand, the council has set up a special committee to investigate the students' reaction to a newly-imposed athletic fee, it may decide to devote the next meeting to hearing the report and discussing its implications. In such a situation, the chairman of the committee may be asked to give a fairly detailed report.

HOME WORK ASSIGNMENT
Writing a Report
Choose some activity about which you know a great deal and in which you are keenly interested, and write a short report (not exceeding two pages) of *one* of the following types:
a) an annual report, b) an evaluation report, c) a progress report.

1. Make a plan in which you list the preliminary decisions under the following headings:

> Type of Report:
> To Whom:
> By Whom:
> Purpose:
> Thesis:
> Topic sentences I will use to develop my thesis:

2. Using these as your guide, write the report in rough.

3. After you have finished the rough draft, revise your copy. Here are some suggestions:

a) Express yourself clearly, so that everyone will understand you. Use words exactly. Avoid the use of words the meaning of which you do not understand. Use as simple language as the subject will bear.

b) Use figurative language sparingly.

c) Prevent monotony of style by: (i) varying the *length* of your sentences: (ii) varying the *kind* of sentences you use—some simple, some compound and some complex; (iii) varying the *structure* of your sentences —frequently putting a phrase or a subordinate clause before the subject of the main clause, so that your sentences will not follow the monotonous pattern of subject-predicate—subject-predicate.

4. Copy neatly in ink the plan and the report.

THE IMPORTANCE OF REPORTS

Almost all organizations require annual reports. Men and women in the business world and in the professions are required at times to make formal reports for specific purposes. Doctors report the results of their research to medical associations and to medical journals. Chartered accountants are engaged to make reports on the financial affairs of business concerns. Presidents of corporations report to shareholders. Heads of departments in a business send reports to the general manager. Often a person's success in his chosen field depends partially on his ability to write lucid reports.

Engineers and geologists particularly should be skilled in writing this kind of exposition. An engineer assigned to accumulate required data on a possible site for a bridge must present this information in the form of a report to those who engaged him. Mining companies and oil companies hire geologists to investigate properties and to report on them.

PUNCTUATION

RECOGNIZING THE APPLICATION OF THE RULES

Senior students are expected to punctuate accurately. In the Appendix (pages 227-34) are given the commonly accepted rules that govern punctuation. Read these carefully, and remember to put them into practice in your own writing.

CLASS DISCUSSION
Recognizing the Application of the Rules

1. In the following passage, (a) state every punctuation rule that has been observed by the writer; (b) cite all instances of punctuation to which none of the rules given in the Appendix applies.

The passage is taken from Sinclair Lewis's novel *Babbit*. Paul Reisling and Babbitt have escaped the hustle and bustle of Zenith and are spending a week-end in Maine.

The Fishing Trip

They had a week before their families came. Each evening they planned to get up early and fish before breakfast. Each morning they lay abed till the breakfast-bell, pleasantly conscious that there were no efficient wives to rouse them. The mornings were cold; the fire was kindly as they dressed.

Paul was distressingly clean, but Babbitt reveled in a good sound dirtiness, in not having to shave till his spirit was moved to it. He treasured every grease spot and fish-scale on his new khaki trousers.

All morning they fished unenergetically, or tramped the dim and aqueous-lighted trails among rank ferns and moss sprinkled with crimson bells. They slept all afternoon, and till midnight played stud-poker with the guides. Poker was a serious business to the guides. They did not gossip; they shuffled the thick greasy cards with a deft ferocity menacing to the "sports"; and Joe Paradise, king of guides, was sarcastic to loiterers who halted the game even to scratch.

At midnight, as Paul and he blundered to their cottage over the pungent wet grass, and pine-roots confusing in the darkness, Babbitt rejoiced that he did not have to explain to his wife where he had been all evening.

They did not talk much. The nervous loquacity and opinionation of the Zenith Athletic Club dropped from them. But when they did talk, they slipped into the naïve intimacy of college days. Once they drew their canoe up to the bank of Sunasquam Water, a stream walled in by the dense green of the hardhack. The sun roared on the green jungle but in the shade was sleepy peace, and the water was golden and rippling. Babbitt drew his hand through the cool flood, and mused.

"We never thought we'd come to Maine together!"

"No. We've never done anything the way we thought we would. I expected to live in Germany with my granddad's people, and study the fiddle." Sinclair Lewis, *Babbitt*

19

2. The following passage is taken from Alan Paton's novel *Cry, the Beloved Country.* Complete the punctuation.

These paragraphs picture an Englishman, Mr. Jarvis, sitting in the library of his son, who had recently been shot in Johannesburg by a young black boy. Ironically, no white man in the city had been doing so much to alleviate the plight of the South African blacks. Over and over the dazed father thought: "Why should it have happened to *him?*"

Young Mr. Jarvis

Jarvis sat in the chair of his son and his wife and Mary left him to return to the Harrisons. Books books books more books than he had ever seen in a house! On the table papers letters and more books. Mr. Jarvis will you speak at the Parkwold Methodist Guild? Mr. Jarvis will you speak at the Anglican Young Peoples Association in Sophiatown? Mr. Jarvis will you speak in a symposium at the University? No Mr. Jarvis would be unable to speak at any of these.

Mr. Jarvis you are invited to the Annual Meeting of the Society of Jews and Christians. Mr. Jarvis you and your wife are invited to the wedding of Sarajini eldest daughter of Mr. and Mrs. H. B. Singh. Mr. Jarvis you and your wife are invited to a Toc H. Guest Night in Van Wyks Valley. No Mr. Jarvis would be unable to accept these kind invitations.

On the walls between the books there were four pictures of Christ crucified and Abraham Lincoln and the white gabled house of Vergelegen and a painting of leafless willows by a river in a wintry veldt.

He rose from the chair to look at the books. Here were hundreds of books all about Abraham Lincoln. He had not known that so many books had been written about any one man. One bookcase was full of them. And another was full of books about South Africa Sarah Gertrude Millins *Life of Rhodes* and her book about Smuts and Engelenburgs *Life of Louis Botha* and books on South African race problems and books on South African birds and the Kruger Park and innumerable others. Another bookcase was full of Afrikaans books but the titles conveyed nothing to him. And here were books about religion and Soviet Russia and crime and criminals and books of poems. He looked for Shakespeare and here was Shakespeare too.

He went back to the chair and looked long at the pictures of Christ crucified and Abraham Lincoln and Vergelegen and the willows by the river. Then he drew some pieces of paper towards him.

The first was a letter to his son from the secretary of the Claremont African Boys Club Gladiolus Street Claremont regretting that Mr. Jarvis had not been able to attend the Annual Meeting of the Club and informing him he had again been elected as President. And the letter concluded with quaintness of phrase— . . . Alan Paton, *Cry, the Beloved Country*

LANGUAGE: THE IDIOM

Idiom is defined in The *Concise Oxford Dictionary* as a "form of expression peculiar to a language". Idioms, in fact, are the idiosyncrasies of a language: sometimes they violate the laws of syntax; often they cannot be literally understood, even in their own language; and they are usually not exactly translatable into any other language. Using them—discriminately—will add naturalness, and often concreteness to your style.

An able discussion of idiom is found in *English Idioms* by Logan Pearsall Smith. In evaluating the effectiveness of idiomatic expressions, Mr. Smith says this: "Idiom is held in little esteem by men of science, schoolmasters and old-fashioned grammarians; but good writers love it, for it is, in Landor's phrase, 'the life and spirit of language'. It may be regarded as the sister of poetry, for like poetry it retranslates our concepts [ideas] into living experiences, and breathes that atmosphere of animal sensation which sustains the poet in his flights."

English Idioms was published in 1923. Nowadays, both scientists and schoolmasters would agree with Mr. Smith that idiom, wisely used, adds vitality and sparkle to writing and speaking.

CLASSIFICATION OF IDIOMS

There are five classes of idioms:

1. *Idiomatic words*: In English, as in other languages, prepositions are sometimes used in a special, idiomatic way.

Examples:
a) We went to Toronto *on* the impulse of the moment.
b) We went to Toronto *at* a moment's notice.
c) My uncle got *in* a train at Paddington Station and *out of* it at Banbury.
   (*English use of idiom*)
d) Mary got *on* the train at Buffalo and *off* at Toronto, Ontario.
   (*These idioms are used both in Canada and the United States.*)

2. *Localisms*: When idioms are definitely associated with a certain *locale* of the country, they are called localisms. In writing, they should be used only in conversation or to impart local colour.

Examples:
a) I saw Mr. Smith going *down street*.
b) Mary *would be* your cousin, wouldn't she?

21

3. *Dialect*: This is a form of speech in which vocabulary and pronunciation are peculiar to a district or a class of people. Examples are the Yorkshire dialect, the Brooklyn dialect and the Cockney dialect, which is characteristic of London's (England) East End. In writing, dialect, also, should be used only in conversation or for local colour.

Examples:
a) "My feyther's place is no more than a bittock ayont twenty-eight miles," he said. "I'll make it by three of the clock, if the Lord's willin'." Edward William Thomson, "Dour Davie's Ride", from *Old Man Savarin and Other Stories (Scotch-Canadian dialect of the Ottawa Valley lumber camps)*
b) "Gin ye sae muckle as touched Wullie d'ye ken what I'd do, James Moore?" asked the little man very smoothly. Alfred Ollivant, *Bob Son of Battle (Dialect of the crofters of Cumberlandshire)*

4. *Slang*: This is probably the most idiomatic form of a language. It is seldom appropriate to written expression in a formal passage, although it may be used in direct discourse, or, on occasion, to achieve sensational or dramatic effects. The more original and vivid of our slang expressions are often accepted, in time, as good usage. Most slang expressions are not used for very long because they soon lose their point of reference. Such expressions tend to "date" writing, and cause it to lose its freshness.

5. *Figurative expressions*: There are, in every language, hundreds of short, figurative expressions, each of which is known as an idiom. Because of their concreteness and aptness, they have been passed down by word of mouth from generation to generation, and have long since become accepted usage. Each one has an interesting history. Perhaps you can guess the origin of some of the following figurative expressions that have become English idioms:

to play second fiddle	to let the cat out of the bag	a feather in his cap
with a grain of salt	to hang out his shingle	the shoe's on the other foot
to broach the subject	to fish in troubled waters	belling the cat
a red herring		

Here are some suggestions in the use of idioms*:
a) use idioms that are appropriate to the subject and the occasion;
b) use sparingly;
c) try to develop a discriminating taste in your use of idioms;
d) notice the effects reputable writers achieve with idioms;
e) try to use some of the idioms that your mother and father use so that you will help to keep alive these colourful expressions.

*If you wish to read the stories behind some of the idioms you use, consult C. E. Funk, *A Hog on Ice,* and E. C. Brewer, *A Dictionary of Phrase and Fable.*

IDIOMS AND CLICHÉS

The writer should be aware of the differences between an idiom and a cliché. By the use of idioms you may improve your style. By the use of clichés you will spoil it. Eric Partridge in his reference book *Usage and Abuses* defines, classifies and exemplifies the cliché:

A cliché is an outworn common-place; a phrase (or virtual phrase) that has become so hackneyed that scrupulous speakers and writers shrink from it because they feel that its use is an insult to the intelligence of their auditor or audience, reader or public . . .

Below are some clichés taken from Mr. Partridge's comprehensive list. However, expressions condemned as clichés by one critic may be acceptable to another. You must use your own judgment to help you identify "ready-made" expressions that seem to indicate lazy thinking on the part of a speaker or writer.

I have no hesitation in saying
ill-gotten gains
earnest desire to make the world a
    better place to live in
explore every avenue
a glorious victory
the grave international situation
the great open spaces
hotly contested
our hour of need
answer in the affirmative

arrive on the scene; arrive at one's
    destination
as good luck would have it
at the psychological moment
the economic factor
full of sound and fury
can safely say
this great country of ours
the burning issues of the day
the destiny of our great democracy

CLASS DISCUSSION

The Use of Idioms

In the following paragraphs, find each of the idioms that the writer has used and put into your own words the idea expressed by it. Notice that the idiom is usually shorter, more concrete or less laborious than your version.

1. The Middle East

Nasser meanwhile had been acquiring enemies nearer at home. His assumption of the role of spokesman for the entire Arab bloc alarmed more conservative Arab leaders. King Saud was beginning to sense that Arabia could be relegated to satellite status if he continued to foot the bills for Nasser's propaganda. He set out to withdraw financial support to Egypt's cause in Syria and Jordan. He made it plain that he did not intend to recognize Red China. He buried the hatchet with King Feisal of Iraq and entertained him at Riyadh for the first time last summer. Anti-Egyptian propaganda was permitted in Arabia, where an army of Egyptian teachers and technicians seemed a little too advanced for Riyadh. Particularly, the appearance of Egyptian labour officials bent on organizing a federation of Arab oil workers in the Persian Gulf caused an anxious flurry there. Editorial, The *Atlantic Monthly*, January, 1957

23

2. The Suez Crisis

It is high time that it was made unmistakably clear to Colonel Nasser that the maintenance of his claim to exercise belligerent rights against Israel is incompatible with peace in the Middle East, and that it will not be tolerated. Editorial, The *Manchester Guardian Weekly*, April 4, 1957

3. Making Decisions

So once more this country [the United States] is going to have to make some basic decisions. It must devise a new policy—which, good or bad, will largely determine the course of history for a long time ahead. (Even if we should do nothing, that would be a decision—probably the worst we could make.)

This is a thoroughly unwelcome task. Already we have been forced into more basic decisions than any people ought to have to make in one lifetime. For most of the eleven months just ahead, therefore, we shall moan and grumble and argue. Congress will stage another Great Debate. Everybody will look around for scape-goats, and there will be plenty of high-octane swearing at (a) the Russians, (b) our allies, (c) foreigners in general, a bothersome lot, and (d) the Secretary of State, whoever that ill-starred wretch may happen to be at the moment. "The Editor's Easy Chair", *Harper's Magazine*, February, 1957

4. Testing Atomic Weapons

Continued pleas from respected citizens and respected scientists asking that the United States, Great Britain and Soviet Russia cease testing atomic weapons because of the dangers of accumulating radioactivity have fallen on deaf ears. The tests go on, and the winds from the Pacific and from Siberia continue to spread those tiny particles that some consider insidious and others insist aren't dangerous. Editorial, *Maclean's Magazine*, June 8, 1957

5. No Money in Culture?

"There's no money in culture," said the cynics, when the Stratford Ontario Shakespeare festival was just an idea in Tom Patterson's head. We wonder whether they have ever been made to eat their hard-headed hats since that festival became a reality. "Comment of the Day", *Saturday Night*, Sept. 26, 1959

HOME WORK ASSIGNMENT
Using Idioms

Using one of the following topic sentences or one of your own choice, write a paragraph. In it, use one or more idioms that you consider appropriate for the subject you have chosen. Underline the idiom or the idioms used.

1. The international situation is brightening (or worsening).
2. My dog is smart!
3. Collecting records can be exciting.
4. Skiing is a dangerous sport.
5. Let's "make the punishment fit the crime"!

IMPROVING STYLE: I

LANGUAGE: IMAGERY

According to *Webster's New Collegiate Dictionary*, the word *imagery* has two meanings:
1. figurative language, especially when used as ornament;
2. mental images (mental representations of sensory experiences).

In this text, the word *imagery* is used in the first sense: figurative language used as ornament. The word *image* is used in the second sense: the reproduction in the mind of a sensation of seeing, hearing, smelling, tasting or feeling.

Figurative language is an intentional departure from the usual way of saying a thing. Its purpose is to lend strength and freshness to an idea; to create pictorial effect; to intensify an emotional effect; to give concreteness to an idea.

If you have no talent for figurative language, you can learn to appreciate imagery used by others. You yourself can learn to create your pictorial and emotional effects by means of concrete words and details, and specific words.

Thrall and Hibbard in their excellent dictionary of literary terms, *A Handbook to Literature,* explain clearly the effects gained by the use of figurative language: "Facts can be recited in a city directory . . . but not until facts are interpreted and given reality through imaginative thought, through the language of imagery, do they take on vividness and reality. An algebraic formula carries truth with it; deft use of figurative language carries a feeling, a convincing, capturing emotion with it. It makes the receptive reader *feel* a truth. Apt imagery gives: a vividness to presentation, colour and warmth for facts and ideas, a suggestion of the concrete and specific (as opposed to the general); a pleasant sense of coöperation, since the reader must read with something of the same imaginative effort with which the poet creates. The artist making use of imagery must, however, avoid two extremes: his imagery must not be trite, or it will fail of its purpose for very staleness; and it must not be too subtle or it will turn into a 'conceit' (*q.v.*) and likewise fail of its purpose because of its very remoteness from the experience of the reader . . . "

25

DEFINITIONS OF FIGURES OF SPEECH

The nine most frequently used figures of speech are: *simile, metaphor, personification, apostrophe, metonymy, hyperbole, oxymoron, irony* and *litotes.*

1. Figures of Speech Based on Comparison

These are: simile, metaphor, personification, apostrophe.

a) *Simile* and *metaphor* compare two things essentially unlike but similar in one respect. When the comparison is direct, the figure is called a simile. The word *like* or *as* introduces the comparison. When, however, the comparison is implied, the figure is called a metaphor.

Examples of Simile:
(i) The train hurtled *like a projectile* through the tube beneath the Hudson River to emerge in the dazzling sunlight of a September afternoon, and now it was racing across the flat desolation of the Jersey meadows. Thomas Wolfe, *You Can't Go Home Again*
(ii) Little clouds that were lost in the dark now came to show *like wisps of flame* in the east. Paul Horgan, *Terror at Daybreak*

Example of Metaphor:
(i) . . . and, continually, you spy little lakes, hidden away, *each a . . . soft jewel.* . . . Rupert Brooke, *Letters from America*
(ii) The tallest of bamboos lean over our low, lazy spread of bungalow; and late this very night, in the full moonlight, I leave my cot and walk down to the beach over *a shadow carpet of Japanese filigree.* William Beebe, "A Jungle Night"
(iii) From the deck of a vessel you may look down, hour after hour, on the shimmering discs of jellyfish, *their gently pulsating bells* dotting the surface as far as you can see. Rachel Carson, *The Sea Around Us*
(iv) On my voyage home I had all the Hilton novels in my gripsack. Everything delighted but nothing surprised me. When *Mr. Chips* [one of James Hilton's novels] was published and its editions *shot skyward* then and then only, his other novels, notably *Lost Horizon, caught fire* and the *Hilton bonfire* was the *blaze* of the year. That *fire* has not died down. Ellery Sedgwick, *The Happy Profession*
(v) And in dank prison cells they [the jailers] give us *to drink.* Of blinding pain . . . Philip Child, *Victorian House*

b) *Personification* is a particular kind of metaphor in which ideas, abstractions, inanimate objects or animals are endowed with human form, character or feelings.

Examples of Personification:
(i) *Born in the East* and *clothed* in Oriental form and imagery, the Bible *walks the ways of all the world with familiar feet* and *enters* land after

26

land *to find its own* everywhere. Henry Van Dyke, *Companionable Books*
(ii) Once the bright days of summer pass by, a city takes on *that sombre garb of gray, . . . wrapt in which it goes about its labours* during the long winter. Theodore Dreiser, *Sister Carrie*

c) An *apostrophe* is a figure of speech in which an abstract quality is personified and directly addressed as if present. Sometimes, an absent person is addressed as though he were present. The apostrophe is a particular kind of personification. It is used chiefly in formal speeches made on patriotic occasions or in reflective lyric poetry. In the hands of a gifted and sincere speaker or writer, this device can be used to produce dramatic and emotional effects. A young writer, however, will find it a difficult figure with which to convey sincere feeling.

Examples of Apostrophe:
(i) Hail to thee, blithe Spirit!
(ii) Milton! thou should'st be living at this hour:

2. Figure of Speech Based on Association

Metonymy is the substitution of a characteristic closely associated with an object to designate the object itself; or the use of a part to suggest the whole.

Examples of Metonymy:
(i) *Grey* hairs should be respected. (A characteristic of the object is substituted for the object.)
(ii) All *hands on deck.* (A part is substituted for the whole.)
(iii) The *pen* is mightier than the *sword.* (An instrument is substituted for the agent.)
(iv) The *kettle* is boiling. (The substitution of the container for the thing contained.)
(v) We are studying *Shakespeare.* (The dramatist is substituted for the plays he wrote.)
(vi) The *pulpit* and the *press* are exerting a strong influence on public opinion.
(vii) Students usually prefer the *classroom* to the *office.*
(viii) Both the *G.I.'s* and the *brass hats* were alarmed by the distant rumble.

3. Figure of Speech Based on Exaggeration

Hyperbole is a deliberate overstatement to achieve an effect.
Used sparingly, hyperbole is an effective device for securing emphasis.

Examples of Hyperbole:

(i) *All the perfumes of Arabia* will not sweeten this little hand. Shakespeare

(ii) The ship battled waves *mountain high.*

4. Figure of Speech Based on Arrangement

Oxymoron is a statement in which words of opposite meaning are combined to achieve a special effect.

Examples of Oxymoron:

(i) His *polite impudence* was amusing.

(ii) The story is, by now, an *open secret.*

(iii) Noel Coward wrote the operetta *Bitter Sweet.*

(iv) The land [in Canada] is virginal, the wind cleaner than elsewhere, and every lake new-born, and each is the first day. The flowers are less conscious than English flowers, the breezes have nothing to remember, and everything to promise. There walk, as yet, no ghosts of lovers in Canadian lanes. This is the essence of the *grey freshness* and *brisk melancholy* of this land. Rupert Brooke, *Letters from America*

5. Figures of Speech Based on Restraint

a) *Irony* is a figure of speech in which one's meaning is expressed in language of opposite meaning.

Examples of Irony:

(i) What a fine friend you are! (If the speaker means the opposite, this remark is ironical.)

(ii) Listen! The wild music of the spheres. (Thomas Mendip, in *The Lady's Not for Burning* by Christopher Fry, used irony to deflate the ego of a stodgy, stupid man, who thinks he has made a profound and imaginative comment.)

(iii) Brutus is an honourable man. Shakespeare (Antony meant the opposite.)

(iv) No doubt but ye are the people and wisdom shall die with you. Bible, "The Book of Job"

b) *Litotes* is a deliberate understatement. This figure of speech is the opposite of hyperbole.

Examples of Litotes:

(i) That was *no small loss.* (With reference to the death of Abraham Lincoln)

(ii) *With no little difficulty,* we persuaded him to join us.

28

ON THE USE OF FIGURATIVE LANGUAGE

Figurative language should be apt. One figure of speech can greatly increase the effectiveness of a description. Sir Winston Churchill's striking metaphor, the "iron curtain", was so apt a description of the barrier between Russia and the West in the period following the Second World War that it seized the imagination of the English-speaking world.

When using figurative language, avoid these pitfalls:

a) hackneyed, or trite, figures of speech, such as: white as snow, glittering like diamonds, a carpet of leaves, Mother Nature, brave as a lion, clear as crystal, busy as a bee, eyes as bright as stars, swift as the wind.

b) mixed metaphors, such as: Mr. James has a hard row to hoe, as he tries to keep his nose above water.

CLASS DISCUSSION
The Use of Imagery

Below you will find passages in which the writers have used figurative language—imagery—for specific effects. Find some of these figures of speech and:

a) identify the figure;

b) tell whether it has been used chiefly for its pictorial or its suggestive effect;

c) state what idea is clarified or what emotion is suggested by means of the figure.

1. Northern Lights in the Arctic

Step out with me under the northern lights. Luminous white serpents are writhing all across the vault of the heavens, ceaselessly coiling, twisting—never for an instant motionless. Suddenly a shimmering iridescence whips across the sky, spanning its arch, a fringe of colour, sea green and delicate rose, rippling continuously from right to left . . . Elizabeth C. Forrest, *Wasted Years?*, The *Atlantic Monthly*

2. The Stars

A vast multitude of stars are wandering about in space. A few form groups which journey in company, but the majority are solitary travellers, and they travel through a universe so spacious that it is an event of almost unimaginable rarity for a star to come anywhere near to another star. For the most part each voyages in splendid isolation, like a ship on an empty ocean, and seldom finds another within hailing distance. Sir James Jeans, *The Mysterious Universe*

3. Lost!

Mixed with the feeling of affront at the scurvy trick that is making a laughing-stock of him for all the forest, is more than a hint of uneasiness,

29

and, taking careful observations, he starts out anew, this time more slowly and coolly. An hour finds him back at the long-dead fire. With a sudden burst of speed in what he hopes is the right direction, he puts this now thoroughly distasteful piece of scenery behind him, tearing and ripping his way through this endless maze, that seems somehow to cover all Northern Canada. He frequently maps out his line of march with a stick in the mud, and spends much time in abstruse calculations; but it is only a matter of time till he returns, torn, exasperated, scarcely believing his eyes, to this hub of the wheel on which he is being spun so helplessly. Grey Owl, "Lost!"

4. Hibernation

First of all, every precaution is taken to avoid loss of heat and to economise the reserves of fuel. The hedgehog wraps himself up warm in a thick blanket of leaves in the heart of a hollow tree-trunk, while bats collect in caves, covering the walls with a kind of velvet tapestry. But that is not enough; they must keep still, for every slightest movement uses up heat. This requirement is scrupulously observed; their immobility is that of the dead. Yet even this is insufficient; respiraton must be reduced to a minimum. Their breathing is so faint that the closest scrutiny can hardly detect it. The faint remnant of life is like the feeble glimmer of a night-lamp husbanding the last drop of oil. So profound is the torpor, so nearly complete the inanition, that were it not followed by an awakening, this state would hardly differ in any respect from death itself. Yet, in fact, this suspension of vitality is the means by which survival is assured. Jean Henri Fabre, *Animal Life in Field and Garden*

5. Nazi Germany

As they [the Germans] look out to-night from their blatant, panoplied, clattering Nazi Germany, they cannot find one single friendly eye in the whole circumference of the globe. Not one! Russia returns them a flinty stare; Italy averts her gaze; Japan is puzzled and thinks herself betrayed . . . Winston Churchill, *Blood Sweat and Tears*

WRITTEN EXERCISE

Using one of the following topic sentences or one of your own choice, write a paragraph in which, at some point, you use figurative language to give concreteness to an idea, intensity to an emotion, or to achieve pictorial effect:

1. Golfers are strange people!
2. A long portage on a hot day in July is no fun!
3. Macbeth's behaviour at the sight of Banquo's ghost must have confirmed the suspicions of the Scottish nobles.
4. Mr. Higgins, the protagonist in Bernard Shaw's play *Pygmalion,* is an eccentric person.
5. Put out your campfire!
6. The blizzard was the worst the city had experienced in forty years.

EXPOSITION: I

ANALYZING EXPOSITION

Any speech or written work, the primary purpose of which is to explain, to make clear, or to inform is called exposition. Skill in exposition will stand you in good stead throughout your life. University students, business and professional men and women, politicians, housewives who are interested in community affairs, all will be more successful in their chosen careers and more useful as citizens if they have mastered the techniques of exposition. The student who has acquired some skill in these techniques is able to reveal, through the numerous essays that are a traditional part of college work, his understanding of the subjects that he has been investigating. The business man, constantly explaining to his staff, business associates and customers, sometimes in the form of written communications, more often orally, will find that some skill in exposition will increase his efficiency. Much of the time of clergymen, teachers and lawyers is spent in explaining! Doctors who have some skill in exposition can, through the medium of medical journals, share their ideas and discoveries. Those who explain clearly and interestingly are obvious assets to any committee. Your value to your firm, to your profession and to your community will be enhanced by a mastery of the skills discussed in this chapter.

CLASS DISCUSSION
The Content of Exposition

1. A newspaper publishes three kinds of articles: news stories, feature articles and editorials.
a) What is the primary purpose of each type?
b) Mention current events that are supplying material for news stories, features and editorials.

2. Magazine editors assume that most people would like to be healthier, wealthier, wiser and happier than they are. Mention an interesting feature article that you have read recently in a newspaper or in a magazine. Explain briefly the specific purpose of the article to which you refer.

3. Read the following feature article written by Bruce West for The *Globe and Mail,* and then use the questions that follow it to discuss its content.

No Need to Drown Yourself

With "cottage opening day" just over, reports are already coming in of drownings in the abundant lakelands of Ontario . . . which should be places for play and healthy relaxation rather than for tragedy.

31

And the greatest tragedy of all is that most of the drowning accidents are the kind that could be avoided by the use of a little common sense. This has been preached again and again, but perhaps one more little sermon on the matter may persuade someone to take that bit of extra precaution that will save a life.

One of the characters who often gets into trouble, of course, is the reckless and dashing dare-devil, who doesn't care how deep the water is when he sets out to slay the gals with a high dive. Quite often, he slays himself, instead. I know of one chap who liked to live dangerously in this manner. He didn't like to look too hard before he dived. Maybe he figured he'd be mistaken for a sissy. One day he dived from a fair height into a river and struck his head on a log that had been lying just under the surface. He never walked again. For the rest of his life he had to be moved about in a wheel-chair.

Another type that often ends up on the hook of a dragline is the lad who sets out to swim to that distant island without an accompanying boat. He feels so full of vim and vigour that he just knows he could swim half way across the ocean if he needed to do so. Sometimes, when he finds out he's made a mistake, there's no one around to help him and another figure is added to the drowning toll. It has long been an established fact that no person in his or her right mind should set out on a long swim alone. Yet every summer a number of people die trying to prove that this is wrong. To those solitary swimmers there should be this word of caution: You may go for a long time without ever needing a helping hand, — but when you do, you'll need it badly.

Apart from the drownings among swimmers, there is also a heavy toll among persons who venture out on the waters in boats of various kinds. Victims dumped from a canoe probably head the list. A canoe is a wonderful craft. Many of us have spent some of the most enjoyable moments of our lives slipping silently along some forest shoreline in a canoe or floating over the quiet waters of some secluded bay. But a canoe has one big drawback. It is as dangerous as dynamite if it is not treated with a great deal of respect. A canoe, which moves along so beautifully on calm waters, can suddenly flip with all the deadly speed of a rattler. No matter how often you've been in a canoe, never let yourself be lulled into the mistaken belief that it is a craft that will put up with any nonsense. Treated with respect, a canoe may bear you thousands of miles without ever causing you to wet your feet. But the moment you start thinking that, because of this, canoes have a certain liking for you and will never let you down, you're headed for trouble.

The margin of safety in a canoe is very finely drawn. Step one inch over the line and you may find yourself floundering in the water. Never try to change places with your partner in a canoe without getting to land. Paddle with your knees planted in the bottom of the canoe as much as possible. If you decide to sit up on the seat for a while to rest your legs, take extra precautions while paddling in this position. Every time you

32

raise the centre of gravity in a canoe, you are increasing the risk of a flip-over. If your partner isn't paddling, insist that he sit in the bottom of the canoe, rather than up on the front seat. If you're fishing and you happen to be wearing heavy boots, slip them off while you're in the canoe. Your feet will be more comfortable; and if you are suddenly dumped, you'll be able to swim a great deal better.

If you're ever thrown from a canoe and you can't swim, remember that a paddle will hold you up indefinitely. Keep calm and reach for a floating paddle; it may save your life by keeping you above the surface until help gets there.

The canoe itself, of course, will float when it's overturned and will hold you up, provided you don't get too eager for a safe haven and try to climb on top of it. The difference between sinking and floating, for the human body, is very small. A firm hold on the edge of the canoe and perhaps a little kicking of the feet will keep you safe and sound.

Don't go overloading small boats equipped with outboard motors. If the water happens to get a little choppy, you may be in for trouble. When the motor of such a boat is running hard, it has a tendency to force down the stern to a dangerous point. A wave may slop over this small amount of free-board and swamp your craft.

If you're out on a lake when a storm comes up, don't try to make it all the way home if the distance is great. Slip into the nearest shore and wait it out. It's better to get a little rain on your head than to have many feet of lake water over it. Bruce West, "No Need to Drown Yourself", The *Globe and Mail,* May 20, 1953

Discussion Questions

1. To whom is the author speaking? What is his thesis?

2. In an exposition, the opening paragraph—called the lead—is used to arrest the attention of the particular group that the writer wishes to inform. Do you think that Mr. West's lead accomplishes this purpose? Give reasons for your opinion.

3. Underline every topic sentence that the author has used. Does each one contribute to the development of the thesis? Give reasons for your opinion.

4. Referring to people in order to illustrate ideas is one method of interesting readers. Which ideas have been elaborated by this means?

5. Contrast is another method that is useful in explaining. Find one contrast that Mr. West has used. What idea is expanded by means of it?

6. The conclusion of an exposition should emphasize, in some imaginative or clever way, the importance, worth or pertinence of the subject that has been discussed. Comment on the effectiveness of Mr. West's conclusion. When evaluating it, keep in mind the specific group he is addressing.

HOME WORK ASSIGNMENT
Analyzing an Exposition

Using the following outline, make a written analysis of "Sport Versus Athletics", an exposition written by a former dean of Princeton University.

Outline for Analysis

1. Title of exposition
2. To whom is the exposition addressed?
3. What is the author's thesis? (State this in one sentence.)
4. Why is he interested in saying this particular thing to this particular group? (Answer in one or two sentences.)
5. Copy, in order, the topic sentences that have been used. Does each one contribute to the development of the author's thesis? Give reasons for your opinion.
6. Underline in every topic sentence the word or phrase used by the author to remind his reader of what has been discussed in the previous paragraph.
7. Has the author arranged his material in a logical sequence? Give reasons for your opinion.
8. Does the last paragraph emphasize the thesis? Justify your opinion.
9. List some of the distinctive qualities of this exposition.
10. What weaknesses, if any, do you find in it? (List them.)

Sport Versus Athletics

Among the countless thousands who flock, the nation over, on a bright Saturday of mid-November to witness a "big" football game in some nearby academic town, there must be a few who, in the interval between the halves, ask themselves, What is this amazing spectacle at which we are assisting? How vast a swarming multitude! Special trains by the score pour out their living freight; the roads of a dozen counties overflow their brims with the converging streams of motors; a battalion of special police keeps the crowds in order; countless hawkers stridently recommend stale edibles or "winning colours". And the occasion of it all is that two and twenty college youths are to play a friendly game of ball. While every autumn sets new records of congregated attendance, there is, I think, a steadily growing sense of something not altogether right and normal in the great edifice of organized college athletics, of which the "big" game is the crowning pinnacle.

What is wrong? It is certainly no cause for regret that the vigorous youth of our universities likes to play manly games. Heaven forfend the contrary! If, then, I have to speak with scant respect of organized athletics, the reader will please understand from the start that I am no enemy of outdoor games. On the contrary, my chief quarrel with the existing state of organized athletics may be summed up in the fact that it is itself an enemy of healthy play. The very word "athletics" suggests such analogous formations as "mathematics" and "dynamics" and "kinematics"; and the very idea of "organization" belongs to the workshop rather than the play-

34

field. What purports to be, and should in fact be, play and a game has been bedevilled into a scientific profession. Our national curse of commercialism has laid a coarse and heavy finger on it. If college records show that football tends to make Jack a dull boy, perhaps the explanation may be that football, as our colleges play it, is all work and no play.

What can be done about it? One can think of several things that might be done. One might, for example, push present tendencies to their logical conclusion, drop all pretense of amateur sport and be frankly professional. Every institution of higher learning would then hire the best players it could find, as it now hires the most skilled professional coach. The boundless enthusiasm of the sport-loving alumnus, that must now be held in check, would then have free play. He could range through all the promising athletic material of the country, and of his bounty present to Harvard or Princeton or Yale the best full-back that money could buy. When money payments no longer made a player ineligible, we should hardly debar him because of his failure in the classroom. Is it not even now intolerable that every season good football players should be ineligible because they are deficient in their academic studies? Why should they even pretend to be students? If it happens that a university student can play football, the fact that he is a student need not disqualify him for the employment. He may thus earn his way through college, provided of course that he does not let his studies interfere with football. Or if, now and then, an athlete professionally resident in the university town should, through some freak of temperament, care to attend an academic lecture or two at hours which do not interfere with practice, there should be no objection. But from all the impertinences of tests and themes and term examinations the normal athlete would be completely exempt. If after many years of association with a university he should covet such a thing as a degree, he might be made Bachelor of Athletics, *honoris causa*, and thus be able to subscribe himself B.A. The degree of B.A. can already be acquired without a syllable of Latin!

The suggestion is a fruitful one. The university which already owned a championship football team might become ambitious to attach to itself the heavy-weight boxing champion. Mr. Dempsey, with the honorary degree of B.Pug. in prospect, would not object to staining his gloves a good gory crimson. Why not a university racing stable, with Yale-Princeton meets at Belmont Park?

But enough of the *reductio ad absurdum!* Is there no remedy that one could suggest in sober earnest? One might, of course, stop by faculty decree all intercollegiate contests. This remedy has often been proposed, and was indeed for a time actually adopted by Columbia. But it would be a pity, even in a relatively unimportant realm of things, to add one more to the "Verboten" signs which are coming to be the mark of American civilization.

35

Outright prohibition is usually an unintelligent way of reforming social abuses. If outdoor games are a desirable element in a young man's life, as everyone admits, it is a pity to deprive him of the added zest which comes from competition beyond the boundaries of the college playing fields. Only let it be an added zest rather than the one and only incentive.

One can think of a number of remedies more intelligent than outright abolition. One might begin by reducing very materially the number of intercollegiate contests in a given season. During October a dozen Yale teams might play football intramurally, and then in November the best of these teams, or some composite of the best, might meet champion teams similarly chosen at Princeton and at Cambridge. One might curtail, or abolish altogether, the professional coaching system. Suppose, for example, Harvard, Yale, and Princeton should agree to retain the skilled trainer, whose business it is to keep the players in perfect physical trim, but leave to the undergraduates themselves the devising of new formations, the training of recruits, and the strategy of the game. One might charge one dollar instead of three for a seat, and so lessen the implication of commercialism which now pervades football, and the lesser organized sports which are its pensioners. The resultant intercollegiate games would no doubt be less brilliant exhibitions of football skill; but amateurs are usually less skilful than professionals. With such a decrease in technical skill, and the players once more amateurs in fact as well as in name, football might be somewhat less interesting to sporting editors, be less prominently displayed in the daily press, and so occupy a less exaggerated place in the national consciousness.

But I have scant faith in any programme of reform, or in any easy nostrum. What we need is, in theological language, conviction of sin and a change of heart. So long as the university world and its multitudinous patrons prefer the great spectacle of professionalized athletics, there is little use in urging mitigations.

But do they so prefer? So far as one can discover, no one in particular is responsible for the present deformation of college sport. It is not the result of conscious choice, but of blind drifting. The professional coaching system, for example, has become more and more professional, more complicated and highly specialized, by the same processes which turned all Europe into a camp of competitive armaments. If one plays a game, one very naturally wishes to win; and a genuinely amateur team would have small chance to win against a professionally trained rival. So, step by step, each would-be champion meets and goes beyond its rival. The best hope for the recovery of amateur methods lies in some Washington Conference of the great athletic powers.

If the will is there, the way is easy. We may yet have a chance to see amateur sport resume the place in our university life so long usurped by the profession of organized athletics. R. K. Root, "Sport Versus Athletics"

INTERESTING THE READER: I

Techniques are the methods or the details of procedure essential to expertness of execution in any art, science, etc. Some of the techniques used by professional writers to interest their readers may be useful to you in expository writing. You will find that they use:

1. an arresting lead—opening paragraph or paragraphs—to arouse the reader's interest in the subject so that he will read on;

2. a paragraph that states and, if necessary, clarifies the thesis;

3. many concrete examples to develop the topic sentences used in the body of the exposition—especially examples that include people;

4. comparisons;

5. contrasts;

6. a conclusion that emphasizes in some clever, imaginative way the thesis of the article.

AN ARRESTING LEAD

A professional writer, aware of the fact that he is competing for the attention of busy people, knows that, unless the opening paragraph catches the reader's attention, his article may not be read. For this reason, such a writer plans very carefully the opening paragraph or paragraphs that will lead the reader into the article.

To capture the reader's attention he may use:

1. a striking statement;

2. a provocative question;

3. an incident (real or fictitious) in which the reader will see himself;

4. a real or fictitious incident that dramatizes the subject to be discussed. People, action and conversation always arouse the reader's interest.

AN EMPHATIC CONCLUSION

Professional writers also know the value of using the conclusion to stress the thesis. For this purpose they may use:

1. a statement that reminds the reader of the lead. This method has the following advantages:

   a) it is a subtle way to emphasize the thesis, and most people prefer the subtle to the obvious;

   b) it helps to give an artistic unity to the exposition.

2. a re-stating of the thesis in some imaginative or clever way;

3. a contrast that emphasizes the thesis;

4. an anecdote that emphasizes the thesis;

5. a well-described incident that emphasizes the thesis.

Leads and Conclusions

Examine each of the following leads and conclusions used by professional writers. Then, for each, answer the following questions:

a) To whom is the article addressed, and what is the author's thesis?

b) How does the author arrest the reader's attention and arouse his interest in the subject?

c) In the conclusion, how does the author stress his thesis?

1. Alan Devoe, a well-known American naturalist, used this paragraph as the lead for his article "Passenger Pigeon, Bird of Yesterday".

The Lead:

On the first day of September, twenty-eight years ago, a slim-winged bird of delicate blue and fawn plumage which had been on exhibition in the Cincinnati Zoological Gardens toppled from its perch and fell dead on the floor of its cage. The incident attracted wider attention than the passing of zoo captives customarily receives. The bird was a passenger pigeon. Precisely, it was *the* passenger pigeon. It was the sole surviving member of that race of "wild blue doves" which once had inhabited our country in such multitudes that the migrating flocks darkened the noonday sky, and the vibrance of rushing wings had the sound, said Audubon, of "a gale passing through the rigging of a close-reefed vessel". What happened on that fall day in 1914 was a good deal more than the dying of a bird in a zoo. What happened, in the eloquent words of the zoologist Hegner, was that "another of our 'inexhaustible resources' had come to an end".

The Conclusion:

That is the story of the going of the passenger pigeons. That is the story of why the word "pigeon"—that once meant hordes of shimmering wings, and a rushing, murmurous music in the American wild places—means now only a dingy fancier-bred bird that creeps on soot-stained feet around the grimy cornices of office buildings.

2. Below you will find the lead and the conclusion of a provocative magazine article entitled "Dowries for Daughters" by LeClerc Phillips.

The Lead:

Yes, I know. The very idea is repulsive to you. It is to the average man and woman in Anglo-Saxon lands. And yet the custom has existed for countless centuries and is still in vogue among some of the most highly civilized races under the sun. Surely there must be something to be said for a practice so widely prevalent as that of dowries for daughters.

You deny it stoutly. You say that a man must stand on his own feet as you yourself have done. You believe that any form of personal subsidy tends to weaken a man's moral fibres and that the institution of such a social system would in time develop a breed of fortune hunters as effeminate and backboneless as the stage picture of the Continental male. You will have none of it. Your daughter's suitors must love her for herself alone. You married your wife without a penny of dowry, and your daughter must go to her husband as penniless as your wife came to you. Afterward, when you are gone—well, then of course, she will have something because you cannot take your money with you.

But by the time your daughter gets this money it is probable that she will be well on in middle life. She will have passed through the fiery furnace of the economic struggle. She will have suffered, and so will her husband. From their point of view, your money will come to them just a little late.

But, you argue, their moral fibres will have remained intact. Well, perhaps; perhaps. But possibly there will be something else that will have been a little bit damaged instead.

The Conclusion:
But his money cannot be a dowry when Mary gets it; it will be her old-age pension.

3. The following passage was used by Stewart Edward White as the lead in one of the chapters of his book *The Forest*. The purpose of this chapter was to give campers instructions on pitching a tent, making a comfortable bed, building a fire and cooking a meal. (The lead for a chapter in a book or for a very long article may be several paragraphs in length.)

The Lead:
But to those who tread the Long Trail, the making of camp resolves itself into an algebraical formula. After a man has travelled all day through the Northern wilderness he wants to rest, and anything that stands between himself and his repose he must get rid of in as few motions as are consistent with reasonable thoroughness. The end in view is a hot meal and a comfortable, dry place to sleep. The straighter he can draw the line to those two points the happier he is.

Early in his woods experience Dick became possessed with the desire to do everything for himself. As this was a laudable striving for self sufficiency, I called a halt at about three o'clock one afternoon to give him plenty of time.

Now Dick is a good, active, able-bodied boy, possessed of average intelligence, and rather more than average zeal. He even had a theory of a sort, for he had read various "Boy Campers", or "The Trapper's Guide", "How to Camp Out", "The Science of Woodcraft" and other able works. He certainly had ideas enough, and confidence enough. I sat down on a log.

At the end of three hours' frustration, heat, worry, and good hard work, he had accomplished the following results: a tent, very saggy, very askew, covered a four-sided area—it was not a rectangle—of very bumpy ground. A hodge-podge bonfire, in the centre of which an inaccessible coffee-pot toppled menacingly, alternately threatened to ignite the entire surrounding forest or to go out altogether through lack of fuel. Personal belongings strewed the ground near the fire, and provisions cumbered the entrance to the tent. Dick was anxiously mixing batter for the cakes, attempting to stir a pot of rice often enough to prevent it from burning, and trying to rustle sufficient dry wood to keep the fire going. This diversity of interests certainly made him sit up and pay attention. At each instant he had to desert his flour sack to rescue the coffee-pot, or to shift the kettle, or to dab hastily at the rice, or to stamp out the small brush, or to pile on more dry twigs. His movements were not graceful. They raised a scurry of dry bark, ashes, wood-dust, twigs, leaves and pine needles, a certain proportion of which found their way into the coffee, the rice, and the sticky batter, while the smaller articles of personal belonging, hastily dumped from the duffel-bag, gradually disappeared from view in the manner of Pompeii and ancient Vesuvius. Dick burned his fingers and stumbled about and swore, and looked so comically pathetically red-faced through the smoke that I, seated on the log, at the same time laughed and pitied. And in the end, when he needed a continuous steady fire to fry his cakes, he suddenly discovered that dry twigs do not make coals, and that his precious operations had used up all the fuel within easy circle of the camp.

So he had to drop everything for the purpose of rustling wood, while the coffee chilled, the rice cooled, the bacon congealed, and all the provisions, cooked and uncooked, gathered entomological specimens. At the last, the poor bewildered theorist made a hasty meal of scorched food, brazenly postponed the washing of dishes until the morrow, and coiled about his hummocky couch to dream the nightmares of complete exhaustion.

The Conclusion:

It is but a little after seven. The long crimson shadows of the North Country are lifting across the aisles of the forest. You sit on a log, or lie on your back, and blow contented clouds straight up into the air. Nothing can disturb you now. The wilderness is yours, for you have taken from it the essentials of primitive civilization—shelter, warmth and food. An hour ago a rainstorm would have been a minor catastrophe. Now you do not care. Blow high, blow low, you have made for yourself an abiding place, so that the signs of the sky are less important to you than to the city dweller who wonders if he should take an umbrella. From your doorstep you can look placidly out on the great unknown. The noises of the forest draw close about you their circle of mystery, but the circle cannot break upon you, for here you have conjured the homely sounds of kettle and crackling flame to keep warm. Thronging down through the twilight steal the jealous woodland shadows, awful in the sublimity of the Silent Places, but at the sentry outposts of your fire-lit trees they pause like wild animals, hesitating to advance. The wilderness, untamed, dreadful at night, is all about; but this one little spot you have reclaimed. Here is something before unknown to the eerie spirits of the woods. As you sleepily knock the ashes from the pipe, you look about on the familiar scene with accustomed satisfaction. You are at home. Stewart Edward White, *The Forest*

1. Using the following outline, make a plan for an exposition on some subject that interests you. This plan is not necessarily the one for the exposition that you will write as a later home work assignment.

Outline for Plan

a) The Preliminary Decisions
   Subject:
   To whom addressed:
   Purpose:
   Thesis:
   Reasons for saying this to those addressed:
b) The Plan for Developing the Thesis
   (i) List the topics that you will discuss in order to develop your thesis.
   (ii) Arrange these topics in some logical order.
   (iii) Turn each of these topics into a topic sentence. Use transitional words or phrases in every topic sentence after the first.

2. Then write: (a) the lead, (b) the conclusion.

EXPOSITION: 1

LESSON THREE

INTERESTING THE READER: II

An expert writer frequently uses concrete examples to illustrate his ideas. Such illustrative material stirs the reader's imagination, because it enables him to visualize people, places and action. Such examples not only keep the reader interested, but also tend to impress upon him the ideas they illustrate. A good rule to follow when writing exposition is to illustrate every generalization with a concrete example.

Experienced writers choose their examples carefully. They know that:

1. historical examples, with their association of ideas and their emotional colour, stir the imagination and feelings of the reader;

2. familiar examples are usually better than unfamiliar ones;

3. examples that include people and action interest all readers.

CONCRETE VERSUS ABSTRACT EXAMPLES

A concrete example is one that can be apprehended by the senses. An abstract example is one that cannot be apprehended by the senses; it denotes, not an object existing in material form, but a quality or a state. The concrete example, therefore, records sensory impressions; the abstract example records thoughts, feelings, state of mind.

Illustrating the Use of Abstract Examples:

The young man sitting on a hill-side in Korea thought of home: the *companionship*, the *good times*, the *pleasure of working.*

(The italicized words are specific examples of the thoughts that come to him, and are, therefore, better than the generalization: he thought of home. However, if these *abstract* examples were replaced by *concrete* examples, the sentence would be more interesting, because the reader could then *see* and *feel* what the young man in his imagination *sees* and *feels.*)

Illustrating the Use of Concrete Examples:

The young man sitting on a hill-side in Korea thought of home: *the long rides down autumn trails with his father; the crowd at the big Queens-Varsity football game in which he scored the winning touchdown; the happy weight of his little black bag as he rushed to the home of old Mrs. Chesley, his first patient.*

The more specific the concrete example, the more effective it is in stirring the imagination and/or the emotions of the reader.

CLASS DISCUSSION I

1. Study the following passages, in each of which two concrete examples have been used to illustrate an idea. In the second passage, the examples are more specific than those used in the first. Notice the increase in pictorial power and in emotional appeal. Find these examples, and account for the effectiveness of the more specific ones.

Free Speech

a) It is not by any means self-evident upon the face of it that an institution like the liberty of speech is right or just. It is not natural or obvious to let a man utter follies and abominations which you believe to be bad for mankind any more than it is natural or obvious to let people interfere with traffic or spread germs.

b) It is not by any means self-evident upon the face of it that an institution like the liberty of speech is right or just. It is not natural or obvious to let a man utter follies or abominations which you believe to be bad for mankind any more than it is natural or obvious to let a man dig up part of the public road, or infect half a town with typhoid fever. G. K. Chesterton, *Robert Browning*

2. In the following paragraph, the author has used two concrete examples, the second one more specific than the first. Find these examples and account for the effectiveness of the more specific example.

One of the Mind's Powers

Among the mind's powers is one that comes of itself to many children and artists. It need not be lost, to the end of his days, by anyone who has ever had it. This is the power of taking delight in a thing, or rather in anything, everything, not as a means to some other end, but just because it is what it is, as the lover dotes on whatever may be the traits of the beloved object. A child in the full health of his mind will put his hand flat on the summer turf, feel it, and give a little shiver of private glee at the elastic firmness of the globe. C. E. Montague, *Disenchantment*

CLASS DISCUSSION II

The Use of Concrete Examples

In each of the following selections, the writer has used one or more examples to impress on his readers the ideas that he is discussing. Use the questions that follow each selection to guide your discussion of the purpose and the effect of some of the illustrations used.

1. *The Use of One Example*:

Advice to a Son

Your mind, like your body, is a thing whereof the powers are developed by effort. That is a principal use, as I see it, of hard work in studies. Unless you train your body you can't be an athlete; and unless you train your mind you can't be much of a scholar. The four miles an oarsman covers at top speed is, in itself, nothing to the good, but the physical capacity to hold out over the course is thought to be of some worth. So a good part of what you learn by hard study may not be permanently retained, and may not seem to be of much final value, but your mind is a better and more powerful instrument because you have learned it. "Knowledge is Power", but still more, the faculty of acquiring and using knowledge is power. If you have a trained and powerful mind, you are bound to have stored it with something, but its value is more in what it can do, what it can grasp and use, than in what it contains; and if it were possible—as it is not—to come out of college with a trained and disciplined mind and nothing useful in it, you would still be ahead, and still, in a manner, educated. Think of your mind as a muscle to be developed; think of it as a searchlight that is to reveal the truth to you; and don't cheat it or neglect it. Edward S. Martin, "A Father to His Freshman Son"

a) For what purpose has Mr. Martin used the example of an oarsman?
b) Is this illustration an effective one? Give reasons for your opinion. Keep in mind the person to whom the author is speaking.

2. *The Use of Several Examples*:

Literature as Revelation

The great difference, intellectually speaking, between one man and another is simply the number of things they can see in a given cubic yard of world. Do you remember Huxley's famous lecture on *A Piece of Chalk,* delivered to the working men of Norwich in 1868, and how the piece of

43

chalk told him secrets of the infinite past, secrets of the unfathomed depths of the sea? The same thing happens with a book. I remember once picking up a copy of *Macbeth* belonging to the great Shakespearian scholar, Andrew Bradley, and reading casually his pencilled notes in the margin. The scene I knew by heart and thought I understood; but his notes showed me that I had missed about a half dozen points on every page. It seems to me that the writers who have the power of revelation are just those who, in some particular part of life, have seen or felt considerably more than the average run of intelligent human beings. It is this specific power of seeing or feeling more things to the cubic yard in some part of the world that makes a writer's work really inspiring. Gilbert Murray, "Literature as Revelation"

   a) What is the main idea in this paragraph?
   b) Explain how the two examples used—Huxley's lecture and Murray's experience with Bradley's copy of *Macbeth*—illustrate this idea.

3. *The Use of Comparisons*:

Liberty

What is liberty?

I have long had an image in my mind of what constitutes liberty. Suppose that I were building a great piece of powerful machinery, and suppose that I should so awkwardly and unskilfully assemble the parts of it that every time one part tried to move it would be interfered with by the others, and the whole thing would buckle up and be checked. Liberty for the several parts would consist in the best possible assembling and adjustment of them all, would it not? If you want the great piston of the engine to run with absolute freedom, give it absolutely perfect alignment and adjustment with the other parts of the machine, so that it is free, not because it is let alone or isolated, but because it has been associated most skilfully and carefully with the other parts of the great structure.

What is liberty? You say of a locomotive that it runs free. What do you mean? You mean that its parts are so assembled and adjusted that friction is reduced to a minimum, and that it has perfect adjustment. We say of a boat skimming the water with light foot, "How free she runs", when we mean, how perfectly she is adjusted to the force of the wind, how perfectly she obeys the great breath out of the heavens that fills her sails. Throw her head up into the wind and see how she will halt and stagger, how every sheet will shiver and her whole frame be shaken, how instantly she is "in irons" in the expressive phrase of the sea. She is free only when you have let her fall off again and have recovered once more her nice adjustment to the forces she must obey and cannot defy.

Human freedom consists in perfect adjustments of human interests, and human activities and human energies. Woodrow Wilson, *The New Freedom*

   a) Put into your own words Wilson's definition of liberty.
   b) Explain clearly how his picture of a great machine illustrates his definition.

c) The picture of the sail-boat also illustrates his concept of freedom. Explain how.

4. *The Use of Contrasting Examples*:

Man's Failure

It is the most trite and tragic of commentaries upon human knowledge to say that it has guided man well except in what relates to himself. He controls many diseases, but has made little progress in controlling crime. He places mighty rivers within bounds, but not his own ambitions, greeds, fears and hatreds. He toils for years to make the desert bloom and then in a brief space turns flourishing regions into wasteland. "Irony of Man and Moon", The *Canadian Editorial Digest,* March, 1945

a) What is the main idea of this paragraph?
b) How do the contrasting examples illustrate this idea?

HOME WORK ASSIGNMENT

This exercise is designed to give practice in writing interesting paragraphs so that the long exposition, which you are being trained to write, will have content that holds the attention of your readers.

Using one of the topic sentences below, or one of your own choice, write an expository paragraph in which you use one or more examples to illustrate your ideas.

1. Driving too fast can be dangerous.
2. Reading comic books can harm a child.
3. Television programmes can be interesting.
4. A good novel deepens a person's understanding of human problems.
5. A good historical novel gives a graphic picture of an interesting era.
6. Advertising on television has gone too far.
7. The billboard advertising that you see while driving along the highway is calling you a fool!
8. Camping provides memorable experiences.
9. Scientists to-day are worried about the after-effects of nuclear explosions.
10. Golf can try a man's nerves.
11. A golf enthusiast lives for golf.
12. Comfort and blueberry picking do not go together.
13. Camp counselling is a rewarding experience.
14. The personality of a man can change the course of history.

PLANNING AND WRITING AN EXPOSITION

Before attempting to write an exposition, plan it carefully. Give some thought to selecting a subject, choosing the group you will address, planning the structure of your exposition and deciding how you can apply the knowledge acquired in Lessons Two and Three, pages 37-45, to interest your reader.

SELECTING A SUBJECT

A writer who has a first-hand knowledge of his subject will be likely to write a more convincing exposition than the one whose knowledge of his subject has been acquired for the occasion.

For example, the young man who, having been a member of a basketball team, has a deep conviction that playing basketball is a very worthwhile experience might be expected to write a more persuasive essay on "School Sports" than the boy who has never played any games and has only an academic interest in their value. Similarly, the person who knows a great deal about racial prejudice and wants well-educated people to crusade against it will write more convincingly about the subject than the person who not only knows little about it, but also thinks it is not an evil.

CHOOSING THE GROUP YOU WILL ADDRESS

Choosing the group to whom you will address your exposition is the second step in your planning. One experience, for example, a trip to a favourite fishing haunt, might be used to convince those who do not like to go fishing that they are missing a pleasurable experience; or to persuade ardent fishermen who have never seen this particular spot that it is a fisherman's paradise; or to present to enthusiastic fishermen an informative article on various baits.

One hobby might provide material for several expositions. If, for example, a person knows a great deal about photography, he might write several articles on this one topic. One article, addressed to other expert photographers, might explain in technical detail the procedures that should be followed to procure a flawless enlargement. Another article, directed to people who do not own a camera, might explain why photography is a fascinating hobby. A third might be written for those who own a camera but do not develop and print their own pictures. The writer, enthusiastic about developing and printing, might try to make the people in his chosen group wiser by pointing out the satisfactions they are missing.

COMPOSING THE THESIS

Having selected your subject and the group you will address, you next compose the thesis that you will develop in your exposition. Below are listed four subjects, each of which is followed by several theses. Any one of these could be developed into an exposition.

Subject	Thesis

a) *Riding*
- (i)   Learning to ride is an unforgettable experience!
- (ii)   Participating in a horse show is an amusing experience.
- (iii)   Owning a horse is fun!
- (iv)   You can persuade your father to buy you a horse!

b) *Conservation*
- (i)   Forest fires can be prevented.
- (ii)   The conservation of our forests is an urgent problem.
- (iii)   Why bother about fires; our forests are inexhaustible.
- (iv)   Soil and water conservation are essential to survival.

c) *The Farm*
- (i)   Living on a farm is fun!
- (ii)   The farm in Spring is an exciting place.
- (iii)   Farming is hard but rewarding work.
- (iv)   Don't live on a farm!
- (v)   Visiting on a farm is a memorable experience.

d) *Music*
- (i)   You can enjoy classical music.
- (ii)   Collecting records is a fascinating hobby.
- (iii)   You will enjoy belonging to an orchestra.
- (iv)   Music can stir the imagination.

LISTING THE PRELIMINARY DECISIONS

When you have decided on a subject, the particular group to whom you will address your exposition, the purpose of the exposition and its thesis, as well as the particular emphasis you wish to give, you will find it helpful to list these preliminary decisions.

Here is an example:

Subject: Photography

To whom addressed: students who would like to have a hobby but do not know what to choose

Purpose of article: to interest them in photography

Thesis: Photography is a fascinating hobby.

Reasons for saying this to hobbyless students: People who know little of photography might think that it means just a dull routine of developing and printing in a dark room.

47

THE REQUISITES OF EXPOSITION

An exposition should have the qualities of unity, coherence and emphasis in the whole and in the individual parts.

An exposition that has unity—singleness of effect—can be summed up in one sentence. Developing *one* thesis gives exposition unity.

An exposition that has coherence—a "sticking together of ideas" —forms a related, linked *whole* rather than a series of unrelated or apparently unrelated ideas. Arranging the individual parts of the exposition in some logical order and linking these parts together by transitional words, phrases or sentences impart coherence.

An exposition that has emphasis impresses on the reader the most important idea: the thesis. Arranging the paragraphs in climactic order, and using the principles of proportion and position, make exposition emphatic in structure.

1. The Overall Structure

The following overall structure, sometimes termed *organization*, will help to impart the qualities of unity, coherence and emphasis to exposition:

a) a lead—one or more paragraphs designed to arouse the reader's interest in the subject the writer is about to discuss;

b) the thesis—one sentence or one short paragraph in which the writer states and if necessary clarifies his thesis;

c) the body of the exposition—the paragraphs used to develop the thesis;

d) the conclusion—one paragraph, the purpose of which is to impress on the reader the thesis that has been developed.

2. The Structure of the Individual Paragraph

Each paragraph of the exposition should have a planned structure. The one most frequently used to make a paragraph unified, coherent and emphatic is:

a) a transitional sentence,

b) a topic sentence,

c) sentences setting forth the ideas that develop the topic sentence, (These are arranged in some logical and emphatic way.)

d) a concluding sentence that emphasizes the most important idea in the paragraph.

3. The Structure of the Individual Sentence

Every sentence also should have an effective structure.

48

4. Content

In addition to unified, coherent and emphatic structures of the whole and of the individual parts, an exposition should have a content that stimulates the reader's thinking.

5. Style

An exposition that is well constructed and has an interesting content might still make dull reading because of the author's awkward or monotonous style. The manner in which a thing is said is a very important element in its appeal. Hence, the final mark of good expository writing is a pleasing style.

CLASS DISCUSSION

Analyzing Students' Expositions

Below are three expository articles written by students on subjects that interested them. Use the following questions to help you analyze and criticize, one at a time, each exposition.

1. To whom is the student speaking? In general, what is he saying to this group and why?
2. In which paragraph has he stated his thesis?
3. In a unified exposition, every topic sentence helps develop the thesis. Is this exposition unified? Give reasons for your opinion.
4. If a lead has been used, is it a good one for that particular article? Give reasons for your opinion. Suggest a possible lead if none has been used.
5. If a conclusion has been used, is it one that emphasizes the thesis? Give reasons for your opinion. Suggest a possible conclusion if none has been used.
6. Which paragraph in the article is the most interesting to you? Why? Which paragraph is the most emphatic structurally? Why?
7. Using the knowledge that you have gained from your study of language, find:
   a) words that are effectively used in context;
   b) examples of good use of figurative language.
8. What is the strongest feature of the article: the overall structure, the content, the style? Give reasons for your opinion.

1. Are Motorcycles Dangerous?

He glanced down at the speedometer and watched the needle push past the one hundred mark. The wind whistled past his head and tugged at his trousers. Trees, pastures, unconcerned cows flashed by as the speedometer registered one hundred and five. He experienced a proud thrill as his great machine barrelled down the road and hugged to a slow curve, pushing one hundred and seven with the throttle wide open. Very gently he eased his machine around the car ahead and screamed by. The two occupants of the car jumped when they heard the staccato roar of

49

the exhaust and watched the powerful motorcycle thunder by and disappear down the road. The man swore; the woman called him a two-wheeled ass, and was sure she would find him embedded in the concrete over-pass five miles ahead.

Was this motorcyclist taking his life in his hands? Was he a speed-happy fool who wanted to ride his way into Kingdom Come at one hundred miles an hour? To the ordinary layman and the motorist, the answer is "yes"; but here are a few facts about motorcycles and cyclists that every person who uses our roads should know before condemning the motorcycle and its rider.

The motorcycle is mechanically safer than a car. Because of the ratio of brake-lining surface and weight, a motorcycle can stop far more quickly than a car. The engine and construction of a motorcycle make it possible to use the engine as a brake. This practice of engine-braking is very seldom used in a car, because it requires expert driving. A motorcycle doing sixty miles an hour can stop in 140 feet, whereas a car travelling at the same speed requires 180 feet to stop.

Furthermore, a motorcyclist has greater control over his machine than a motorist has over his car. In order to drive a motorcycle, one must know his mount thoroughly. He must have timing and co-ordination completely perfect; he must know his machine's capabilities and incapabilities; he must know his machine's temperament and mood before he even dares to take it out on the road. The motorcyclist knows the purpose and function of every part of his cycle. The average motorist knows only how to shift gears and press a gas pedal. Just ask any woman driver the compression ratio of her car, and it will be obvious how much she knows about mechanics and driving!

The motorcyclist takes great pride in the condition and running order of his mount. He has to. Since there are no garages that service a motorcycle, it must be greased, de-carbonized, completely maintained by its owner. He takes immaculate care of his machine, because he knows any mechanical failure could cause great embarrassment. In short, he knows about the scratch on his fender, the tightness of the big ends, the chipped needle-valve, and even the nail he used to replace a broken cotter pin in the rear brake coupling.

So the next time a conscientious motorcyclist overtakes and passes you, don't swear, don't curse, say a silent prayer for him. Don't condemn him as a speed-happy fool; just keep your eyes on the road and quietly murmur, "There goes a fellow who knows what he's doing!" Rudy K.

2. An Old Book Forever New

A book may be of interest to each successive generation at a certain age; or it may be of continued interest to a person all through his life; or it may be of continued interest to each succeeding generation.

The Bible, a book that is forever new, falls into the last category. For succeeding generations to find interest in a book, it must be founded on

50

eternal truths; it must portray the picture of human nature that is common to all men in all generations. Such is the Bible. In its stories we are told of situations that are frequent occurrences to-day: the story of Esau selling his birthright for a mess of pottage; of the Prodigal Son, who was welcomed home and forgiven by his father; and of the king who lived hundreds of years ago, but whose cry of "Absolom, Absolom, my son Absolom, would God I had died for thee" has been echoed down the ages by thousands of despairing fathers. Again, in the parables, we find truths that are still truths to-day. The man who passed by on the other side is still passing, and the sower is still sowing with the same results. Finally, the sayings of Solomon are as full of meat and wisdom to-day as ever they were. "As the dog returns to his vomit, so does the fool to his folly"; and "the way of an eagle in the air, the way of a ship amidst the waters of the sea, the way of a man with a maid" are still marvellous to behold.

As well as containing everlasting truths, a book, to be enduring, must give man hope and inspiration. To those who have experienced despair—and who has not—the Bible gives strength to shoulder the burden and to continue on their weary way. To the downtrodden, to the poor, and to the afflicted, the teachings of the *New Testament* are like "The shadow of a rock in a weary land"; to a troubled spirit the Beatitudes are as dew to the thirsty earth; and to how many has the simple message of the Twenty-third Psalm been of lasting comfort? But the Bible not only raises us from the depths of despair; it also shows us an attainable goal to strive for. Peter, the best-beloved disciple, denied his Christ thrice; David sinned; and Paul was once Saul of Tarsus; but these men were loved by God, which examples give hope to every man that, in spite of his failings, he may yet reach the Kingdom of Heaven.

A book to be continually new to a man within his own lifetime must be not only a source of truth and hope, but must, each time he reads it, be a source of new interests, and new ideas. When he is young, the Bible is a source of fascinating tales: Jacob and Rachael, Joseph and his brethren, and, best of all, the story of the First Christmas. A child is interested only in thrills and adventures; but as he matures, becomes a man, and gains an experience of life, the hidden meaning in the seemingly simple stories is revealed to him. It is the quality of having always a new thought in store for one as his insight in life grows that makes the Bible truly an old book forever new. Hugh C.

3. Fragments from a Ten-Year Span—The Fifties

Oh, it was busy. Oh, how those years flowed, and how we scurried and skipped and stumbled and strove along with them. Shunted from brink to brink, fad to fad, era to era. But the movement lacked rhythm, and the energy lacked a source. It was hollow activity. And far beneath it lurked a fear, the fear that all our doing had no meaning, all our lives had no purpose. The whole melee of the fifties was a desperate attempt to avoid the problem of existence posed by an age of revolution.

The years before had brought so much, uncovered such fields, that they threatened to destroy all conventional values, all previous meaning. Science confronted religion; psychology defied faith. A madman mutilated a people of six million souls, and goodness seemed an anachronism. The universe minimized mankind, and mankind plunged into a perilous, unknown whirlpool. We needed to search out new questions and new destinations. But in the fifties we did not. We stuck our heads in the sand and pretended there was no basic issue. We struck the question "Why?" from our vocabulary. We went on blithely inventing and organizing. But beneath the veneer lay despair and emptiness. Our lives pointed here and aimed there, but found nothing to focus on. Our lives had lost meaning; and rather than face this, we retired into activity and hid in outwardness. Precisely because we did not know why we were doing, we did so much. For some reason, we thought that by speeding up, we could avoid getting anywhere, or getting to the roots. And out of this contradiction in human terms emerged the fifties.

At least this is what emerged in Forest Hill Village, in Toronto, in Canada. And this is how we saw it from the prep schools, and from the junior high, and from the collegiate.

When the decade arrived, there was a war in a very far-off place called Korea. It was a strange war, like a game of Capture the Flag. You could shoot your opponents with a fifty-calibre bullet, but you were not allowed to threaten him with a five-megaton bomb. You could plunder and murder and burn, but only within the boundaries. It was a silly war; no one knew why it was there. And that, of course, marked most of the events of the fifties.

Some would say Korea was a microcosm of the Communist-Capitalist macrocosm. But what was the substance of the much publicized ideological conflict? Or did we ever get to it? Did we not spend our time on television spy programmes and on propaganda *coups* and on diverting senate sub-committees instead of on looking the Marxian challenge in the eye? The United States built bases all around the Communist nations, and in so doing skirted the subject completely.

Somewhere during those ten years, they tossed a monster called rock n' roll at us. Primitive, hairy creatures with primitive, stringy instruments bellowed primordially. And the kids screamed like animals. The sociologists had a field day. — " . . . a throw back, right to the jungle". But when adult society sneered, it would have done well first to examine its own situation. The frenzy of rock n' roll was only an amplification of the "hustle and bustle" of Western society at large, an aspect of the activity that tries to avoid the ultimate fears. And what better release from the intellectual search than the physical reaction to the beat of the drum?

Rock n' roll was the most successful of a multitude of fads, as the public dashed from one preoccupation to another, from hula hoop to adult Western, from three-button suit to pizza pie. Try anything once, was the motto, and if it doesn't keep you busy, try anything else once.

Every generation has its idols. The personality cult seems timeless. But

52

it remained to the fifties not only to elevate the personality, not only to make the personality representative of the movement, but to replace entirely the movement with the personality. What did the president of the United States stand for? Nothing. He was what he was: friendly, agreeable and non-committal, just "a guy". Why did this estrangement from principle occur? Why did it become necessary for the president of the leading nation of the Western world to avoid a platform completely? Because platforms are ideas and ideals, and ideas and ideals are too close to ultimate questions, with the fear of an opacity of ultimate answers. Partly, at least, because of this.

"All hail the return to religion", cried the papers. And statistics seemed to confirm this. Was there not indeed an unprecedented rise in religious affiliation and in church construction? Mind you, don't scan too closely the religious nature of a society that largely shunned the starving half of a world. But at least people were going to church. Yes, they were going. And what were they doing there? Why, they held raffles and bingo games and brotherhoods and fashion shows and community projects, and once in a while they attended services. Yet there remained a basic fear of the ultimate questions, in this case those of religion. Probably the most vital religious issue of the fifties was the very vitality of religion; that is, was the source of religious activity, that source being God, a vital, living source? It came to a question of being basically religious or basically humanitarian. And characteristically, with a flurry of activity, in this case church-centred activity, the problem was disposed of, or swept behind a pew in the back row. The so-called "return to religion" was, in truth, the oddly manifested flight from religion.

Finally, in France, a group took the dilemma by its horns. They were called Existentialists, though they meandered far intellectually from the founders of that movement. And their conclusion almost justified the Western refusal, generally, even to consider the deeper problems. What some of these gentlemen said, in effect, was that life indeed has no meaning, the world is hostile, and Man is alone. But in a courageous manner, they resolved to live and fashion their own code in spite of this depressing fact. Yet even this movement was distorted by the Western world.

For out of a deformed Existentialism, came the Beat Generation. They sought to face the hard, existential truth. But somehow the Beats developed their own conventions and fetishes. The refusal to dress neatly seems the beatnik counterpart to church bingo. The process turns back on itself. But this time, in the face of fact, rather than in its absence, Man retreats. It is a frightening prospect, but not, on that account, the only prospect.

"Daddy, can I go out and play with the kids?"

"Shut up and deal."

The sick joke has been the most recent addition to Western culture. It seems a particular form of humour which would appeal only to a small number of people. Yet that appeal has been near-universal. In its morbidity, the sick joke seems almost an implication that, at last, man is facing his ontological foe. But this is unlikely. More probably, this is a timid

53

projection of man's fear of what the truth is. Rather than a discovery of that truth, it is a poor, prejudiced guess. But the sick joke is, in a sense, a broad analogy of the fifties themselves.

The fifties have been sick. The fifties have been fearful. The fifties have been futile. To the pessimist, in his own eyes the dire realist, the fifties have been all these. To his mind, Man, in his surge forward, has managed only to recede. This is a harsh judgment of humanity. It seems wiser to say that part of human progress, or part of the human drama, is to experience not only the exultation and the joy of advance, but, also, the trepidation and terror of the unknown. Either can precipitate the other. Both can exist simultaneously. Life can proceed *sans* neither.

It is no simple game, this Life. It is far more complicated than Capture the Flag, far more dangerous than Korea, far more exciting than rock n' roll. But if any image can be drawn of the fifties, it would have to be the grotesque caricature of Mankind, thrashing wildly to get out of the wilderness, but refusing to open his eyes and find the road. Rick S.

HOME WORK ASSIGNMENT

Write a fairly long exposition (from 500 to 1,000 words) drawing your thesis from a subject in which you are very much interested and of which you have first-hand knowledge. A list of suggested subjects is found opposite.

DIRECTIONS

1. Make a list of the preliminary decisions. (See page 47.)
2. Use the following overall structure (organization):
   a) the lead (one paragraph),
   b) the thesis (one paragraph and usually only one sentence),
   c) the body of the exposition (the paragraphs that will develop your thesis),
   d) the conclusion (one short paragraph).
3. Make a detailed plan:
   a) indicate what you will use as a provocative lead,
   b) use a diagram to indicate the topics you will discuss in the body of your exposition in order to develop the thesis. Here is an example:

Para. 1	*Para. 2*	*Para. 3*	*Para. 4*
State Topic	State Topic	State Topic	State Topic

   c) Compose a suitable topic sentence for each topic developed in the body of the exposition.
   d) Indicate what you will use as an arresting conclusion.
4. Write the exposition in rough. Then revise it carefully, trying to improve it by using specific and concrete examples.

54

5. When you feel you have done your best work, copy into your note-book: the list of preliminary decisions, the topic sentences used to develop the thesis and the finished exposition. Write on every other line or, if you type your exposition, double space it.

Suggested Subjects for an Exposition

Democracy	Wild Animals	Birds
Freedom	Pets	School Traditions
Dictatorship	Hunting	Bird Enemies
An Interesting Person	Politics	Riding
Football	Advertising	A Favourite Author
Horses	Wild Flowers	Automobiles
Farming	Photography	School Sports
Fishing	Parents	Planes
Religion	Citizenship	Boats
Science	Historical Novels	Mountain Climbing
Music	Ballet	Reading
Current Affairs	Theatre	A Current Problem
Camping	Trains	Childhood
Small Boys	Conservation	

CRITERIA BY WHICH EXPOSITION MAY BE JUDGED

1. *Credit*

Merits: To be worth a pass, an exposition must have merit in structure and in content. The whole exposition must be unified, coherent and emphatic in structure; and every paragraph must be unified and coherent. The content must be fairly good: the student must know his subject and be enthusiastic about it; and he must give accurate information to the reader.

Flaws: The flaws that prevent this exposition from receiving a higher grade are:
a) *unemphatic paragraph structure;*
b) *uninteresting content*: few or no concrete examples to illustrate ideas; dull lead and conclusion;
c) *immature style*: language and sentence structure are still poor.

2. *Third-Class Honours*

Merits: To be worth third-class honours, an exposition must possess all of the above merits in structure and in content, and, in addition, the following:
a) *well-constructed paragraphs*: emphatic as well as unified and coherent;
b) *interesting content*: effective concrete examples; a lead and a conclusion that would interest the group to whom the exposition is addressed.

Flaws: This student has mastered the techniques of expository writing but has not yet learned to write a pleasing style. He shows little sensitivity to words and has little skill in sentence structure.

3. *Second-Class Honours*

Merits: This exposition has all of the merits possessed by the third-class one, and an additional merit: sensitive use of words.

55

Flaw: This student has not yet mastered the art of writing well constructed sentences.

4. First-Class Honours

The first-class exposition has merit in structure, content and style. It differs from the second-class exposition in one respect: sentence structure. This student has learned to write unified, coherent and emphatic sentences, and to vary his sentence structure in order to prevent monotony.

EXPOSITION: 1

LESSON FIVE

CHOOSING THE BEST EXPOSITIONS WRITTEN BY STUDENTS

Evaluating exposition written by your classmates will develop your critical faculties so that you will be able to criticize intelligently your own writing. Hearing the best expositions read aloud will remind you of the methods that can be used to interest readers.

PROCEDURE

Divide into groups of three, each group choosing a chairman and a recorder.

The duties of the chairman are:
1. to read his own essay aloud, and to call on the other two members of his group to read theirs;
2. to direct the discussion in which the group will choose the best essay.

The duties of the recorder are:
1. to make a brief memorandum of the comments made on each essay;
2. to attach this information to the essay;
3. to hand essays with attached memoranda to the teacher;
4. to give the teacher the name of the student whose essay was judged best.

This group discussion accomplishes two important purposes:
1. it gives every student a clear idea of how successful he has been in interesting a group of intelligent and critical readers;
2. it affords the group itself valuable practice in critical analysis.

When each group has chosen its best exposition, the authors may be asked to read theirs aloud to the class. If the teacher appoints a chairman to call upon these students and to handle any discussion that may arise, the person chosen will gain experience in an important skill, chairing a meeting.

At the conclusion of the reading, this question might be discussed: *What qualities make these expository articles interesting to the reader?*

IMPROVING STYLE: II

EMPHATIC SENTENCES: I

Joseph Pulitzer, the distinguished editor of The *New York World*, was so convinced of the importance of style that he read critically every editorial that appeared in his paper and sent his penetrating and often biting comments to the editorial assistant responsible for it. As a result, many young men trained by him became outstanding journalists. His genuine concern for the written word was reflected in his will, which established a fund to award annual prizes for outstanding literary accomplishment by United States writers.

The student who has mastered the techniques of writing unified and coherent sentences has gone a long way towards improving his style. However, since the ability to write forcefully enables a person to hold the attention of his reader or his listener and to drive home salient ideas, skill in writing emphatic sentences is also important. The closing sentence of Lincoln's Gettysburg Address—"And we are here resolved that government of the people, by the people and for the people . . ."—is far more emphatic (and more memorable) than: *And we are here resolved that government of the people, by them and for them* shall not perish from the earth.

Rhetorical device is the name given to each of a number of techniques used to make writing and speaking effective. In these lessons on improving style, the term is confined to techniques used to make sentences emphatic.

All good writers, to arrest the attention of their readers and to stress important ideas, use the eight rhetorical devices that are discussed in the following pages.

1. position	3. repetition	5. parallelism	7. antithesis
2. climax	4. periodicity	6. balance	8. chiasmus

Mastery of these rhetorical devices will improve your style considerably. If you write a sentence that seems weak, you will know how to turn it into a compact and forceful one. If you wish to emphasize a particular idea, you will know how to use sentence structure to achieve your desired effect.

1. POSITION

Position is the name given to the rhetorical device of placing an important idea where it will catch the attention of the reader or the listener. Use the following suggestions for emphasizing by means of position.

1. Psychological tests show that people tend to remember longest what they hear first and what they hear last. You may capitalize on this psychological fact by placing one important idea at the beginning of the sentence and another at the end. Winston Churchill used this device memorably when paying tribute to the young airmen who fought in the Battle of Britain.

> "*Never* in the field of human conflict was so much owed by so many to so *few*". (By placing his most important words in the two best places—first and last—he emphasized the magnitude of the contribution made by a handful of men. An alternative way of saying this is not nearly so emphatic: *In the field of human conflict so much was never owed to so few by so many.* The key positions here have not been used for the most important words.)

2. Placing some part of a sentence out of its expected place will attract attention to this part. Note the two examples that follow.

a) The city, full of noise, *strident and discordant,* grated on John's nerves. (Here the use of position—placing the two adjectives out of their natural position—has stressed the qualities that made John dislike the city.)

b) After the equinoctial gale had somewhat subsided, *the rescuers launched their boats.* (Placing the main clause last stresses the thought it contains.)

EXERCISE I: ORAL

Recognizing the Device of Position

In each of the following sentences, the device of position has been used to emphasize some idea.

a) Read aloud the part of the sentence that has been stressed by the use of position.

b) Explain clearly what idea each author has emphasized by position.

1. God brings men into deep waters, not to drown them, but to cleanse them. Aughey

2. If you wish to be a writer, write. Epictetus

3. To Egypt she [Cleopatra] was a wise and capable ruler, and in Egypt for long her memory was cherished. John Buchan, *Augustus*

4. The enduring bequest of the East was to spring half a century later, not from the effete successors of the old monarchies, but from the bare Palestinian Hills. John Buchan, *Augustus*

5. Of all metals, gold is the most negotiable.

EXERCISE II: WRITTEN

Making Sentences Emphatic

Each of the following excerpts is a rearranged version of a passage

58

taken from the work of a professional writer. In the original, position was used to secure emphasis of one or more ideas.

In each of these rearranged texts:

a) *decide* what idea or ideas you think should be stressed;

b) using the rhetorical device of position to emphasize it or them, *rewrite* each sentence;

c) *underline* the idea or ideas you have emphasized by this device.

1. The green, gladed, unbroken, beautiful forest lay between. (Re-arranged from Hervey Allen, *The Forest and The Fort*)

2. The bayou, circling, coiling, curving, curling, moves without a ripple through wildernesses of fantastic beauty. (Re-arranged from Lafcadio Hearn, "The Garden of Paradise")

3. The agencies that dehumanize man are: propaganda which endeavours to make men think alike or not to think at all; political movements whose form and method suppress the need for decision; philosophies which demand unquestioning acceptance of a body of "truth" . . . Those who are aware of the nature of humanity are ranged against all these influences. Freedom is all essential to them. (Rearranged from an editorial, "Dehumanizing Humanity", The *Globe and Mail*)

EXERCISE III: WRITTEN

Using One Emphatic Sentence

The use of even one emphatic sentence will add force to the paragraph as a whole.

Each of the following excerpts from the work of professional writers is a rearranged version of a passage that was forceful in style. Find *one* sentence that might be more emphatic in structure. Then, using the rhetorical device of position, rewrite the sentence so that its structure stresses an important idea. Underline, in your version, the idea you have emphasized by means of position.

1. Born in the East and clothed in Oriental form and imagery, the Bible walks the ways of all the world with familiar feet and enters land after land to find its own everywhere. . . . Its great words come to us uncalled above the cradle and beside the grave. Henry Van Dyke, *Companionable Books*

2. Browning nowhere shows his native strength more clearly than in his treatment of love. . . . It may even be admitted that there are poets whose verses have echoed more faithfully the fervour and intoxication of passion and who have shown greater power in interpreting it in the light of a mystic idealism. But Browning stands alone in one thing. Henry Jones, *Browning as a Philosophical and Religious Teacher*

3. To love, he repeatedly tells us, is the sole and supreme object of man's life; it is the one lesson which he has to learn on earth; and love once learnt, in what way matters little, "it leaves completion in the soul". We dare not miss love. Henry Jones, *Browning as a Philosophical and Religious Teacher*

2. CLIMAX

Arranging words, phrases or clauses in ascending order of importance or emotional force will make a sentence climactic.

Example:

A word from his lips might influence their passions, might change their opinion, might affect their destiny. (Notice that each imagined result is more important than the previous one.)

ORAL EXERCISE
Climactic Sentences

By using the rhetorical device of climax, change each sentence into an emphatic one. Explain, in each case, why you have arranged the ideas in this particular order.

1. Susan's reply enraged her husband, angered her mother and annoyed her brother.
2. The congregation respected Mr. Hunter for his scholarship, revered him for his saintliness and liked him for his friendly manner.
3. Macbeth seemed untouched by the agonies, the lamentations, the tears of his suffering kingdom.
4. Shakespeare was deeply interested in the potentialities of man: his glory, his power, his greatness.
5. Hanson reflected bitterly on the events of the past two months: nothing but hollow friendship, violated faith, ungenerous enmity.
6. Hamlet realized that his uncle was a murderer, that his mother was a victim of her own sensuality and that Polonius was a pompous fool.

3. REPETITION

Although unintentional repetition is to be avoided, an effective way to secure emphasis is to repeat a word or a phrase or a clause that you wish your reader or your listener to remember.

Example:

Men are born into the State, are members of the State, must obey the laws enacted by the State, in time of danger must come to the defence of the State, must, if necessary, hazard their lives for the State. Lyman Abbott

WRITTEN EXERCISE

Compose three sentences in each of which you deliberately repeat a word or a phrase or a clause to emphasize an important idea.

Suggested Subjects

The International Situation
Good Basketball Players
Good Hockey Players
A Poor School Band
A Poor Chairman

EMPHATIC SENTENCES: II

Sentences may be classified in three ways: according to their structure, as simple, compound, complex and compound-complex; according to their function, as declarative, imperative, interrogatory and exclamatory; according to their rhetorical effect as periodic or loose.

4. PERIODICITY

The rhetorical device of periodicity (a special use of position) is the placing of the bare subject or the bare predicate (verb) or the bare object or the bare complement at the end of the sentence. The effects achieved by periodicity are suspense, and emphasis on the main statement.

THE PERIODIC SENTENCE

A periodic sentence withholds its complete meaning until the last word.

Examples of Periodic Sentences:

1. Over the sleeping city thundered six jet *planes.*
2. When Claudius and the Queen had arrived, and Hamlet and Laertes had both chosen their foils, the exhibition duel *began.*
3. After Brutus had convinced the mob that he had killed Caesar for the good of Rome, and that he had the same dagger for himself if Rome would benefit from his death, he quietly left the *Forum.*
4. Macbeth, when he learned that Fleance had escaped and that Macduff had fled to England, was *distraught.*

THE LOOSE SENTENCE

A loose sentence is one in which a complete statement is made before the last word is reached.

Examples of Loose Sentences*:

1. A boy paddled his canoe / down the river / flowing past his home.
2. The chairman called the meeting to order, / and then the debaters entered the hall.
3. The lawyer continued his argument / in a quiet and dignified manner, / which surprised the jury.

THE PARTLY PERIODIC SENTENCE

A sentence may also be partly periodic. A partly periodic sentence is a compound or compound-complex sentence in which one part is periodic and the other part loose. The effect gained is the

---

*In the examples a light line (/) indicates where the sentence might terminate and still make sense.

emphasis of the main statement in the part of the sentence that is constructed in periodic form.

Example of a Partly Periodic Sentence:

After greeting the Queen and Claudius and choosing one of the foils from the table, Hamlet paused; then he bowed to the waiting Laertes and apologized for "the madness that is poor Hamlet's enemy". (This sentence is periodic in form as far as the semi-colon—periodicity having been used to stress the drama of Hamlet's pausing; the second part of the compound sentence is loose. This construction seems an appropriate one to describe Hamlet's two *equally* gracious actions, *bowing* and *apologizing*: the loose structure gives equal importance to both actions.)

In the seventeenth and eighteenth centuries, the periodic sentence was used more frequently than it is to-day. Edward Gibbon, author of *The History of the Decline and Fall of the Roman Empire* (1776-88), and Thomas Carlyle, whose works include *The French Revolution* (1837), achieved memorable climactic effects with their many periodic sentences. To-day, good writers seem to prefer to use many loose sentences and the occasional periodic sentence. The loose construction gives ease and flow to their style; the periodic provides emphasis.

CLASS DISCUSSION

In the following two paragraphs taken from F. S. Smythe's *British Mountaineers,* you will find nine loose sentences and one periodic. For what purpose has he used the periodic sentence?

Mountaineering

From the earliest times mountains have been regarded as mysterious and aloof from the ordinary affairs of plain and city. Our ancestors looked upon them with awe and fear. Gods, devils, dragons, the spirits of the damned dwelt on their inaccessible summits ready to wreak vengeance on the rash intruder. They refused the plough, interposed barriers between peoples; they were of no commercial value; they were ugly.

Yet as man slowly and painfully freed himself from his primeval fears and superstitions, a spirit of enquiry gained ascendency. What was to be found on these lonely summits where lightning played and the blizzard had its lair? Fearfully a few bold spirits began to cross mountain ranges and climb mountains, at first for the sake of commercial enterprise or for military reasons. The Alpine passes, for instance, were opened up for both purposes, from the time when Hannibal drove his elephants across them to the time when immense tunnels were driven to link Italy with France and Switzerland. Slowly men lost their repugnance for mountains, and began to realise that to view them and adventure upon them was an inspiring experience. In that moment was born the spirit of mountaineering as a sport. F. S. Smythe, *British Mountaineers*

EXERCISE I: ORAL

Identifying Periodic and Loose Sentences

From each sentence, read aloud the bare subject, the bare predicate, the bare object or the bare complement (if the sentence contains one); and then use the definitions given on pages 61 and 62 to determine which sentences are periodic, loose or partly periodic.

1. Work is the law. Like iron that lying idle about degenerates into a mass of useless rust, like water that in an unruffled pool sickens into a stagnant and corrupt state, so without action the spirit of man . . . loses its force. . . . Joseph Conrad, *The British Merchant Service*
2. Nevertheless adventures have their uses in social progress. William Bolitho, *Twelve Against the Gods*
3. Crouching so he was almost sitting back on his skis, trying to keep the centre of gravity low, the snow driving like a sand-storm, he knew the pace was too much. Ernest Hemingway, "Cross Country Snow"
4. In 1929, in the great slump, disaster fell. H. E. Bates, "Trees and Men"

EXERCISE II: WRITTEN

Turning Loose Sentences into Periodic Sentences

This exercise will afford you practice in changing loose sentences into periodic so that, when you wish, you can deliberately use a periodic sentence to break the monotony of a series of loose sentences, or to emphasize some idea that you wish to impress on your reader.

a) Turn each of the following loose sentences into a periodic sentence by rearranging its parts so that the bare subject, the bare verb, the bare object or the bare complement of the main clause comes last.

b) When you have written your periodic sentence, underline the last word in it.

1. Many people are bored if they have to wait half an hour for a bus.
2. The movies widen man's knowledge by enabling him to see what the world is like.
3. Insects eat our food before it is ripe.
4. From all parts of the United States and Canada, people interested in the theatre visit the Stratford Shakespearean Festival every year.
5. He accomplished the feat alone.
6. Exultant and deafening cheers arose from the stadium.
7. We saw the whole fishing fleet moored in the harbour when we came down the hill into Lunenburg.
8. At the first audience given by the new king of Denmark, Hamlet was a conspicuous figure, clad in black from head to foot and standing apart from the gaiety of the court.
9. American and Canadian newspapers will send their best reporters to Chicago when the Democrats or the Republicans hold a convention there to nominate a candidate for the presidency of the U.S.A.

The Use of One Periodic Sentence in a Paragraph

In the original text of each of the following passages, the writer used one periodic sentence to emphasize an important idea. In each of these versions, all sentences are loose.

a) In each paragraph, decide what idea you wish to emphasize.

b) Secure emphasis for this idea by changing to periodic form one sentence in each paragraph.

1. The ballot is the agent by which we participate in democracy and set our country's destiny, and it is given to all. The vote of the poor man weighs as much in a democracy as the vote of the rich, and the vote of the fool is in no way inferior to the vote of the scholar. . . We must be obeyed when we speak, whether we are right or wrong. Frank Tumpane (Rearranged from an article in The *Globe and Mail*)

2. The sombre stretch of rounds and hollows seemed to rise and meet the evening gloom in pure sympathy, the heath exhaling darkness as rapidly as the heavens precipitated it. And so the obscurity in the air and the obscurity in the land closed together in a black fraternization towards which each advanced halfway. The place became full of a watchful intentness now; for the heath appeared slowly to awake and listen when other things sank brooding to sleep. Thomas Hardy (Rearranged from *The Return of the Native*)

3. There are faces everywhere, thousands of faces, vivid, sometimes startling, in this dramatic top-lighting. Voices can be heard even above the screeching and hammering and rasping of metal on metal. Thoughts are busy, dreams glow and fade behind the eyes that stare at the lathes and presses, at tiny gears and tangles of insulated wire, at great curved flanks of aircraft. J. B. Priestley (Rearranged from *Daylight on Saturday*)

EXERCISE IV: WRITTEN

The Use of Two Periodic Sentences in a Paragraph

In the following paragraph, find the two periodic sentences. What ideas has Dr. Kittredge emphasized by means of periodicity?

The Canterbury Tales

Chaucer's own birth and station, as I reminded you in my opening lecture, had brought him into easy contact with both high and low; and his experiences as burgher, soldier, courtier, office holder, and diplomatic agent had given him unparalleled opportunities for observation, which his humorously sympathetic temperament had impelled him to use to the best advantage. Mankind was his specialty. He was now a trained and practised writer, with a profound sense of the joy and beauty, the sadness and irony, of human life. . . . Now, at length, in this Canterbury Pilgrimage, with its nine-and-twenty contemporary human creatures, he has recognized his crowning opportunity. G. L. Kittredge, *Chaucer and His Poetry*

IMPROVING STYLE: II

EMPHATIC SENTENCES: III

Intelligent and imaginative use of the rhetorical devices called parallelism, balance, antithesis and chiasmus will improve both the clarity and the force of your sentences.

5. PARALLELISM

Parallelism in a sentence is the placing in similar grammatical form of the several parts of a compound construction. Two consecutive sentences similarly constructed and closely allied in meaning are also parallel in structure. Here is an example of Robert Louis Stevenson's use of parallelism:

Youth is the time to go flashing from one end of the world to the other in body and in mind; to try the manners of different nations; to hear the chimes at midnight.

To stress the folly of Europe, Winston Churchill used two consecutive sentences that were parallel in structure:

But there was no unity. There was no vision.

CLASS DISCUSSION I
The Use of Parallelism
In each of the following sentences:
a) find *compound constructions* in parallel constructions;
b) state the function of each of these parallel constructions;
c) explain what idea the author has emphasized by the use of parallelism.

1. . . . a wise and frugal government, which shall restrain men from injuring one another, which shall leave them otherwise free to regulate their own pursuits of industry and improvement, and shall not take from the mouth of labour the bread it has earned—this is the sum of good government. Thomas Jefferson

2. We must hope that the campaign will be brief, that oil may be found, and that bitterness will eventually be obscured by social change. The *Manchester Guardian Weekly,* August 8, 1957

6. BALANCE

Balance is another device that may be used to emphasize an idea. When a writer repeats in a sentence or in consecutive sentences an *arrangement* of words, he is using the device of balance. *Examples:*

1. *The fickleness of the women I love* is only equalled by *the infernal constancy of the women who love me.* George Bernard Shaw, *The*

Philanderer (Shaw has used balance for humorous effect: to stress the conceit of the philanderer.)

2. To pity distress is human; to relieve it is godlike. Horace Mann (This compound sentence, with the conjunction *but* understood, is perfectly balanced: the subject of each clause is an infinitive phrase; the verb in each clause is the same; and the subjective completion in each is one predicate adjective. Balance is used to stress the importance of translating an admirable sentiment into action.)

7. ANTITHESIS

If the balanced parts of a sentence contain ideas that are in *contrast*, the device is called *antithesis*.

Example:

Prosperity pampers the mind; privation trains and strengthens it. William Hazlitt (Antithesis has been used to emphasize a disadvantage of prosperity and an advantage of privation.)

8. CHIASMUS

Chiasmus is a cross arrangement in two successive groups of words. The order in the second group of words is an inversion of that followed in the first.

Example: He saved *others; himself* he cannot save. Matthew, xxvii, 42

CLASS DISCUSSION II

Balance, Antithesis, Chiasmus

a) Read aloud the parts of each sentence in which balance, antithesis or chiasmus has been used.

b) What idea has the author stressed by means of the device he has used?

1. The unhappy truth is that everyone wants to stop tests of hydrogen bombs which he has just finished, while no one wants to stop tests which he is about to embark upon. The *Manchester Guardian Weekly*

2. A witty woman is a treasure; a witty beauty is a power. George Meredith, *Diana of the Crossways*

3. Peter loved mountain-climbing; horse-back riding he detested.

CLASS DISCUSSION III

Parallelism and Balance

In some of the following sentences, the writer has used parallelism, in some balance, and in some both parallelism and balance.

a) From each sentence read aloud the parts in which these devices have been used, and identify the device or devices.

b) In each sentence, what idea has been stressed by means of the rhetorical device or devices?

1. They [the coolies] had been ranged closely, after having been shaken into submission, cuffed a little to allay excitement, addressed in gruff words of encouragement that sounded like promises of evil. Joseph Conrad, *Typhoon*

2. He had to compel himself to release her hand, to take his eyes away from her face, and to speak, to her and Mrs. Muriven indifferently, the polite openings of conversation. Charles Morgan, *The River Line*

3. To me it is a happy memory that although we differed, sometimes sharply, on most questions of public policy, our personal relations were never disturbed, and that from first to last, although I was obliged to own him as a political foe, I was proud to hold him as a personal friend . . . Sir Robert Borden, address delivered at the unveiling of the monument to Sir Wilfrid Laurier, at Ottawa, August 3, 1927

4. Stream-lining is only one of several problems connected with attaining greater speeds on the road and on the rails. For example, higher speeds are not much use if the train is liable to leave its rails, or if it must slow down at curves. . . . Professor A. M. Low, *Recent Inventions*

5. A race of free men would be converted into a race of state-aided beggars. Robert Lynd, "I Tremble to Think"

6. Upon Sir Wilfrid Laurier's magnetic personality, his wonderful gift of intellect, imagination, and compelling eloquence I need not dwell; nor upon the splendid distinction and achievement of his great career. Rather would I speak of his great personal charm . . . Sir Robert Borden, address delivered at the unveiling of the monument to Sir Wilfrid Laurier, at Ottawa, August 3, 1927

HOME WORK ASSIGNMENT

1. Describe one (or more) of the following experiences in three sentences that are emphatic because you have used the rhetorical device of position: an exciting moment while skating or while playing football or hockey; an impressive moment at the symphony concert, ballet or theatre; an exciting moment at a corn roast or on a camping trip.

2. Compose three climactic sentences, each on a different topic. Use one of these sentences to picture the cumulative effect of some mighty natural force; another, to impress upon your reader the corrosive effect of selfishness; the third, to stress the destructive effect of Macbeth's vaulting ambition or of Hamlet's procrastination.

3. Compose a sentence in which you use parallelism to stress some important ideas about one of the following: a good basket-ball player, a good novel, a good ballet dancer, a good car, a good boat.

4. Compose three sentences in each of which you use the rhetorical device of balance. Use each one to emphasize some idea that interests you. In one of them, try for a clear-cut contrast (antithesis). If you cannot think of a contrast, here are some suggestions:

love—hate	men—women	sail boat—motor boat
war—peace	school—holidays	American automobiles—
		English automobiles

5. Compose two sentences in each of which you use the rhetorical device of chiasmus to stress some contrast.

EXPOSITION: II

PLANNING AND WRITING EXPOSITION
(WITH THESIS DEVELOPED BY NARRATIVE)

Sometimes a writer illustrates his thesis or part of his exposition by means of a narrative.

Your next home work assignment (page 72) will be to write an essay in which you narrate an incident that will illustrate the thesis.

CLASS DISCUSSION
Analyzing Students' Expositions

Below you will find two essays, in both of which the students have used the narrative approach to exposition. Use the questions that follow each essay to discuss its purpose, content and structure.

1. The Modern Barber Shop

The era of the haircutting barber shop has passed into history. In the old days one entered a barber shop for the sole purpose of getting a haircut; no more was expected of him. To-day if one escapes the chair with a mere haircut and with full possession of all his mental faculties, he is indeed fortunate.

The preliminaries are much the same as before. You enter, remove hat and coat and sit down to await your turn. There is still a great pile of magazines and comic books to choose from. There all similarity ends. Once the barber has you safely in his chair your trouble begins.

"Brush cut, sir?" he asks.

"No thank you; just a trim."

As you lean back in the chair to indulge in a bit of delightful daydreaming, some sweet young thing in a spotless white uniform and long, fluttering eyelashes asks in a sultry voice:

"Manicure, sir?"

You would not mind having her hold your hand for fifteen minutes, but after all you are not a millionaire, so you answer:

"No thanks; just a trim."

Just as you pick up your daydream where you left off, another voice asks:

"Shoe-shine, sir?"

You open one eye wide enough to glare at the young lad with the shoe-polish. You sigh slightly and repeat:

"No thanks; just a trim."

Again when you reach the point in your daydream where you are about

68

to approach that new girl that moved into the district and ask her for a date, the barber breaks in with:

"Massage, sir?"

With a gruff edge to your voice, you reply:

"No thanks; just a haircut."

The whirr of the clippers is a soothing sound, and you forget all your worries and cares. You are drifting on a pink cloud and basking in the warm sunlight.

"Shave, sir?"

You awake with a start, and grasping both arms of the chair to prevent yourself from indulging in physical violence, you look the barber in the eye and shout:

"No!"

The barber, of course, assumes the most hurt expression imaginable and continues with your hair. Before you realize what is happpening, however, he has the back of your neck covered with hot soap. To-day's barbers are endowed with a mania for shaving. If you do not want to pay to have your face shaved, they will scrape the back of your neck for nothing. Out of the corner of your eye you can see the ominous tip of the straight razor as it descends upon your neck in a long arc. With a shudder you close your eyes and wait for your life-blood to flow. Somehow he manages to miss severing any major arteries, and another ordeal has been passed.

Finally it is all over; and as you lean back waiting for the barber to remove the cloth, a bottle of hair-oil suddenly appears in his hand.

"I see you have a little dandruff. May I suggest a bottle of . . ."

There is something in your expression that makes him replace the bottle and crank the chair down. Maybe it was your bulging eyeballs or the frothing at the mouth.

You search in your pocket for the dollar you have saved to be able to undergo this luxury; and as you give it to the barber, his left hand steals behind the cash register and emerges clutching a book of lucky draw tickets, a hopeful gleam in his eye.

Flesh and blood can stand only so much, and as you run out into the street with a cry, his voice calls after you:

"How are you set for razor blades?"

Yes, even the lowly barber shop has become big business. No longer is one able to be completely refreshed and revived for a nominal fee. One no longer hears even the latest gossip in a barber shop. Barbers are too busy figuring ways to extract the money from the customer to bother talking about current events. Now he must hoard all his loose change to afford a haircut and also build up his nervous system so that he will not suffer a complete mental breakdown after one visit. (Essay written by student for Ontario Departmental Examination in English Composition, 1952)

1. a) What is the thesis of this essay, and where is it stated?
   b) What method has the student used in his lead to arouse the reader's interest in the subject?
2. Does the incident narrated illustrate the student's thesis? Give reasons for your opinion.
3. What methods has the student used in the last paragraph to impress on his reader the thesis of the essay?
4. a) What overall structure has the student used?
   b) Suggest another overall structure he might have used.
5. By what means does he make the incident realistic?
6. For each of the following excerpts taken from the essay, tell: (a) *what* effect the student wished to gain; and (b) *how* he gained this effect:
   a) . . . some sweet young thing in a spotless white uniform and long, fluttering eyelashes asks in a sultry voice:
   b) With a gruff edge to your voice, you reply:
   c) The whirr of the clippers is a soothing sound, and you forget all your worries and cares.
   d) You are drifting on a pink cloud and basking in the warm sunlight.
   e) Out of the corner of your eye you can see the ominous tip of the straight razor as it descends upon your neck in a long arc.
   f) With a shudder you close your eyes and wait for your life-blood to flow.
7. If you find weaknesses in this essay, point them out and suggest how they might be eliminated.

2. Training A Horse

In the middle of a circular track about forty feet in diameter, flattened with a brush jump on one straight-away and an ordinary high jump on the other straight-away, stands a little, grizzled, grey-haired man. In one hand he is holding a long lunging-line, on the other end of which is a big, black mare; and in the other hand and held to his side is a long, black buggy-whip. The mare is midnight black with delicate white stockings, high hind-quarters, long, straight back and a narrow neck, on which is proudly perched a chiselled head. The man has been working her very hard, for she is covered in a heavy, white foam; and her nostrils are dilated several times their normal size.

He approaches her quietly, talking all the time, gives her a pat and sends her into motion: first a quick trot that would make the heart of any horselover jump as she keeps her head high, perks her ears forward and puts down her feet in a piston-like motion; then into a smooth-rocking canter as she takes the brush jump. Her ears perk up even more as she notices the towering six-foot bar. Her eyes focus on it as she gathers more and more speed, pushing off her powerful hindquarters. Suddenly, yet smoothly, she gathers herself and sails over the bar like a *petite* ballerina, fore and hind legs tucked in, head and neck slightly extended; and she lands without a sound.

This performance is repeated two or three times. Then there is a decided change: she becomes sloppy when taking the brush and seems not to have the same exuberance. This time she hits the bar. What happened? She is too sloppy, too self-assured. The grizzled old master pulls her in, but meanwhile an assistant has replaced the light wooden bar with a heavy steel tube. She is sent on her way once more with no apparent change. One stride from take-off—crack goes the whip on her rump. THUD—she piles into the tube and comes down heavily on her knees, then slowly struggles to her feet. Without a rest she is sent on her way with another sharp crack.

An inexperienced observer thinks this treatment is cruel and may even query, "Doesn't that hurt her?" He is answered on the next jump as she sails cleanly and gracefully over the bar. David S.

Discussion Questions

1. The purpose of this essay is expository, but the method used to achieve this purpose is narrative. What is the specific purpose of the essay?
2. For what purpose has the student used each of his four paragraphs?
3. How does he make the trainer and the horse interesting to the reader?
4. For each of the following excerpts from the essay, tell: (a) *what* effect the student wished to gain; and (b) *how* he gained this effect:
   a) . . . stands a little, grizzled, grey-haired man.
   b) The mare is midnight black with delicate white stockings, high hindquarters, long, straight back and a narrow neck, on which is proudly perched a chiselled head.
   c) Suddenly, yet smoothly, she gathers herself and sails over the bar like a *petite* ballerina, fore and hind legs tucked in, head and neck slightly extended; and she lands without a sound.
   d) The grizzled old master . . .
   e) One stride from take-off—crack goes the whip on her rump. THUD—she piles into the tube and comes down heavily on her knees . . .
   f) He is answered on the next jump as she sails cleanly and gracefully over the bar.
5. If you think the essay could be improved, suggest how.

71

HOME WORK ASSIGNMENT

Using one of the following theses or one of your own choice (see suggested subjects below), write an essay in which you narrate as effectively as you can a real or an imaginary incident that will illustrate the thesis you have selected.

Theses

1. Sailing can be dangerous.
2. A canoe trip often provides strange (interesting, frightening) experiences.
3. Fishing can be be very exciting.
4. Collecting (stamps, records or coins) sometimes leads a person into unexpected situations.
5. My grandfather is an interesting (clever, original) man.
6. Grandmothers are understanding people.
7. The man working in a service station (the bus driver or the policeman or the family doctor) sees human nature at its worst.

DIRECTIONS

1. Compose your thesis as clearly and as effectively as you can.
2. Choose an incident that will be a good illustration of your thesis.
3. Decide how you can end your essay effectively.
4. Select a definite place and time for the incident you narrate, and try to make your readers visualize the place, the time of year, the time of day, the kind of day.
5. Give your readers a clear visual image of each character when you introduce him. This is one technique with which to gain an impression of reality.
6. Frequently, *throughout* the story, include a detail that will force your readers to visualize some aspect of the setting and to visualize the people. This is a second technique of securing a realistic effect.
7. Try to reveal to your readers the dominant character trait or traits of the people involved. This is a third technique with which to gain an impression of reality.
8. Try to make the dialogue—if you use it—sound natural. This is a fourth technique you may use to create an impression of reality.
9. Punctuate correctly. (Pay particular attention to the punctuation of the dialogue.)

Suggested Subjects

Art	Farming	Photography
Birds	Fishing	Plays
Camping	Football	Radio
Canoeing	History	Sailing
Cars	Horses	Science
Cats	Movies	Swimming
Dogs	Music	Television
Examinations	Novels	Travelling

IMPROVING STYLE: III

RHYTHMICAL SENTENCES

A regular rise and fall of accented and unaccented syllables, so regular that it can be measured, is one of the distinguishing features of certain kinds of poetry. Good prose also has rhythm, although generally not so strongly marked as that found in poetry. Lincoln's "Gettysburg Address", for instance, is memorable prose, not only because it voices in a simple and moving way the noble sentiments of a dedicated man, but also because it expresses them rhythmically.

After you have written a piece of prose, read your work aloud and listen to its *sound*. If you do so, you will perhaps become aware that you have written an occasional sentence that sounds abrupt or jerky. By adding a word, a phrase or a clause, or by rearranging or reconstructing the sentence, you can produce one that is rhythmical.

In addition to depending on your ear to help you write rhythmical prose, try consciously to use these three rhetorical devices:

1. parallelism;
2. a group of three words, phrases or clauses;
3. cadence.

PARALLELISM

Parallelism, which you have already studied, adds not only clarity and force to a sentence, but also rhythm. If the parallel parts of the sentence are, in addition, balanced, the rhythmic effect is intensified.

Examples:

1. *Not Rhythmical*

In the dramatic monologue "My Last Duchess", Browning portrayed an Italian duke of the Renaissance, a man who admired the beautiful; and his collection of exquisite works of art delighted him.

Rhythmical

In the dramatic monologue "My Last Duchess", Browning portrayed an Italian duke of the Renaissance, a man who admired the beautiful, and who collected, for his own pleasure, exquisite works of art. (Each characteristic of the duke is discussed in a similar construction, an adjectival clause modifying the *same* noun, *man*. This parallel structure makes the sentence rhythmical.)

73

2. Not Rhythmical

To err is human; but the man who forgives possesses one of the attributes of God.

Rhythmical

To err is human; to forgive divine. Alexander Pope (By using a balanced structure, Pope has written a sentence that has a marked rhythm.)

GROUP OF THREE PHRASES OR THREE CLAUSES

A group of three phrases or three clauses imparts rhythm to a sentence. If the third phrase or clause is somewhat longer than either preceding one, the rhythm is particularly satisfying.

The following sentences are rhythmical because they contain clauses in parallel structure; but the second sentence is more rhythmical than the first because of its *three* parallel constructions.

Examples:

Fairly Rhythmical

Mark Antony exultantly congratulated himself: here was a Roman mob ashamed of its own ingratitude and enraged by the incredible treachery of Brutus. (The parallel structure of the two adjectival phrases makes the sentence rhythmical.)

More Rhythmical

Mark Antony exultantly congratulated himself: here was a Roman mob ashamed of its own ingratitude, enraged by the incredible treachery of Brutus and inflamed by the sight of Caesar's bleeding and mutilated body. (The addition of the third phrase makes this sentence even more rhythmical than the preceding one.)

Fairly Rhythmical

Hamlet brooded over the fact that his father had been murdered and that his uncle had cleverly fooled the Danish people.

More Rhythmical

Hamlet brooded over the fact that his father had been murdered, that his uncle had cleverly fooled the Danish people, and that his mother had married so hastily that the entire court was deeply shocked. (The use of three noun clauses, the last clause longer than either of the preceding ones, gives to the sentence a particularly satisfying rhythm.)

CADENCE

A cadenced sentence may be likened to the flight of a bird that rises from the ground high into the sky, maintains a level flight for a time, and then glides smoothly down to earth. When a sentence is so constructed that it contains a rise in thought to a climax, then a level flight, and concludes with a gentle fall, we say that it is cadenced. The quiet fall at the end is called a cadence. The last clause in the "Gettysburg Address" is beautifully cadenced: ". . .

and that government of the people, by the people, for the people (the rise to a climax) shall not perish (the level flight) from the earth (the cadence)." The final line in Wordsworth's sonnet "On Westminster Bridge" contains an impressive cadence: "And all that mighty heart (the rise) is lying (the level flight) still (the cadence)."

CLASS DISCUSSION

Below is reproduced "The Gettysburg Address". Read it aloud and listen for its rhythm. Then find sentences that you consider particularly rhythmical and explain how Lincoln achieved this effect.

The Gettysburg Address

Fourscore and seven years ago our fathers brought forth on this continent a new nation, conceived in liberty, and dedicated to the proposition that all men are created equal.

Now we are engaged in a great civil war, testing whether that nation, or any nation so conceived and so dedicated, can long endure. We are met on a great battlefield of that war. We have come to dedicate a portion of that field as a final resting-place for those who here gave their lives that that nation might live. It is altogether fitting and proper that we should do this.

But in a larger sense, we cannot dedicate—we cannot consecrate—we cannot hallow this ground. The brave men, living and dead, who struggled here, have consecrated it far above our poor power to add or detract. The world will little note nor long remember what we say here, but it can never forget what they did here. It is for us, the living, rather to be dedicated here to the unfinished work which they who fought here have thus far so nobly advanced. It is rather for us to be here dedicated to the great task remaining before us—that from these honoured dead we take increased devotion to that cause for which they gave the last full measure of devotion; that we here highly resolve that these dead shall not have died in vain; that this nation, under God, shall have a new birth of freedom; and that government of the people, by the people, for the people, shall not perish from the earth.

IMPROVING STYLE: III

VARIETY IN SENTENCE STRUCTURE

In order to improve your style, use the techniques you have studied to vary the pattern of your sentences. Every paragraph you write should have a pleasing variety in sentence structure. Most inexperienced writers use too many sentences of one kind and of approximately the same length. Some students use long, rambling, compound sentences. Others use only short, simple sentences, each one beginning with the subject. Such sentence structure will not attract a reader's interest to what you are saying.

Make a practice of reading critically every essay you write and improve it by varying the sentence structure.

Below you will find seven rules to help you in this revision:

1. Vary the length of your sentences. Keeping in mind the specific effects you wish to achieve, make some sentences quite long, some only fairly long and some quite short.

2. Vary the type of sentences you use. Do not *over-use* any one kind, as for example, the compound sentence or the short, simple sentence.

3. If a sentence seems to be unduly long for your purpose, either turn it into a periodic or partly periodic sentence, or use parallel structure to give it coherence and emphasis.

4. Use the rhetorical device of position to improve the emphasis of your sentences. (It is surprising how many sentences can be improved by using this one device.)

5. Use climax, repetition and balance to give point to key ideas.

6. A balanced sentence, a climactic sentence or one in which repetition, antithesis or chiasmus is well used will often make an emphatic conclusion for a paragraph.

7. To impart rhythm to your sentences, use parallelism; words, phrases or clauses in groups of three; and cadence.

CLASS DISCUSSION

Variety in Sentence Structure

Below are three paragraphs, concerned with very dissimilar topics and having a range in date of composition of almost one hundred years. In each paragraph, however, the author has used the loose sentence to give his style an easy flow, the periodic sentence and the balanced sentence to emphasize important ideas.

Use the following questions as a guide in discussing the sentence structure of these paragraphs.

a) What is the central thought in each paragraph?
b) How many loose and how many periodic sentences has each author used?
c) What idea has been stressed by the periodic sentence?
d) Which sentences contain parallel structure? What ideas are stressed by the parallelism?
e) Which sentences are balanced? Prove, and state the effects achieved.

1. The Celt

As the individual Celt was easily turned into a soldier, so a tribe of Celts was easily turned into a battalion of soldiers. All that was necessary was that the military organisation should be conformed to the patriarchal organisation, with the Chief at the apex, and the clan became at once a regiment. From the first moment exact order and prompt obedience were found. Every man, from highest to lowest, was in his proper place, and knew that place perfectly. There was no danger of mutiny or of desertion. That very homesickness which in regular armies impels recruits to abscond kept the Highlander loyal, for to desert was to separate himself forever from his family. Thomas Babington Macaulay, *A History of England* (1848)

2. O'Neill Into Opera

Twenty times last week a strapping, coffee-coloured man in a baby-blue wrapper went out in front of the curtain of Manhattan's Metropolitan Opera House to bow right and left in a shattering storm of applause. Ten times there appeared with him a stocky, wavy-haired man . . . who stood and looked bewildered. The coffee-coloured man was baritone Lawrence Tibbett, the bewildered one, Composer Louis Gruenberg. Because Gruenberg had been fascinated by a short, stark play of Eugene O'Neill's called *Emperor Jones,* because he had hunted O'Neill out one midnight in Paris two years ago, got permission to set the play to music and then proceeded potently to do so, New York had witnessed the première of the most exciting U.S. opera yet written. For Baritone Tibbett the moment was a career's fine crown. Courtesy *Time*, copyright Time Inc. (1933)

3. The Machine

A certain type of flimsy romantic has been too ready with abuse of a mechanical age, just as a certain type of imaginative writer with a smattering of science has been too gross in his adulation. The machine, when mastered and directed by the human spirit, may lead to a noble enlargement of life. Enterprises which make roads across pathless mountains, collect the waters over a hundred thousand miles to set the desert blossoming, build harbours on countless harbourless coasts, tame the elements to man's uses—these are the equivalent to-day of the great explorations and adventures of the past. So, too, the patient work of research laboratories, where to the student a new and startling truth may leap at any moment from the void. Those who achieve such things are as much imaginative creators as any poet, as much conquerors as any king. If a man so dominates a machine that it becomes part of him, he may thereby pass out of a narrow world to an ampler ether. The true airman is one of the freest of God's creatures, for he has used a machine to carry him beyond the pale of the Machine. He is a creator and not a mechanic, a master and not a slave. John Buchan, *Memory Hold-The-Door*, (1940)

WRITTEN EXERCISE I
Improving Sentence Structure
Do *one* of the following exercises:

1. Select from your recent writing one fairly long paragraph in which you have used little variety in sentence structure. Improve the style of this paragraph by:
a) using some of the techniques you have studied to improve your sentences;
b) deliberately varying the *length* of your sentences to achieve specific effects.

Then copy into your note-book (i) the original version and (ii) the revised version of your paragraph.

2. Using *one* of the topic sentences suggested below, or one of your own choice, write an expository paragraph in which you use:
a) a periodic sentence;
b) a sentence containing parallel structure;
c) a climactic sentence;
d) a balanced sentence;
e) a sentence in which you have used position effectively.

The paragraph should be at least one-half page in length. Underline the sentences in which you have used the above rhetorical devices, and in a footnote indicate which sentence contains which rhetorical device.

Suggested Topic Sentences
1. Our basketball team is not getting the support it deserves.
2. The Athletic Directorate is a useful organization in our school.
3. Some television programmes are excellent.
4. Studying for examinations is an exasperating experience.
5. Skiing can be dangerous.
6. Handle a canoe (or a gun) with care.
7. Mussolini and Hitler held somewhat similar ideas.
8. .... is an absorbing novel.

WRITTEN EXERCISE II
An Appreciation of Sentence Structure
a) By which rhetorical device has each of the following sentences been made effective?
b) What idea is emphasized by the device used?

1. The storm broke with the fury of a jungle king, with the ferocity

of a wounded tiger, with the destructiveness of a stampeding elephant. Michael G.

2. The snow-capped mountains dipped low to the valley, slung far to the west, and searched for the heavens. Bernie F.

3. A soloist must have evenness in vibrato, clarity in attack, and brilliance in tone. Jim D.

4. Throughout the home season, the number of penalties has been few; the number of fights, fewer. The success of the Canadian hockey team has been mainly due to their high-scoring offence, and their careful defence. Their past play has excited the hometown fans; their future play will thrill the world. Paul S.

5. Covering the world with white beauty, bringing joy into the life of the young child, and jamming traffic for miles, silently the snow fell. Larry S.

6. As he trundled round the corner with his wheelbarrow of turnips, he knocked over a portly, cigar-smoking, grey-haired gentleman. Marian L.

7. To enjoy the bite of the cold wind in your red-hot face, to sense the flying snow beneath your feet, to feel the thrill of an aviator as you fly down the hills, to glory in the strength and control of your own body, these are the joys of skiing. Laurence S.

8. If one hogs the ball and scores for that reason in double figures, if one displays a fancy flashiness that is unnecessary, if one appears disgusted and proves it by anguished facial expressions when an easy shot is missed, he is said by the ignorant to be a star. Martin S.

9. As the moon disappeared behind the ghostly clouds, and the stars stood as great candles out in endless space, he sighed. Bernie F.

WRITTEN EXERCISE III
a) What is the author's main idea in each of the following passages?
b) Illustrating directly from the passage, show by what devices of clausal *arrangement* the author makes plain his idea.
c) Illustrating directly from the passage, show by what devices of clausal *construction* the author makes plain his idea.

1. . . . The government has bought health for the masses out of taxes; the government has engaged in the care of the poor, of the defective, and has organized opportunity in a score of ways undreamed of in other times and places. But with all this public activity, with all the political distribution of wealth, with all our legislation, with all our constitutional prohibition of hereditary caste, vast inequities still remain. . . . William Allen White, "The Dynamic Man", *Harper's Magazine,* 1927

2. . . . but while we are praising what our government has done we should not deny that government also is the shield for special privilege, that government does make it possible for the rich to enjoy privileges in our courts which are denied to the poor, that government does at times act with stupidity, and at times with cupidity . . . William Allen White, "The Dynamic Man", *Harper's Magazine,* 1927

LITERARY CRITICISM OF EXPOSITION

EVALUATING THE STRUCTURE OF EXPOSITION

Criticism is the term used to designate the evaluation of any art form. In city newspapers, you will find criticisms of current theatrical productions, movies, musical events and ballet performances, and of recently published books. Literary criticism is that branch of critical writing that appraises literature.

The purpose of literary criticism is to evaluate an author's success in achieving his aim or to appraise some specific aspect of the work under survey or to judge a piece of literature by certain standards. The first two kinds of evaluation are known as thesis criticism; the third is referred to as judicial criticism. For example, one writer, criticizing *Julius Caesar,* might evaluate Shakespeare's success in achieving his aim. The thesis of this criticism might be: *Shakespeare is successful in creating his desired effect: that of arousing the audience's pity for the idealistic Brutus, unable to cope with the practical and unscrupulous Cassius.* Another writer might evaluate, not the overall effect aimed at, but one aspect of the play, for instance, Shakespeare's use of the soliloquy. The thesis of this criticism might be: *Shakespeare makes skilful use of the soliloquy to acquaint the audience with the natures of Brutus and of Cassius.* Both of these critiques would be thesis criticism. A third writer might judge *Julius Caesar* with reference to a generally accepted definition of tragedy. He would be writing judicial criticism.

A first-rate piece of criticism is a well-organized and well-written exposition composed by a person who, because of his knowledge of literature, his sound judgment and his good taste, is an authority on the subject about which he is writing.

The purpose of these lessons in literary criticism is to train you in the techniques of critical writing. Students who have studied literature seriously for several years should be able to recognize the merits and faults of the plays, novels, essays, short stories and poetry that they read; and, therefore, should be able to evaluate intelligently an author's work.

CLASS DISCUSSION I
Criticism in the Newspapers

1. In the modern newspaper, some of the most popular features are the criticisms of current plays, musical productions, movies and books. Account for this popularity.

2. Criticism is exposition for a special purpose. To whom is it addressed and what are its purposes?
3. Newspaper criticisms are frequently signed by the writer. Why?
4. What qualifications make a successful literary or music critic?
5. Why is criticism a difficult kind of writing for students?

CLASS DISCUSSION II
Evaluating the Structure of an Expository Passage

Using the questions you will find at the end of the following excerpt taken from Henry Van Dyke's *Fisherman's Luck,* discuss the structure of the passage and also the structure of each paragraph.

Who Owns the Mountains?

What is property, after all? The law says there are two kinds, real and personal. But it seems to me that the only real property is that which is truly personal, that which we take into our inner life and make our own forever, by understanding and admiration and sympathy and love. This is the only kind of possession that is worth anything.

A gallery of great paintings adorns the house of the Honourable Midas Bond, and every year adds a new treasure to his collection. He knows how much they cost him, and he keeps the run of the quotations at the auction sales, congratulating himself as the price of the works of his well-chosen artists rises in the scale, and the value of his art treasures is enhanced. But why should he call them his? He is only their custodian. He keeps them well varnished, and framed in gilt. But he never passes through those gilded frames into the world of beauty that lies behind the painted canvas. He knows nothing of those lovely places from which the artist's soul and hand have drawn their inspiration. They are closed and barred to him. He has bought the pictures, but he cannot buy the key. The poor art student who wanders through his gallery, lingering with awe and love before the masterpieces, owns them far more truly than Midas Bond . . .

We measure success by accumulation. The measure is false. The true measure is appreciation. He who loves most has most. Henry Van Dyke, *Fisherman's Luck*

Discussion Questions

1. To whom is Van Dyke speaking, what is he saying, and why?
2. For what purpose does Van Dyke use the first paragraph? The second paragraph? The third paragraph?
3. One of the marks of good paragraph structure is *unity.* An expository paragraph is unified if it develops one central idea. Is the second paragraph unified? Justify your opinion.
4. If an expository paragraph is to have *coherence,* the ideas in it must be presented in some orderly way. Divide the second paragraph into its units of thought and then decide whether or not Van Dyke has arranged his ideas in a logical order.
5. A well-constructed paragraph also has *emphasis.* This is gained by impressing on the reader the central idea in the paragraph. A writer may

81

use the structure of a paragraph to emphasize his central idea. He may use: *position*—placing the most important idea at the end of the paragraph; *proportion*—devoting to this idea a larger part of the paragraph than he devotes to any other idea; *repetition*—repeating the idea that he wishes to stress; *climax*—arranging his ideas in ascending order of importance. What methods has Van Dyke used in the second paragraph to stress its central idea?

HOME WORK ASSIGNMENT

Read the following two paragraphs (from "Inaugural Address" by Woodrow Wilson) and answer in writing the questions that follow them. Ignore the brackets in your first reading; their insertion is explained in the questions.

We see that, in many things, that life is very great. It is incomparably great in its material aspects, in its body of wealth, in the diversity and sweep of its energy, in the industries which have been conceived and built up by the genius of individual men and the limitless enterprise of groups of men. It is great, also, very great, in its moral force. Nowhere else in the world have noble men and women exhibited in more striking forms the beauty and the energy of sympathy and helpfulness and counsel in their efforts to rectify wrong, alleviate suffering, and set the weak in the way of strength and hope. We have built up, moreover, a great system of government, which has stood through a long age as in many respects a model for those who seek to set liberty upon foundations that will endure against fortuitous change, against storm and accident. Our life contains every great thing, and contains it in rich abundance.

But the evil has come with the good, and much fine gold has been corroded. (With riches has come inexcusable waste. We have squandered a great part of what we might have used, and have not stopped to conserve the exceeding bounty of nature, without which our genius for enterprise would have been worthless and impotent, scorning to be careful, shamefully prodigal as well as admirably efficient.) (We have been proud of our industrial achievements, but we have not hitherto stopped thoughtfully enough to count the human cost, the cost of lives snuffed out, of energies overtaxed and broken, the fearful physical and spiritual cost to the men and women and children upon whom the dead weight and burden of it all has fallen pitilessly the years through. The groans and agony of it all had not yet reached our ears, the solemn, moving undertone of our life, coming up out of the mines and factories and out of every home where the struggle had its intimate and familiar seat.) (With the great Government went many deep secret things which we too long delayed to look into and scrutinize with candid, fearless eyes. The great Government we loved has too often been made use of for private and selfish purposes, and those who used it had forgotten the people.) Woodrow Wilson, "Inaugural Address", March 4, 1913

Questions

1. To whom was Woodrow Wilson speaking? In general, what was he saying? Why did he wish to say these things on this particular occasion?
2. What is the main idea developed in the first paragraph?
3. What method did Wilson use to impart unity to this paragraph?
4. Define coherence in paragraph structure. Name and exemplify three methods used to impart coherence to the structure of the first paragraph.
5. Name and illustrate two methods used to make this paragraph structurally emphatic.
6. State in one sentence the main idea developed in the second paragraph.
7. The three examples used to develop the main idea have been bracketed. Are these arranged in some logical order? Give reasons for your opinion.
8. Show that Wilson has used contrast within each example to impart coherence to the paragraph structure.

COMPARING TWO STUDENTS' CRITICISMS OF STRUCTURE

Below you will find reproduced two short essays in which two students attempted to write a criticism of: (a) the thought developed in the passage taken from Van Dyke's essay "Who Owns the Mountains?"; (b) the overall structure of the passage; and (c) the structure of each paragraph.

Use the discussion questions that follow each criticism to guide your discussion of its effectiveness as a piece of expository writing.

First Criticism

1. In this passage Henry Van Dyke is defining true ownership. He is speaking to all those who think that to own something beautiful, they must buy it; and to those who, having bought beauty, think they own it. His aim is to make clear to them his definition of ownership, in the hope that they will enrich their own lives by accepting it.

2. Mr. Van Dyke has written a unified, coherent and emphatic passage.

3. The whole passage is an artistic unit, coherent and emphatic. Mr. Van Dyke uses a short paragraph to give in general terms his own definition of ownership. He develops this idea by means of one concrete example placed in a paragraph by itself. The concluding brief paragraph is used to emphasize his theme. Thus, because the three paragraphs develop the one idea, that real property "is that which we take into our inner life and make our own forever", the passage is unified; because the arrangement of the ideas is orderly—a statement of the thesis, a development of the thesis and a restatement of the thesis—the passage is coherent; and, because the conclusion has been used to emphasize the thesis by means of a striking statement, the passage is emphatic.

4. The first paragraph, which states and explains the thesis of the passage, is well constructed: unified, coherent and emphatic. It has one central idea—real property is that which "we take into our inner life and make our own forever"—developed in a logical way: Van Dyke asks a question—what is property?—and answers with two definitions, the dictionary one

83

and his own. The author emphasizes his own definition by placing it last and elaborating it.

5. The second paragraph is beautifully constructed. The central idea is that the real owner of a painting is the man who appreciates it. The author develops this idea by means of one concrete example that illustrates his thesis: Midas Bond—note the suggestive power of his name—bought valuable paintings but does not understand them; the art student understanding them and loving them is the true owner. Since the whole paragraph develops this one illustration of the thesis, the paragraph is unified. A logical pattern of thought lends it coherence. Van Dyke pictures Midas Bond the real owner; and proceeds to prove that the poor artist truly owns them. This paragraph is also emphatic. Van Dyke wishes to emphasize that the poor artist who understands the pictures is the real owner. To stress this idea, the author closes his paragraph with a detailed picture of the art student "lingering with awe and love before the masterpieces". By leaving this picture with his readers, he emphasizes his theme: he who loves most has most. Because the paragraph is unified, coherent, and emphatic, it is well constructed.

6. The last paragraph is also well constructed. It, too, has one central idea—he who loves most has most—developed in an orderly way: the false definition of success—accumulation—and Van Dyke's definition—appreciation. By devoting the last two of the four sentences to his own definition, the author has emphasized it.

7. Mr. Van Dyke's thesis is an interesting one. A great many people do not understand that real happiness comes, not from *possessing* beauty, but from *appreciating* it. We live at a time when the advertisers, through newspapers, radio and television, are telling us we must *possess* to be happy. Mr. Van Dyke's definition provides an antidote for this materialism.

8. Mr. Van Dyke has written a unified, coherent and emphatic definition of property. Because of the effective structure of the entire passage and of each paragraph, the reader will remember for a long time this little philosophical essay. Eva W.

Discussion Questions

1. For what purpose has this student used each of the paragraphs in her criticism?
2. In paragraph 5 of this criticism, what opinions advanced by the student have been illustrated by reference to the original passage?
3. Is this criticism unified, coherent and emphatic? Give reasons for your opinion.

Second Criticism

1. Mr. Van Dyke's passage is unified, coherent and emphatic, and each of the paragraphs is also unified, coherent and emphatic.
2. The author is in this essay defining property.
3. The whole passage is well constructed. Mr. Van Dyke develops one thesis, arranges his material in an orderly way and ends by stressing his opinion about property.

4. The first paragraph is a well-constructed paragraph. In it the author defines property.
5. Van Dyke's second paragraph is unified. It has no irrelevant ideas. The author describes Midas Bond as the real owner of a gallery of art treasures. He then says that the art student who understands the pictures is the one who owns them. The paragraph is coherent. Every sentence follows in order. The paragraph is easy to understand. He leaves his most important idea for the conclusion and he elaborates it and also he uses repetition. This makes an emphatic paragraph that impresses the reader. All in all, Van Dyke has written a well-constructed paragraph that is a masterpiece.
6. The last paragraph is unified, coherent and emphatic. It impressed me very much.
7. The whole passage has a remarkably fine style.

Discussion Questions

1. For what purpose has this student used each of the paragraphs in his criticism?
2. In paragraph 3, what opinions advanced by the student have not been illustrated by reference to the original passage?
3. a) The topic sentence of paragraph 5 in this criticism is unsuitable. Compose one that will prepare the reader for the ideas discussed in the paragraph.
   b) In paragraph 5, what opinions have not been illustrated by reference to Van Dyke's passage?
4. Criticize the content of paragraph 6.
5. Show that the conclusion of the appreciation is off-topic.
6. In what respects is the first appreciation better than the second?

HOME WORK ASSIGNMENT
Writing a Criticism of Paragraph Structure

Write a criticism of the structure (the unity, coherence and emphasis) of the following paragraph. Your criticism is to consist of one paragraph.

The Hudson's Bay Company

The English Hudson's Bay Company founded in 1670 to exploit the fur-trade of the north has proved to be the most virile survivor of the chartered companies of the seventeenth century. The East India Company, vaster in its day, is hardly a shadow of its old self, while this younger rival, still the greatest dealer in furs in the world, carries on from the Atlantic to the Pacific an enormous trade in general merchandise and remains the owner of many thousands of acres of land in Canada. While across the continent in wild regions are scattered dozens of its posts, its commerce is not merely to these remote places. In Montreal, in Winnipeg, in Vancouver and other centres the great stores of the Hudson's Bay Company are as ready to supply to urban populations delicate fabrics in silk as to equip a distant post with kettles and blankets for the swarthy natives who bring to it their furs. George M. Wrong, *The Rise and Fall of New France*

LITERARY CRITICISM OF EXPOSITION

EVALUATING THE STYLE OF EXPOSITION

According to *The Concise Oxford Dictionary*, style is the *"manner of writing, speaking, or doing, especially as opposed to the matter to be expressed or the thing done"*. In this lesson you will be given practice in evaluating an author's language (diction — choice of words to express ideas — and imagery) and command of sentence structure.

CLASS DISCUSSION I

Evaluating Diction and Imagery

Read aloud the paragraph entitled "The Uncommon Man". Then use the questions that follow it to evaluate the author's diction and imagery.

The Uncommon Man

I believe that the coming age will be that of the Uncommon rather than of the Common Man, and have two reasons for believing this: first, that the concept of the Common Man is as false, inhuman and fictitious as the once prevalent notion of the Innocent Savage; second, that my experience of men and women has taught me that they love their differences, their separate identities, and will not tolerate the sea-green regimenters who, in the name of social equality, seek to impose upon them a grey sameness of the soul . . . Whoever has had genuine experience of life outside a social-betterment committee or a statistical bureau and has worked with the so-called masses instead of grinding a political axe on their backs; whoever has kept watch on a bridge or served in an engine-room or gone away with a boat's crew or fought in trenches or made long marches or been a prisoner for long months in close company, or been sunk in the North Sea, or has been done or suffered all these things—whoever, that is to say, has learned his fellow-creatures outside the sheep-pens of the social dogmatists knows that each one of them is an uncommon man and is incapable of thinking of himself or of the man next him in any other terms. A ship's company is not a herd—nor, for that matter, except for our ignorance of animals, is a herd itself! Woe betide the priest who looks for the Common Parishioner and not for the Child of God, or the captain who is not a distinguisher of sailors, or the midshipman whose cutter's crew is for him an Average multiplied by twelve! The boat is called away at night. The shore is distant by a long spell under oars. The dip of the blades, the click-clock of the crutches, the steady body-swing, the dim monotony of twelve faces half hidden, half revealed: might not the midshipman on his dickey almost be lulled into supposing himself confronted by a dozen specimens of the Common Man? Not when shore is reached and the boat waits, tied up to a wall, and pipes are lighted. Then each man is distinct; alone in his

86

case of flesh as all spirits are, as Nelson was; with a sense of association, never of sameness, and, ultimately, incommunicable. Look in the twelve faces: the Common Man is not there, nor any awareness of him. Charles Morgan, *Reflections in a Mirror* (First Series)

Discussion Questions

1. To whom is Mr. Morgan speaking, what is his thesis, and why does he feel impelled to say this particular thing to this particular group?
2. From the paragraph, select words, phrases and figures of speech that you consider effective. Give reasons for your choices.
3. Find one idiom used by Mr. Morgan and point out the effect he achieves with it.
4. Find one use of onomatopoeia in the paragraph. What effect is achieved by its use?
5. Point out any words you think are ineffectively used, and tell why.

CLASS DISCUSSION II
Evaluating Sentence Structure

Read aloud the following paragraph taken from a speech broadcast by Winston Churchill in Rochester, N.Y., June, 1941, before the United States had entered the war against Nazi Germany. To help you appraise Sir Winston's use of sentence structure in achieving his aim, consider the questions that follow the paragraph.

The Time Is Short

But what is the explanation of the enslavement of Europe by the German Nazi régime? How did they do it? It is but a few years ago since one united gesture by the peoples, great and small, who are now broken in the dust, would have warded off from mankind the fearful ordeal it has had to undergo. But there was no unity. There was no vision. The nations were pulled down one by one while the others gaped and chattered. One by one, each in his turn, they let themselves be caught. One after another they were felled by brutal violence or poisoned from within by subtle intrigue, Sir Winston Churchill, *The Unrelenting Struggle*

Discussion Questions

1. To whom was Churchill speaking, what was his thesis and why did he feel impelled to say this particular thing to this particular group?
2. Experienced writers and speakers do not make every sentence the same length and the same type. What kinds of sentences has Churchill used in order to help him achieve his aim?
3. What rhetorical devices has Churchill used to make his sentences emphatic? In each case, tell what idea is stressed by the device.

LITERARY CRITICISM OF EXPOSITION

PLANNING AND WRITING A LITERARY CRITICISM OF AN EXPOSITORY PASSAGE

A good literary criticism, as stated on page 80, is a well-organized piece of exposition. Like all good exposition, it includes a lead, a statement of the critic's thesis, a logical development of this thesis and a conclusion.

The opening paragraph, the lead, explains briefly the purpose of the selection being appraised, and states to whom the writer is speaking, what he is saying, and why he wishes to say this particular thing to this particular group.

The second paragraph contains the critic's thesis: his opinion of the effectiveness of the selection he is evaluating.

The paragraphs that comprise the body of the criticism develop this thesis. Each of these paragraphs has a topic sentence that contributes to the development of the critic's thesis. When expanding each topic sentence, the critic usually makes specific references to the passage in order to illustrate his opinions. A good critic usually avoids sweeping generalizations. He supports his assertions with specific illustrations.

The concluding paragraph stresses the critic's thesis.

An examination of criticism written by senior students will focus your attention on the techniques of critical writing.

CLASS DISCUSSION
Analyzing a Student's Criticism

Students were required to write a criticism of the paragraph structure, the diction and the sentence structure of "The Time Is Short", reprinted on page 87. Read the criticism and then use the questions that follow it to guide your discussion of its effectiveness.

A Criticism of the Paragraph "The Time Is Short"

1. This paragraph is taken from a broadcast in which Churchill was trying to persuade the United States to join in the fight against the Nazis.
2. An effective expository paragraph must be so constructed that it is unified, coherent and emphatic. In addition, diction and sentence structure must be employed in some original and imaginative way that aids the author in developing his thesis. Since the paragraph "The Time Is Short", contains all these elements and is written in Churchill's own powerfully distinctive style, the paragraph is completely successful in developing Churchill's thesis: that the free nations must unite or perish.

3. Churchill's exclusion of any material that is not relevant to his thesis has made the paragraph unified. The topic sentence states that the subject will be an "explanation of the enslavement of Europe by the German Nazi regime". Nowhere in the paragraph does Churchill stray from the topic: he speaks of the lack of unity, the lack of vision, the tragic indecision on the part of the free European nations. All these are part of his explanation of the downfall of the democracies of Europe. Thus Churchill's strict adherence to his topic sentence gives the paragraph unity.

4. Churchill's arrangement of the ideas that develop his topic sentence in an orderly, and in this case somewhat chronological way, lends coherence to the paragraph. He begins by speaking of the pre-war days when "one united gesture" would have stopped Hitler's brazen march of aggression. By means of phrases such as "each in his turn" and "one after another", Churchill then gives a chronological suggestion of the manner in which the smaller nations were swallowed by the Nazi terror. Since he has begun with a situation and then listed reasons for the situation, Churchill has succeeded in giving the paragraph coherence.

5. Churchill's use of a climactic contrast at the end of the paragraph gives it structural emphasis. By contrasting two different ways in which nations were destroyed by the Nazis—"brutal violence" from without, "subtle intrigue" from within—Churchill has left a vivid picture in the minds of his listening audience. This "double-barrelled" threat to the security of democracy, Churchill has realized, will make a deep impression on his listeners in the United States.

6. In order to convince the Americans that they should join the free nations in the fight against Nazi Germany, Churchill uses rhetorical devices to make his sentences emphatic. He begins his paragraph with two rhetorical questions designed to direct the attention of his audience to the explanation he is about to offer. He then answers these two questions in one fairly long complex sentence that he makes emphatic by placing an important contrast—great and small—out of its natural position. He thus uses the rhetorical device of position to highlight the need for unity. He follows this explanation with two very short sentences similarly constructed. This parallelism stresses the folly of Europe: "But there was no unity. There was no vision". In the last two sentences, Churchill again uses position, this time to emphasize his thesis, that lack of unity caused the enslavement of Europe. By placing the words "one by one" at the beginning of sentence 7, and the words "one after another" at the beginning of sentence 8, he forces on the attention of his audience Europe's incredible folly. In these last two sentences, he uses another rhetorical device, balance, to underline the twin methods used by the Nazis: "felled by violence", or "poisoned" from within "by subtle intrigue".

7. The diction in this paragraph also suits the purpose of the paragraph. The noun "enslavement" is very effectively used to suggest the helplessness of the conquered European countries. The adjectival phrase, "broken in the dust", also pictures weak, ruined, conquered nations. Like the two just-mentioned examples, "fearful ordeal", which describes the horrible reality of the conquest of these countries, would make his listeners dread German

89

invasion and want to unify to prevent it. The specific verbs, "gaped" and "chattered", describe the amazement of the free nations and their trivial and useless talking by which no one benefited. "One by one" and "each in his turn" stress the idea of the disunity that made it possible for Germany to conquer these countries by fighting only one nation at a time. The adverbial phrase "by subtle intrigue" vividly describes the clever German propaganda, which was very effective in some places in converting people to the Nazi beliefs. These last three examples show the mistakes that the still-free nations can be spared from making by unifying. Thus, the language in this paragraph would help persuade the free people to unite.

8.   This paragraph, then, because of its good structure, its imaginative use of words, and its striking sentence structure would impress on the United States the folly of isolation. Michael S.

Discussion Questions

1.   What is the thesis of this piece of literary criticism?
2.   Is the student always on-topic? Give reasons for your opinion.
3.   Are paragraphs 3, 4, 5, 6 and 7 unified? Give reasons for your opinion.
4.   A good critic offers evidence to support his opinions. In paragraphs 3, 4 and 6 what opinions has the student illustrated?
5.   If you think the student might have expressed himself more effectively in certain parts of this criticism, point out the weaknesses and suggest how they might be eliminated.

HOME WORK ASSIGNMENT I

Below are three expository passages. Write a literary criticism of any *one* paragraph. Discuss the author's paragraph structure, his diction, his imagery and his sentence structure.

1. The Sea Around Us

Nowhere in all the sea does life exist in such bewildering abundance as in the surface waters. From the deck of a vessel you may look down, hour after hour, on the shimmering discs of jellyfish, their gently pulsating bells dotting the surface as far as you can see. Or one day you may notice early in the morning that you are passing through a sea that has taken on a brick-red colour from billions upon billions of microscopic creatures, each of which contains an orange pigment granule. At noon you are still moving through red seas, and when darkness falls the waters shine with an eerie glow from the phosphorescent fires of yet more billions and trillions of these same creatures.

And again you may glimpse not only the abundance but something of the fierce uncompromisingness of sea life when, as you look over the rail and down, down into water of a clear, deep green, suddenly there passes a silver shower of finger-long fishlets. The sun strikes a metallic gleam from their flanks as they streak by, driving deeper into the green depths with the desperate speed of the hunted. Perhaps you never see the hunters, but you sense their presence as you see the gulls hovering, with eager, mewing cries, waiting for the little fish to be driven to the surface. Rachael Carson, *The Sea Around Us*

2. Magic

Any grove or any wood is a fine thing to see. But the magic here, strangely, is not apparent from the road. It is necessary to leave the impersonal highway, to step inside the rusty gate and close it behind. By this, an act of faith is committed, through which one accepts blindly the communion cup of beauty. One is now inside the grove, out of one world and in the mysterious heart of another. Enchantment lies in different things for each of us. For me, it is in this: to step out of the bright sunlight into the shade of orange trees; to walk under the arched canopy of their jade-like leaves; to see the long aisles of lichened trunks stretch ahead in a geometric rhythm; to feel the mystery of a seclusion that yet has shafts of light striking through it. This is the essence of an ancient and secret magic. It goes back, perhaps, to the fairy tales of childhood, to Hansel and Gretel, to Babes in the Wood, to Alice in Wonderland, to all half-luminous places that pleased the imagination as a child. It may go back still farther, to racial Druid memories, to an atavistic sense of safety and delight in an open forest. And after long years of spiritual homelessness, of nostalgia, here is that mystic loveliness of childhood again. Here is home. An old thread, long tangled, comes straight again. Marjorie Rawlings, *Cross Creek*

3. Challenge and Response

Is there such a thing as an excessive challenge? We have not yet encountered an example of such, and there are several extreme cases of the operation of challenge-and-response which we have not yet mentioned. We have not yet cited the case of Venice—a city, built on piles driven into the mud banks of a salt lagoon, which has surpassed in wealth and power and glory all the cities built on *terra firma* in the fertile plain of the Po; nor Holland—a country which has been actually salvaged from the sea, but yet has distinguished herself in history far above any other parcel of ground of equal area in the North European plain; nor Switzerland, saddled with her portentous load of mountains. It might seem that the three hardest pieces of ground in Western Europe have stimulated their inhabitants to attain, along different lines, the highest level of social achievement that has as yet been attained by any peoples of Western Christendom. Arnold J. Toynbee, *A Study of History*

HOME WORK ASSIGNMENT II

Below are two expository passages. Write a literary criticism of *one* of them. Discuss the overall structure of the passage; the structure of any two paragraphs; the diction, the imagery and the sentence structure of these two paragraphs.

1. Speed

New York is a city of many beauties, and with a reckless prodigality she has done her best to obscure them all. Driven by a vain love of swift traffic, she assails your ear with an incessant din and your eye with the unsightliest railroad that human ingenuity has ever contrived. She has sacrificed the amenity of her streets and the dignity of her buildings to the false god of

91

Speed. The men of New York, as they tell you with insistent pride, are "hustlers", but the "hustling" probably leads to little enough. Haste and industry are not synonymous. To run up and down is but a form of busy idleness. The captains of industry who do the work of the world sit still, surrounded by bells and telephones. They show themselves furtively behind vast expanses of plate-glass, and move only to eat or sleep. It is the common citizen of New York who is never quiet. He finds it irksome to stay long in the same place. Though his house may be comfortable, even luxurious, he is in a fever to leave it. And so it comes about that what he is wont to call "transportation" seems the most important thing in his life.

Movement, then, noisy and incessant, is the passion of New York. Perhaps it is the brisk air which drives men to this useless activity. Perhaps it is an ingrained and superstitious habit. But the drowsiest foreigner is soon caught up in the whirl. He too must be chasing something which always eludes him. He too finds himself leaving a quiet corner where he would like to stay, that he may reach some place which he has no desire to see. Charles Whibley, *American Sketches*

2. The Greatest Man in the World

If we are asked who is the most important man in the world, we can all guess; but one thing is pretty certain—we shall all guess wrong. The most important man in the world is somewhere, but he will not be known until he is dead and we are all dead with him and posterity has given its verdict.

If ever it might have been expected that the chief of men could be picked out with certainty, it would have been while Augustus Caesar reigned at Rome over the whole known world. He was so supreme that he seemed less a man than a god. But down in a little province of his vast empire there was a Boy growing up who was destined to change the whole face of the world and to outshine Augustus as the sun outshines a rush-light. The magnificence of Augustus and his empire is an empty memory of nineteen centuries ago, but Christianity is still the mightiest force in the affairs of men . . .

Take another illustration. The end of the eighteenth century was a time of great men. We should have been puzzled then to decide between Pitt and Burke, Nelson and Napoleon, and a host of others. None of us would have thought of looking for him in the person of a certain gentle, unassuming instrument-maker—James Watt. He inaugurated the Age of Steam. He released the greatest power that the ingenuity of man has ever invented, and the train that thunders through the land, the ship that ploughs the sea, and the engine that drives a thousand looms are among the prolific children of his genius.

And so, no one can know the greatest man in the world. The people who make the greatest noise in the world rarely do anything that matters to posterity. The most important man is probably making no noise at all. His noise will come late like the sound of a great gun heard from afar. But it is a noise that will echo down the ages. A. G. Gardiner, *Alpha of the Plough*

ARGUMENT

ANALYZING A PERSUASIVE EDITORIAL

When exposition is used for the purpose of convincing, it is called argument.

Argument is an appeal to the reasoning powers of those whom you are trying to convince. For instance, a journalist concerned about slum clearance might try, through the editorial pages of his newspaper, to *prove* to his fellow citizens that replacing the city's rickety and unsanitary tenements with municipally-owned apartment blocks would be less costly than paying for the delinquency and the crime that may be bred in these unsavoury parts of the city.

Often those who wish to elicit the active support of others combine an appeal to their readers' emotions with an appeal to their reason. For example, the above-mentioned journalist, after attempting to convince his readers that his plan was economically sound, might also appeal to their pity for other human beings compelled by unfortunate circumstances to live in squalid quarters. The purpose of this appeal to the emotions would be to make his readers *want* to help eliminate slum areas in the city.

In *Julius Caesar,* Marc Antony's speech to the Roman mob is an excellent example of the effectiveness of argument linked with emotional appeal. Antony first *convinced* the citizens that Caesar was not ambitious, the one reason Brutus had given for the assassination; and then deliberately aroused *their pity for Caesar* and *their hatred for the assassins.* This speech resulted in the *action* Antony desired—an angry mob rushing out of the Forum to kill Caesar's murderers.

If you can arouse strong emotions, such as pity, shame, pride, guilt, you can probably make people *want* to act in the way you wish them to. An appeal to the emotions, whether used as Lincoln and Churchill used it, to awaken man's nobler instincts, or as Hitler used it in his later days, to stir man's baser instincts, is a powerful device in the hands of a skilful speaker or writer.

The editorial pages of our newspapers constitute a forum used to influence public opinion. William Allen White, of The *Emporia Gazette,* and William Dafoe, of The *Winnipeg Free Press,* are examples of intelligent and dedicated editors whose writings affected the thinking and the actions of a great many people. If you want to read able argumentation and persuasion, turn to the editorial pages of good newspapers.

Although statisticians estimate that only ten percent of the population reads editorials, nevertheless this group is an influential one, because it is composed for the most part of intelligent and articulate people.

THE PRESENTATION OF EFFECTIVE ARGUMENT

1. The thesis must be clearly enunciated.
2. Any terms that might be misunderstood must be defined.
3. The proof must be sufficient.
4. The finished argument must be unified: the writer or speaker must develop only *one* thesis, though it may have a number of components.
5. Any emotional appeal must be appropriate in kind and intensity to the group addressed.
6. The action that the writer or speaker wishes his readers or listeners to take should be stated in *specific terms.*

CLASS DISCUSSION

1. a) Mention a recent current event that has aroused controversy in your country or in your community. Explain why the event has divided public opinion.
   b) Suggest a thesis that might be used for an editorial argument on the subject.
2. a) Mention a local problem that you think could be solved with the active support of interested people. What action would solve it?
   b) How could you prove that this problem exists?
   c) To what emotion could you appeal to make others *want* to help solve the problem?

WRITTEN EXERCISE

After reading silently this editorial, reprinted from The *New York World,* answer in writing the questions that follow it.

Celia Cooney

For some months now we have been vastly entertained by the bobbed-haired bandit. Knowing nothing about her, we created a perfect story standardized according to the rules laid down by the movies and the short-story magazines. The story had, as the press agents say, everything. It had a flapper and a bandit who baffled the police; it had sex and money, crime and mystery. And then yesterday we read in the probation officer's report the story of Celia Cooney's life. It was not in the least entertaining. For there in the place of the dashing bandit was a pitiable girl; instead of an amusing tale, a dark and mean tragedy; instead of a lovely adventure, a terrible accusation.

In the twenty years she has lived in this city she has come at one time or another within reach of all the agencies of righteousness. Five years before she was born her father was summoned to court for drunkeness and neglect; the charities department recommended then that her older brother and her sisters be committed to an institution . . . Celia herself, the youngest of eight, came at four years of age into the custody of the Children's Society. Six months later, on the recommendation of the Department of Public Charity, she was turned back to her mother, who promptly deserted her.

She was taken to Brooklyn to her aunt, and for ten years or so attended school. At the age of fourteen her mother brought her back to New York, took her to a furnished room, stole her clothes and deserted her. A year later, aged fifteen, Celia became a child labourer in a brush factory in Brooklyn, and was associating at night with sailors picked up on the waterfront. At sixteen Celia was back in New York, living with her mother, working as laundress for a few months at a stretch in various hospitals. At twenty she was married, had borne a child, had committed a series of robberies, and is condemned to spend the rest of her youth in prison.

This is what twentieth-century civilization in New York has achieved in the case of Celia Cooney . . . Fully warned when she was still an infant, society allowed her to drift out of its hands into a life of dirt, neglect, dark basements, begging, stealing, ignorance, poor little tawdry excitements and twisted romance. The courts had their chance and missed it. The church had its chance and missed it. The schools had their chance and missed it. The absent-minded routine of all that is well-meaning and respectable did not deflect by an inch her inexorable progress from the basement where she was born to the jail where she will expiate her crime and ours.

For her crimes are on our heads too. No record could be clearer or more eloquent. None could leave less room for doubt that Celia Cooney is a product of this city, of its neglect and its carelessness, of its indifference and its undercurrents of misery. We recommend her story to the pulpits of New York, to the social workers of New York, to those who are tempted to boast of its wealth, its magnificence and its power.

Questions

1. To whom is the editorial addressed?
2. What is the editor saying, and why does he feel impelled to say this particular thing to this particular group?
3. The opening paragraph of an editorial should arouse the interest of the group to whom the editorial is addressed. What methods does the writer use to arouse interest?
4. The editor is trying to convince his readers that a serious problem exists.
   a) What is the problem?
   b) What facts does the editor use to convince his readers that such a problem exists?
5. The editor uses an emotional appeal to make his readers want to help solve the problem.
   a) To what emotions does he appeal?
   b) Does the emotional appeal go too far? Give reasons for your opinion.

95

6. A persuasive editorial is one that tries, not only to win its readers over to a cause, but also to influence them to take definite action.
   a) What action does this editor wish his readers to take?
   b) In the last sentence, what is the purpose of the reference to New York's "wealth, its magnificence, and its power"?
7. In one sentence state the thesis of this editorial.
8. The style of an editorial has a great deal to do with its power to convince and to persuade. What are some of the characteristics of this editor's style? Cite examples from the text to substantiate your opinions.

HOME WORK ASSIGNMENT I

Study carefully the editorial reprinted below. Then answer in writing the questions that follow it.

Stronger Than Any Bomb

There is little reason to accept the theory, put forward in Formosa, that Mao Tse-tung's retirement as Chairman of the Chinese People's Republic represents an ouster or a demotion. He remains head of the Chinese Communist Party, and that is the key position in any Communist State. The official Peking explanation is probably perfectly correct: Mr. Mao is withdrawing himself from the daily responsibilities of office in order to concentrate on the problems of developing a Communist society in China.

There is something highly significant about this move. We do not encounter its like in the West. British Prime Ministers do not retire to seclusion to study the fundamental problems of the parliamentary system of government. United States Presidents do not leave the White House at intervals to meditate on the strengths and weaknesses of the U.S. Constitution. But Communist leaders—Lenin, Stalin and now Mao Tse-tung—have regularly taken time off from the day-to-day business of government in order to think through basic problems in the light of Mar-xist doctrine, and, where necessary, to re-formulate the doctrine itself.

There is more than one reason for this difference. One is that the principles of Anglo-Saxon democracy are old and generally accepted, while Marxism is a new, experimental system which requires frequent revision to conform to hard facts. But it is also true that Communist leaders have a far greater belief in the power of ideas than their opposite numbers in the West; and in this they are eminently right.

An idea—even a wrong idea—which is fervently held by a great number of people is the strongest force in the world, far exceeding the power of guided missiles or hydrogen bombs. We have only to consider the explosive and revolutionary effects of the 95 Theses which Martin Luther nailed to the church door in Wittenberg, or of the American Declaration of Independence. In our own time we have seen the concept of nationalism shatter ancient empires as if they were glass.

But the power of ideas has never been more strikingly illustrated than by the progress of Commun-

96

ism, which, from its obscure origin in a London slum less than a century ago, has now seized and utterly transformed the two largest countries on earth. The Russian and Chinese revolutionaries found their ideology was their strongest weapon; they are wise to keep it bright and sharp.

There is, however, another factor at work. Mao Tse-tung is not only the dictator of China; he is also something very close to the high priest of the whole Communist religion. Since Stalin's death, there has been no other leader, in Russia or elsewhere, who comes anywhere near matching him in authority and prestige.

His influence is especially great in Asia and Africa. The new nations emerging there are facing the same problems of backwardness, poverty and overpopulation as bedevil China, and they are increasingly impressed by the earnestness and apparent success with which the Chinese Communists are grappling with these handicaps. Because of this, and because the Chinese are Asians, it is the Chinese version of Communism, rather than the Russian, which has the greater appeal to the colored peoples of the world.

It may very well be that Mr. Mao's retirement is a calculated effort to increase his prestige and influence. It is in the great tradition of Asian sages and prophets, all of whom—Buddha, Mohammed, Zoroaster, Confucius, Lao-Tze—went into seclusion before emerging with their new gospels. We may be certain that when Mr. Mao returns with a new formulation of Communism, it will be most carefully and respectfully studied throughout Asia and Africa.

It is a pity that Western leaders do not take a leaf from the Communist book. Our cause might be more secure if those who govern our affairs could take a little time off, now and then, to study the basic principles of freedom and democracy. The *Globe and Mail,* December 19, 1958

Questions

1. What is the editor's thesis? Where is it stated?
2. To whom is the editor speaking, and why does he wish to call attention to the retirement of Mao Tse-tung?
3. List, in order, the reasons the editor gives to prove his thesis.
4. Copy each topic sentence the editor has used. Underline, in each topic sentence after the first, the transitional word or phrase he uses to remind his readers of the content of the preceding paragraph. What quality does the use of this device impart to the editorial?
5. For what purpose does the editor use the last paragraph?
6. Does this editorial make an appeal to the reader's emotions? Give reasons for your opinion.
7. Find three examples of the editor's use of: (a) concrete (and very specific) examples, and (b) figures of speech. What idea is clarified by each example you have selected?
8. This editor often uses verbs to good effect. Cite three examples of this and explain why you think these verbs are used effectively.

Below you will find the first part of an address made to the graduating class of a medical college in Springfield, Illinois, by Adlai Stevenson, twice Democratic candidate for the office of the president of the United States. Read it carefully and then write answers to the questions that follow it. (The paragraphs are numbered for convenience in discussion.)

1. Commencements are traditionally, perhaps even properly, a time for viewing with alarm, for oratorical anxiety over these tender young things about to attack the grisly old world in search of a secure foothold. And then the orators inevitably end up on a note of rugged confidence and spiritual exhilaration. Distasteful as it may be to both of us, I shall probably do the same, but with, I suspect, somewhat more disorder and confusion of thought than is conventional on such solemn and orderly occasions.

2. I am so old I can even remember when ministers had texts for their sermons. My text is from *King Henry IV*, Part 1, Act ii, Scene 3, where Hotspur says: "But I tell you, my Lord fool, out of this nettle, danger, we pluck this flower safety". In the nettle, danger, lies the flower, safety. Can we pluck it out? Can we identify the nettle? The flower? Can we agree what the danger is; can we agree what safety is; can we agree where it lies? Perhaps it has never been more difficult. But we must try, and keep on trying to identify our dangers and our goals. If most of us can't agree what's good and what's bad, then our destiny is not nobility and peace, but impotence and disaster.

3. Perhaps you in the health professions, who have an urge to cure the ills of man, and an education to identify the nettles, the dangers, in the human body, are well equipped to press the search for the nettles and flowers of humanity as well as humans. And that—the quest for truth— after all, is the essential purpose of all education.

4. But are you educated? Are you without precocity on the one hand and backwardness on the other? Are you balanced mortals? I know you will shortly hold diplomas and graduate degrees from one of the great universities of the modern world. But I remind you that John Milton's test of a complete education—"that which fits a man to perform justly, skilfully and magnanimously all the offices, both private and public, of peace and war"—is as good to-day as it was three hundred years ago . . .

5. And because there are few really educated, completely balanced people on earth; because there are few specialists with the versatility of Leonardo da Vinci, or Thomas Jefferson, I am bold enough to suggest that you professional people especially should beware of any complacent idea that to know your own field well is enough. Unfortunately, an education, so-called, which should only be an introduction to humility and further enquiry, is too often an introduction to pride and mental paralysis.

6. So, with that brief plea for a restless, unsatisfied mind always open to everything except fear and prejudice, which, so far as I've been able to detect, is the only remedy for the humanist deficiencies of scientific education, I would like to mention some nettles and dangers in which lie sorrow and safety alike . . .

7. Has something happened to our morals and ethics? Is this the century of cynicism? Has the black bag with the pay-off money become the national emblem? Is the fix more influential than the Bible? It begins to look that way. Of course having lived only one life of which I have any distinct recollection, I have no basis of comparison, and I don't know whether things are any worse than they used to be. But I do know they are pretty bad. We have heard much about the alliance of crime and politics. Hoodlums and racketeers dominate whole sections of our cities. Public officials are corrupted for protection of gambling. By muscle and money racketeers take over legitimate businesses and ruin honest men. The revelations of the Kefauver investigations about the extent and power of organized crime shocked many of us. Evil influences creep into high places. The shakedown is a common-place. For a little money a business man can save a lot of trouble. Lobbies for every special interest, good or evil, are an institution in all legislative halls. Gamblers bribe athletes to fix games. Colleges hire athletes who are not bona-fide students. Two-legged jackals peddle narcotics to children on our street corners. Respectable citizens protest loudly about lawlessness and venality but don't hesitate to fix a traffic ticket. A lot of overweight trucks are punishing our roads this very day because it pays to violate the law. To-morrow someone will commend my efforts to enforce the gambling laws, but, he will add, of course, the private clubs and lodges should be exempted. And then there are the unscrupulous for whom anything goes if it is within the letter of the law, or not too far outside; the numerous kind to whom legality and morality are the same. The defiant, "Well, ain't it legal!" has become a part of our language.

8. I could go on and on, and so could you, adding to the evidence that something has happened; that the distinction between right and wrong is blurred; that cynicism and materialism are eating away at morals and ethics.

9. Unless you and your likes all over the country resist the corruption and corrosion of our times, you will pluck no flowers of safety from this ugly nettle of moral danger, because whatever the apostles of the easy way, whatever the heralds of cynicism say, the inexorable law, the inescapable fact remains that whatever we sow we reap. And no man, nor nation, nor civilization has been able to beat that rap yet—if I may use a vulgarism in such exalted company. *Representative American Speeches,* 1952

1. In general, what is Mr. Stevenson saying to this class graduating in medicine?
2. Why does he feel impelled to say this particular thing to this particular group?
3. How does Mr. Stevenson, in the first two paragraphs of his address, attempt to arouse the interest of his audience in his subject?
4. To what emotion does he appeal in paragraphs 3, 4 and 5?
5. What is the purpose of paragraph 6?
6. Would the omission of paragraphs 7 and 8 improve the address? Give reasons for your opinion.
7. For what purpose has Mr. Stevenson used his last paragraph?
8. Name and illustrate some of the characteristics of Mr. Stevenson's style.
9. Is Mr. Stevenson convincing? Persuasive? Give reasons for your opinions.

ARGUMENT

LESSON TWO

PLANNING AND WRITING A PERSUASIVE EDITORIAL

In order to write an effective persuasive editorial:
1. choose a subject in which you are interested and of which you have an intimate knowledge;
2. address the editorial to people of your own age;
3. decide what thesis you wish to prove and what action you want your readers to take;
4. marshal convincing proof of your thesis;
5. decide to what emotion (s) you will appeal;
6. plan the overall structure of your editorial.

THE OVERALL STRUCTURE OF A PERSUASIVE EDITORIAL

The overall structure of argument is usually the same as that of exposition: a lead, a statement of the thesis, the proof of the thesis and a conclusion.

An editorial argument frequently uses as a lead some current event. The editor relates this incident as concisely and forcefully as he can and then states his thesis. In the body of the editorial he marshals, in logical order, what he considers to be sufficient proof of his thesis; in the conclusion, he emphasizes in some clever or imaginative way the thesis he has been developing. Such an arrangement of material results in an argument that is unified, coherent and emphatic in structure.

When planning an editorial that not only will convince people but also will influence them to take action, a journalist may choose one of three overall structures. He may make his emotional appeal after the lead and a statement of the thesis, and then launch into his proof, after which he concludes by telling his readers, as specifically as possible, exactly what action he wants them to take. This structure is the one that Abraham Lincoln recommended to all who would influence others to take action. A writer may, however, reverse this order of proof and emotional appeal; or he may weave the two together.

An inexperienced writer has a tendency to devote too large a part of his editorial to the emotional appeal and too small a part to the argument. Such a lack of appropriate proportion may alienate thoughtful readers.

CLASS DISCUSSION I
Planning an Editorial

Below you will find the preliminary decisions made by a student who chose to write his persuasive editorial on traffic accidents. Use the discussion questions that follow to make a plan for this editorial.

Preliminary Decisions

Subject:	Traffic Accidents
To Whom Addressed:	Teen-aged boys
Purpose:	To *convince* them that reckless driving is dangerous not only to themselves but to others, and to *persuade* them to obey the traffic rules
Why:	A great many teen-aged boys think that it is "smart" to break these rules.
Thesis:	Reckless driving is dangerous not only to yourself, but to others.

Discussion Suggestions

1. The lead in this type of editorial is usually a reference to a current event. Its purpose is to give the reader definite evidence that a problem demanding solution exists. Suggest possible leads for the above editorial.
2. The thesis to be proved in this editorial contains two ideas. What are they, and in what order would you discuss them? Why?
3. The two paragraphs following the lead might contain the necessary evidence to convince teen-aged boys that many of them drive recklessly. Suggest concrete examples that you might use for this purpose.
4. Having attempted to convince teen-aged boys that their driving is reckless, you should now make them *want* to become careful drivers. Suggest an emotion to which you might appeal with some hope of success. Give reasons for your choice.
5. In the conclusion, you must tell them exactly what action you wish them to take. What specific suggestions can you make to impress on them the

101

importance of the rules that they may have enjoyed breaking? Remember that vague generalities, such as "Obey the traffic laws", are *not* as effective in influencing people as are specific suggestions, such as "The next time you feel an urge to slide through on a yellow light . . ."

Analyzing Persuasive Editorials Written by Students

The following editorial, written by a student interested in public affairs, would have been improved by the addition of topic sentences. Read the editorial, and answer in writing the questions that follow it. The paragraphs are numbered for convenience in discussing.

Good Citizenship

1. Our municipal elections were held on January third. Newspaper reporters, radio announcers, and civic-minded citizens were but a few of those who were disappointed and shocked by the exceedingly poor voting turnout. There was no flood, no tornado, no snow-storm, no severe epidemic, no atomic explosion. Yet eligible voters did not come to the polls.

2. Now that all the returns have been counted, the city clerk has estimated that only one-quarter of the eligible voters took advantage of their privilege and voted for the man they wanted to see in office. John Smith, who was not even expected to place in the voting results, was elected mayor for a two-year term. Now, for the next two years, we shall be forced to listen to the complaints of the supporters of his opponent, James Jones, who will, in all probability, dislike Smith's method of running civic affairs. The majority of the adults in our city will be discontented because, perhaps, the new library will not be built, nor the football stadium modernized. They have no one to blame for this discontent but themselves. They had the power to elect their favourite, but they were unable to do so. Why? Because they did not vote!

3. According to time-honoured custom, both Smith and Jones made it possible for their supporters to go to the polls with as little difficulty as possible, by having automobiles call at the homes of the voters to drive them to and from the polls. The weather was fair on that day in January, and even if the voters had to walk, they would have enjoyed the exercise, had they taken advantage of their opportunity! Executives of large firms were requested to arrange a shift system so that all their employees might have the necessary time to mark their ballots. Advance polls were arranged to allow those who would be out of town to vote. Nevertheless, this year's elections were marked, and will be noted for, the smallest voting turn-out since 1902, when a severe epidemic of influenza prevented many from voting.

4. The franchise is a right not possessed by all the countries in the world to-day. In some Communist-controlled nations you may vote, but all the candidates are from one party. We are dissatisfied if, as a result of our elections, our cousin is not elected, or if the roof of the town hall is not painted a colour we like, or if our taxes are a few cents higher than they

were so that the new street-lights can be paid for. Think how much worse it would be if you lived in Communist-"governed" Russia! You could not attend the church of your choice. Instead, you would be forced to elect, to obey, almost to worship as gods, the men whom the party chose. Thank God we have the right to elect whom we wish! We should use that right. Indeed, the exercising of your franchise is not only a right and a privilege; it is a necessity, an obligation, an absolute must! Sheila F.

Discussion Questions

1. To whom is this editorial addressed and why?
2. What are its purposes?
3. What facts does the writer use to convince her readers that a serious problem exists?
4. To what emotions does she appeal in order to persuade them to take action?
5. The editorial would be more coherent and forceful if the writer had used topic sentences. Compose an appropriate topic sentence for each of the following paragraphs: 2, 3 and 4.
6. Correct the errors that the student made in the following sentences:
    a) John Smith, who was not even expected to place in the voting results, was elected mayor for a two-year term.
    b) Smith and Jones made it possible for their supporters to go to the polls with as little difficulty as possible, by having automobiles call at the homes of the voters to drive them to and from the polls.
    c) Nevertheless, this year's elections were marked, and will be noted for, the smallest voting turnout since 1902 . . .
7. Name and exemplify some of the characteristics of this student's writing.
8. Would this editorial influence its readers to take action? Give reasons for your opinion.

CLASS DISCUSSION III

The following persuasive article was written by a student who had returned recently from a visit to England. Use the questions that follow it to evaluate its effectiveness. The paragraphs are numbered for convenience in discussing.

Justice

1. The measured tread of your footsteps, and those of the men walking beside you, rings out against the polished steel floor with a horrible monotony. A few seconds later you arrive at the end of a long, dimly-lit corridor. A grinding screech makes your teeth grate, as a steel key turns in a steel lock, and a steel door swings open. A big uniformed man yanks at the steel manacles connecting your wrist to his, and you move slowly into another room. Here you are photographed, finger-printed, and given a dull, grey uniform to wear. Then you are on the move again. This time you walk through two tremendous doors into a sombre, grey yard, where a group of sombre, grey-clad men are performing various tasks. There is a very loud bang behind you, as the two great doors close. You do not think too much about that clang at the moment, but you will remember it. It will begin

103

coming back to your mind, day after day. You will hear it while sitting alone in your cell; you will hear it outside, whether working or exercising; you will hear it when you are eating your meals, washing your face, combing your hair; you will hear it in nightmares when you are asleep; you will never forget it! For it is the final clang that shuts you off from your world. It is the clang that changes you from a name to a number, from an individual to a tiny member of a great, grey body of men, from a citizen to a ward of the government. You are a convict!

2. The alarm clock jangles. You wake up from your bad dream. You are relieved, but the dream makes you stop and think. "Well," you say, "things have changed. We're civilized now; prisons are no longer the horrible things they used to be." Or are they? Suppose we consider objectively for a moment.

3. If a criminal is given a sentence of over two years, he is taken to a federal penitentiary. Here, in a large, spacious building, he serves his time; and much effort is expended to rehabilitate him. If, however, his sentence is less than two years, he goes to a provincial "pen"; and things are different.

4. Here exist almost unbelievable conditions that go back practically to the mediaeval dungeons: old, crumbling stone buildings, which should have been levelled years ago. And what of conditions inside? One of these institutions, our Don Jail, has been condemned as the "Black Hole of Calcutta" by every investigating team for the last fifty years. In many places jails are worse. Some are so dirty that a farmer would not keep a good sow there. And to add to these conditions come the horrors of overcrowding. In one community there is even a waiting list to get into jail! This building, originally built to hold forty men, now houses a hundred and forty; and new convicts must be kept under guard in the community until a vacancy occurs. These, then, are the conditions in which men and boys with sentences of under two years live. In most cases the punishment of living in these quarters is too great for the crime committed. What kind of justice is it that sends men to an atmosphere where the mind festers, the conscience corrodes, and the prisoner returns to society with a deadly hate for it? Remember that most of these prisoners are young boys being punished for their first offence. Since they are extremely impressionable, sending them here is practically condemning them to a life of crime. However, in many cases nowadays the local magistrates are upping the sentences over the two-year mark, in order that youths may be sent to federal penitentiaries, where they get a decent chance.

5. What is to be done about this problem? First and foremost there must be a change in public opinion. In one town, where one of the very worst of these prisons was located, the public attitude was one of "Well, it's good enough—and better than the ones that go in there deserve!" The man who expressed this opinion was a very strong church worker in the community. If he had read his own Bible, he would have found the passage, "Love thy enemies . . ." Christ said this because he knew that loving his enemies is the only way a person may change them from being enemies. So to-day society must take a different view of its enemies. By the eternal

104

standards of justice a person must be punished for his crimes. But what is the use of punishing him in a way that will bring on more crimes and make him for his whole life a thorn in the side of the community?

6. Once public opinion has changed, the next thing is to improve our penal system. In the federal penitentiaries better conditions exist. Here, kept under decent conditions, the prisoner meets psychiatrists, church workers, and social workers, all with a genuine interest in helping him. The old, hardened criminals are separated from the younger ones. Prison is no longer a crime school, but a rehabilitation centre. Even so, of our federal inmates who are released, one out of two comes back.

7. There is, however, a better system than this one. In Britain, almost without exception, a first offender is not imprisoned, but placed on probation. This entails going on living in the community under the guidance of a trained social worker. The effects of this system are astounding. At the turn of the century when probation was introduced there were one hundred and eighty thousand criminals in Britain's jails. Last year, despite the tremendous rise in population over a half century, there were only thirty-four thousand people in prison. Here we may compare Britain, with a population of forty-five million and thirty-four thousand convicts, to Canada, with a population of fourteen million, and ninety-eight thousand convicts.

8. Justice has always been pictured as being blindfolded. In Canada, one must believe she is cross-eyed as well. We punish our prisoners on one hand for going against us; and on the other hand, incense them with hatred for society and all that it stands for, so that they will return to plague us again and again. Our provincial penitentiaries must be cleaned up, probation must be adopted in a large-scale fashion, and above all, the public must learn to want prison reform, and to campaign for it. George M.

Discussion Questions

1. To whom is this article addressed?
2. Of what does the writer wish to convince his readers?
3. To what emotions does he appeal?
4. a) What action does he wish his readers to take?
   b) Keeping in mind the people to whom he is speaking, comment on the practicability of the suggestions made in the last paragraph.
5. Comment on the effectiveness of the lead in arousing the reader's interest in the topic.
6. Are paragraphs 4, 5, 6 and 7 unified? Give reasons for your opinion.
7. Are these paragraphs emphatic in structure? Give reasons for your opinion.
8. What are some of the characteristics of this student's style? To support your opinion, refer to specific sentences that the student has used.
9. If you think that this article has weaknesses, point them out, and suggest how they can be eliminated.

105

ON EDITORIAL STYLE

As you are planning the structure of your editorial, plan also to put your best writing into the finished work. Perhaps some of you will choose editorial work for a career. If so, you will find that journalism exacts at all times your best efforts. You must be aware of the life and issues about you; you must be able to see the story behind the fact, the bizarre in the commonplace. You must be able to use words as tools. The following excerpts, taken from *Editor and Editorial Writer* by A. Gayle Waldrop contain many good suggestions with examples by outstanding journalists; these passages show, in addition, something of the "adventure" that working with words can bring to you.

Excerpts from
Editor and Editorial Writer

In *An Adventure with a Genius,* Alleyne Ireland tells of hearing Joseph Pulitzer propound a dozen times his theory of editorial writing. Pulitzer called for three cardinal qualities: brevity, directness and style.

He watched the style of each man with the closest attention, examining the length of the paragraphs, of the sentences, of the words, the variety of the vocabulary, the choice of adjectives and adverbs, the employment of superlatives, the selection of a heading, the nicety of adjustment between the thought to be expressed and the language employed for its expression. He was never content that a man should stand upon his record; growth and development were the chief aims of his discipline.

In a foreword to the editorials of Frank I. Cobb, Pulitzer's most distinguished "pupil", Woodrow Wilson wrote: "I recognized in him a peculiar genius for giving direct and effective expression to the enlightened opinions which he held". Not forgetting that Cobb's "sturdiness of character and clear vision of duty" had much to do with his forceful editorials, we should not discount the value of the style devices of which he was master.

Cobb knew well the importance of the strong title, the direct opening paragraph, and of circling back from the final paragraph to the first. His titles reveal use of strong words, of questions, of contrast, of alliteration. ... He often aroused attention by starting his editorials with short and simple sentences, and left a final echo in the closing sentences or paragraph ...

The repetition of the same idea in the same words or by variation was one of Cobb's chief style weapons. It is not enough to

106

make a point clear only once. The emphasis of repeated phrases, repeated quotations, is essential to leading thought and inspiring action. The businessman who advertises relies on repetition, not on brilliancy or wit or great variety. "The courtship which culminates in marriage consists largely of the repetition of the same sentence millions of times", Arthur Brisbane once wrote. "It sounds dull to outsiders, but it brings results". Supplementing the important weapon of repetition, Cobb used the auxiliary arms of parallel structure and culmination; figures of speech, to appeal to the visually-minded; contrast, which simplified issues; questions, ably framed; alliteration, with a careful regard for sense as well as sound; an occasional epigram, short and quotable. He used allusions, literary and historical. He included a wealth of concrete details. Occasionally he used the lie direct, paradox, deadly parallel, paraphrase, personification. Often he used quotations, at the beginning, in the body, in the last paragraph. . . .

It is significant that Winston Churchill made use of repetition, questions, contrast, alliteration, and figures of speech in his great prewar and wartime addresses. He ranged through natural history and common experiences in his picture-making appeals, from the Biblical "locust years" to the homely "pulling their wagon out of the ditch" . . .

Churchill asked questions singly and in series. He used the device of repetition, before the war, especially with five subjects: "redress of the grievances of the vanquished should precede the disarmament of the victors"; "the only defence is an adequate air force"; "business as usual"; "the lack of a united front"; and "rubbing this sore of the Disarmament Conference until it has become a cancer". The addresses of Winston Churchill were spoken editorials. Because his nouns were pictures and his verbs worked, a study of his style will reward the editorial writer. In Pulitzer prize-winning editorials you will find the same style devices that Cobb and Churchill used, and some others, including direct address, aphorisms, the intensification and the softening of the negative, and understatement.

Make a detailed plan and then write a 500-word editorial in which you try: (a) to convince your readers that a problem exists and (b) to persuade them to take action. Revise your first draft so that your editorial will be as clear, forceful and persuasive as you can make it. Hand in both the plan and the editorial. A list of suggested subjects and an example of a detailed plan are found below.

Subjects for Persuasive Editorials

Basketball
Bus Drivers
Camera Club
Charity
Comic Books
Current Affairs Club
Drama Guild
Extra-Curricular Activities
Fishing
Flood Control
Football
Forest Conservation
Forest Fires
Freedom
Glee Club
Going to Church
Good Citizenship
Good Manners
Hockey

Join Our Club!
Juvenile Delinquency
Morning Devotions
Politics
School Bus
School Library
School Magazine
School Spirit
Science Club
Selling Advertising for the
    School Magazine
Student Council
Summer Camp
Summer Camp for Underprivileged
    Children
Track and Field
Traffic Accidents
Trashy Novels
Winter Sports

Example of a Detailed Plan for a Persuasive Editorial

Below is a detailed plan made by the student referred to on page 101. Study this plan carefully before making your own.

1. *Preliminary Decisions*

To whom addressed: driving teachers and inspectors who grant new drivers their licences

Purposes of Editorial:

a) to convince these people that many traffic accidents are caused by drivers who have been inadequately taught, and who have received their licenses only because of the laxity of the inspectors and administrators;

b) to show these people that their carelessness has caused many traffic accidents; I want to make them so ashamed of their poor work that they will want to improve it;

108

	c) to show them that their duty as citizens, teachers and human beings is to raise the standards of their work in order to eliminate many needless accidents.
Thesis:	Many traffic incidents have been caused by incompetent drivers.

2. *The Structure of the Editorial*

Lead:	accident, and interview with the man who caused it
Body of Editorial:	a) lack of competent teaching (I will cite evidence to prove.) b) shame teachers and inspectors (my emotional appeal.)
Conclusion:	Challenge these two groups to do something

3. *The Detailed Plan*: Topic Sentences

a) In the body of the editorial:	(i) This lack of competent teaching and this carelessness in testing is an ever-increasing problem in our city. (ii) Teachers and inspectors should realize the heartache and tragedy caused by their laxity. (iii) As citizens, teachers and human beings, you should consider it your duty to raise the standards of your work.
b) In the conclusion:	The lives of many people are in your keeping.

CRITERIA BY WHICH A PERSUASIVE EDITORIAL MAY BE JUDGED

1. *Credit*

Merits: To be worth a credit, a persuasive editorial must have merit in structure and in content. Structurally, the editorial must be unified, coherent and emphatic; and every paragraph must be unified, coherent and emphatic. In content. it must have an argument, an effective emotional appeal, and suggestions for action.

Flaws: The flaws that prevent a persuasive editorial or article from receiving a higher grade are:

a) *unconvincing argument*: the writer does not cite enough facts and/or examples to be convincing: relies on his own *opinion* rather than on facts;

b) *weak conclusion*: the suggestions for action are either impracticable or so general that the reader does not know what action he can take;

c) *immature style:* diction and sentence structure are still poor.

109

2. Third-Class Honours

Merits: To be worth third-class honours, a persuasive editorial or article must possess the above merits in structure and in content, together with the following:

  a) *convincing proof*: plenty of facts and/or concrete examples to substantiate opinions given:

  b) *a lead* that would attract the attention of the group to whom the editorial or article is addressed;

  c) *intelligent conclusion*: practicable and specific suggestions.

Flaws: The writer of such an editorial has mastered the techniques of effective persuasion but has not yet learned to write a pleasing style. He shows little sensitivity to words, and he has not learned to construct effective sentences.

3. Second-Class Honours

Merits: To receive this grading, an editorial must have all of the merits listed as necessary for a third-class grading, and must show, in addition, that the writer has used words sensitively.

Flaw: The one weakness in the second-class editorial is poor sentence structure. The student has not yet mastered the techniques of writing good sentences.

4. First-Class Honours

The first-class persuasive editorial must have merit in structure, content and style. It differs from the second-class composition in one respect; sentence structure. The author has learned to write unified, coherent and emphatic sentences, to vary his sentence structure in order to prevent monotony, and to use rhetorical devices for specific effects.

ARGUMENT

LESSON THREE

CHOOSING THE BEST EDITORIALS WRITTEN BY STUDENTS

Follow the procedure outlined on page 56.

For discussion at the conclusion of the reading of the best editorials, the subject might be: *What are some of the merits of these editorials?*

Refer to specific editorials to illustrate your opinions.

DESCRIPTION

THE AIMS OF DESCRIPTION

A description is a verbal portrayal of a person, an animal, an object or a scene.

CLASS DISCUSSION I

1. Name three purposes for which a novelist may use descriptive passages. Illustrate each purpose by a reference to some novel you have read recently.
2. Name three purposes for which you might use description in an exposition.
3. For what purposes might you use description in an argument?
4. In the following excerpt taken from the Preface to *The Nigger of the Narcissus,* Joseph Conrad explains his aim in writing:

> To arrest, for the space of a breath, the hands busy about the work of earth, and compel men entranced by the sight of distant goals to glance for a moment at the surrounding vision of form and colour, of sunshine and shadows; to make them pause for a look, for a sigh, for a smile—such is the aim, difficult and evanescent, and reserved only for a very few to achieve. But sometimes, by the deserving and the fortunate, even that task is accomplished. And when it is accomplished—behold!—all the truth of life is there: a moment of vision, a sigh, a smile . . .

   a) According to Conrad most people do not really look at the world intently enough to enjoy its beauty, to sigh at its pathos, to smile at its humour or its irony. What prevents them from being aware of these interesting aspects of life?
   b) Put into your own words Conrad's aim in writing. Illustrate, if possible, by reference to a passage from a good novel you have read.

CLASS DISCUSSION II

Read aloud the article reproduced below, and then use the questions that follow it to discuss its content. (When the writer was a student at Harvard University, he studied English with a professor who required his first-year pupils to write a daily theme.)

The Daily Theme Eye

When I was an undergraduate at Harvard our instructors in English composition endeavoured to cultivate in us a something they termed "the daily theme eye". This peculiar variety of optic, I fear, always remained a mystery to a majority of the toilers after clearness, force, and elegance. Clearness, force and even a certain degree of elegance, may be acquired; but the daily theme eye, like the eye for the sights of a rifle, may be dis-

111

covered, developed, trained—but not acquired. It comes by the grace of Heaven, not of the Harvard or any other English department, and its possession is often one of the marks of the man whose destiny compels him to write . . .

The fairy who stood over my cradle, though he forgot the gold spoon and much else besides, at least bestowed the gift of this wonderful optic. It brought me my college degree; for when other courses failed—which means when I failed in other courses—there was always English; it has brought me a living since; but more than all else it has brought me enjoyment, it has clothed the daily walk with interest, the teeming, noisy town with colour and beauty, "the society of my contemporaries", to use Emerson's big phrase for my little purpose, with stimulating excitement. It has turned the panorama of existence into a play, or rather a thousand plays, and brought after sorrow or pain the great comfort of composition.

Daily themes in my day had to be short, not over a page of handwriting. They had to be deposited in a box at the professor's door not later than ten-five in the morning. A classmate of mine, when an epigram was called for, once wrote, "An epigram is a lazy man's daily theme written at ten-three a.m." And because of this brevity, and the necessity of writing one every day whether the mood was on you or not, it was not always easy —to be quite modest—to make these themes literature, which, we were told by our instructors, is the transmission through the written word, from writer to reader, of a mood, an emotion, a picture, an idea . . .

. . . Well, the effort of those of us who were sincere and comprehending in our pursuit of the elusive power to write was to make our themes literature as often as possible; and to do this the first essential was the choice of a subject. Not everything one sees or does or thinks can take shape on a page of paper and reproduce itself for the reader. Selection was the first requirement.

It became needful, then, to watch for and treasure incidents that were sharply dramatic or poignant, moods that were clear and definite, pictures that created a single clean impression. The tower of Memorial seen across the quiet marshes against the cool, pink sky of evening; the sweep of a shell under the bridge and the rush of the spectators to the other rail to watch the needle-like bow emerge, and the bent, brown backs of the crew; the chorus girls, still rubbing the paint from their cheeks with a tiny handkerchief wrapped over the forefinger, coming out of a stage entrance into the snow; the first sharp impression of a book just read or a play just seen,— these were the things we cherished, for these we could put on a page of paper with a beginning, a middle, and an end, and with some show of vividness. What we came to do, then, was to keep a note-book of our impressions, and when in June our themes were returned to us we had a precious record for the year. By training the daily theme eye, we watched for and found in the surroundings of our life, as it passed, a heightened picturesqueness, a constant wonder, an added significance. That hardened cynic, the professional writer, will smile and say, "You saw copy". Yes, we saw copy; but to see copy is to see the significant, to clarify what the ear and heart and eye receive, to add light and shadow to the monochrome of life.

My college room-mate, a blessed boy full of good humour and serious purpose, was as incapable of acquiring the daily theme eye as a cat of obeying the eighth commandment. His idea of a daily theme was a task, not a pleasure. If there was no chance to write a political editorial, he supplied an anecdote of his summer vacation. Once he described a cliff he had seen in Newfoundland, and, determined to be pictorial, he added, "tumbling waterfalls" and "sighing pines". Unfortunately, the instructor who read it had also been in Newfoundland, and he pointed out that his investigations of the cliff in question had failed to disclose either "tumbling waterfalls" or "sighing pines". My room-mate treated the matter as a joke; he could not see that he had been guilty of any fault. And yet he is a much more moral man than I, with a far more troublesome conscience. Truth to his principles he would die for. But truth to the picture his mind retained and his hand tried to portray in the medium of literature, to him so trivial and unimportant, he could not grasp. What did it matter? So it would never occur to him to record in his themes the fleeting impressions of his daily life, to sit up half the night trying to pack into the clumsy frame of words the recollection of a strangely innocent face seen suddenly in the flash of an opened door down a dark, evil alley where the gusts of winter swirled. He went to bed and never knew a headache or jumpy nerve. Yet I could not help thinking then that there was something in life he was missing besides the ultimate mark in our composition course. And I cannot help thinking that there is something in life he misses still. Walter Pritchard Eaton, "The Daily Theme Eye", The *Atlantic Monthly*

Discussion Questions

1. What is a "daily theme eye"?
2. Why does the author value such a talent?
3. What does he think his room-mate is missing in life?
4. Mr. Eaton says: "Not everything one sees or does or thinks can take shape on a page and reproduce itself for the reader. Selection was the first requirement". What kind of an incident, what kind of a mood and what kind of a scene make good "copy"? Give one example of each.

CLASS DISCUSSION III

Read and discuss the following description taken from Thomas Wolfe's novel *Of Time and the River*.

The Race

As the train was pounding north across New Jersey, another train upon the inside track began to race with it, and for a distance of ten miles the two trains thundered down the tracks in an even, thrilling, and tremendous contest of steel and smoke and pistoned wheel that blotted out everything, the vision of the earth, the thought of the journey, the memory of the city, for all who saw it.

The other train, which was bound from Philadelphia, appeared so calmly and naturally that at first no one suspected that a race was on. It came banging up slowly, its big black snout swaying and bucking with a clumsy movement as it came on, its shining pistons swinging free and loose, and with short intermittent blasts of smoke from its squat funnel. It came up so slowly and naturally, past their windows, that at first it was hard to understand at what terrific speed the train was running, until one looked out of the windows on the other side and saw the flat, formless and uncharactered earth of New Jersey whipping by like pickets on a fence.

The other train came slowly on with that huge banging movement of the terrific locomotive, eating its way up past the windows, until the engine cab was level with Eugene and he could look across two or three scant feet of space and see the engineer. He was a young man cleanly jacketed in striped blue and wearing goggles. He had a ruddy color and his strong pleasant face, which bore on it the character of courage, dignity, and the immense and expert knowledge these men have, was set in a good-natured and determined grin, as with one gloved hand held steady on the throttle, he leaned upon his sill, with every energy and perception in him fixed with a focal concentration on the rails. Behind him his fireman, balanced on the swaying floor, his face black and grinning, his eyes goggled like a demon, and lit by the savage flare of his terrific furnace, was shovelling coal with all his might. Meanwhile, the train came on, came on, eating its way past, foot by foot, until the engine cab had disappeared from sight, and the first coaches of the train drew by.

And now a wonderful thing occurred. As the heavy rust-red coaches of the other train came up and began to pass them, the passengers of both trains suddenly became aware that a race between the trains was taking place. A tremendous excitement surged up in them, working its instant magic upon all these travellers, with their gray hats, their gray, worn city faces, and their dull tired eyes, which just the moment before had been fastened wearily on the pages of a newspaper, as if, having been hurled along this way beneath the lonely skies so many times, the desolate face of the earth had long since grown too familiar to them, and they never looked out windows any more.

But now the faces that had been so gray and dead were flushed with color, the dull and lustreless eyes had begun to burn with joy and interest. The passengers of both trains crowded to the windows, grinning like children for delight and jubilation.

Eugene's train, which for a space had been holding its rival even, now began to fall behind. The other train began to slide past the windows with increasing speed, and when this happened the joy and triumph of its passengers were almost unbelievable. Meanwhile their own faces had turned black and bitter with defeat. They cursed, they muttered, they scowled malevolently, they turned away with an appearance of indifference, as if they had no further interest in the thing, only to come back again with a fascinated and bitter look as their accursed windows slid by them with the inevitability of death and destiny. Wolfe, *Of Time and The River*

Discussion Questions

1. What episode is Mr. Wolfe describing, and why did he find it an interesting one?
2. a) What is the dominant mood of this description?
   b) How did the author establish it?
3. For what purpose has the author used each of his paragraphs?
4. What was Mr. Wolfe's aim in writing this description?
5. Point out some of the characteristics of Mr. Wolfe's style.

CLASS DISCUSSION IV

In the following description published in *News,* September 29, 1945, Judith Robinson depicts the return to a small Ontario town of young men who had been fighting in far places. Read the description aloud, then use the discussion questions on pages 116-7 to guide your analysis of it.

The Basin

The garageman at The Basin looked new since last year. He wasn't, he said. Just been away for a while.

Far away?

Oh, middling. England and Italy and a spell in Holland. Nice being home, the garageman said.

The brown dog that lies in front of the store when it isn't lying in front of the bakery got up and lounged across the road to lie in front of the bakery. The shadow of the big maple beside the bank had reached as far as the wooden stoop in front of the store. In front of the bakery the pavement was still warm and unshadowed.

Four o'clock on a September afternoon and on Main Street in The Basin the brown dog was the only traffic. The garageman said he didn't notice it slow. Couldn't be too slow to suit him for a spell.

A high-seat jalopy, towing a high-wheeled waggon came tutting up the gravel road from the wharf and stopped by the gas pump. An old oil drum was in front of the waggon box. The man in the jalopy leaned out and jerked his head towards the drum. Put in eight, Al, he said. Pay you Sat'day. Al put in eight. Car and waggon went away again, slewing in the new gravel at the turn, tutting back to the wharf.

A pattern of leaf-shadows slid from the top of the jalopy down the curve of the black drum and along the waggon box, then dropped to the road again to lie quiet as before.

It'll do me this way, the garageman said, for quite a long spell.

This side of The Basin on the Bay Shore, where the little yellow house was built for spotters from the bombing school to sit, watching the target across the sunny water, there was nothing. The little house was clean gone, the flat rock bare as your hand between the green of the road-edge and the willow shrubs along the water. No roar of engines sounded over it. The ripples broke along the shelving stone as lightly as though the day had never been when a bomber dived too low on a target there and could not pull out.

115

The water had forgotten that horror of destruction, the air brought no shuddering whisper of it across the brightness of the bay.

The mail-car stopped by the box across the road from the flat rock, and went on again. A young man in khaki came down the lane from the farmhouse, carrying a little girl on his shoulder. He was a tall young man and he carried the child high, so that she had to stoop to miss the lowest branches of the tree by the mail box. As she stooped, she steadied herself, a small arm around the back of the young man's head, a hand on his cheek. She leaned down; he looked up, and they smiled half shyly to one another.

That'd be the Gorman's son-in-law home, Lizzie said when she heard about him. They'd been expecting him these last three boats. Never seen the little girl till now, and her five next birthday. Seems queer, don't it? Lizzie said.

Next day, on the Fifty-foot, the Gorman's farm truck passed, going to the back sixty. A big young man was driving it. He wore a faded battle-blouse, with the shoulder patches still up, above a pair of new blue overalls. They looked all right together, and the Gorman's son-in-law looked as though they felt all right, too.

For peace has come back to the Bay Shore. The price of freedom having been paid anew, The Basin has accepted deliverance with its accustomed calm. But of those who, loving it, went out to save it, some will not come back.

The Basin, which is old and has outlived many battles and many sorrows, holds their spent youth whole in its quietness, as in enchantment. So that all of their days, which were so few on this loved shore, return now to touch and transmute . . .When the sun strikes aslant through driven clouds, it wakens for that moment, the light of a gaiety as swift and bright and unforgettable. So, when a shout echoes across from the point, it calls to another echo, deeper and sweeter, that waited only to be called . . .

So the tumble-down barns and the rickety little milk-can platforms along the Bay Shore road, and the mean tourist cabins by the ferry too, being all part of the dear remembrance youth took with it, for a strength in far and perilous places, shine now in reflected radiance. The Bay Shore is bright in that reflection; the unfading after-light of a happiness that, being lost, remains forever lovely and forever young.

Yet lost. The sun that was bright on The Bay goes down behind the pine ridge, and over The Basin, night sorrows uncomforted for the youth that will not grow old. *News*, September 29, 1945

Discussion Questions

1. From whose point of view is the village described? Give reasons for your opinion.
2. At what time of year, time of day, and on what kind of a day is the village described?
3. What is the dominant atmosphere of the village? Prove by referring to the details in the description.

116

4. Explain: "So the tumble-down barns and the rickety little milk-can platforms along the Bay Shore road, and the mean tourist cabins by the ferry being all part of the dear remembrance youth took with it for a strength in far and perilous places, shine now in reflected radiance".
5. What is emphasized by the visual detail with which the description concludes?
6. Why did Miss Robinson think this simple scene was worth describing?
7. What was her aim in this description?

DESCRIPTION

LESSON TWO

THE CLASSIFICATION OF DESCRIPTION

Description may be classified according to its *purpose* as scientific or literary.

Scientific description is that in which the writer has two aims: (a) to evoke images and (b) to inform the mind.

Literary description also has two aims: (a) to evoke images and (b) to convey someone's emotional response to the thing described.

Some scientific description combines the aims of scientific and of literary description. In Rachel Carson's *The Sea Around Us* and Sir James Jeans's *The Mysterious Universe* the authors' aims were not only to evoke images and to inform the mind, but also to convey their own feelings towards the things described.

Both literary and scientific description are subdivided according to their *subject matter* into individualized and generalized description. When a writer chooses to depict a particular scene, event, person, animal or object, viewed by a specific person at a specific time, he is writing individualized description—such as, for example, the McGill-Varsity football game, October 11th, 1958, viewed by a McGill fan. However, when a writer selects as his subject, not a specific football game, but rather football games in general or some aspect of football games, he is writing generalized description.

CLASS DISCUSSION

1. Classify each of the following four descriptions as:
   a) scientific generalized;
   b) scientific individualized;
   c) literary generalized;
   d) literary individualized;
   e) scientific and literary description combined.
2. Give reasons for your classifications.

117

1. Wading

He was warm from his jaunt. The dusky glen laid cool hands on him. He rolled up the hems of his blue denim breeches and stepped with bare, dirty feet into the shallow spring. His toes sank into the sand. It oozed softly between them and over his bony ankles. The water was so cold that for a moment it burned his skin. Then it made a rippling sound, flowing past his pipe-stem legs, and was entirely delicious. He walked up and down, digging his big toe experimentally under smooth rocks he encountered. A school of minnows flashed ahead of him down the growing branch. He chased them through the shallows. They were suddenly out of sight as though they had never existed. He crouched under a bared and overhanging live-oak root where a pool was deep, thinking they might reappear, but only a spring frog wriggled from under the mud, stared at him, and dove under the tree root in a spasmodic terror. He laughed.

"I ain't no 'coon. I'd not ketch you," he called after it.

A breeze parted the canopied limbs over him. The sun dropped through and lay on his head and shoulders. It was good to be warm at his head while his hard calloused feet were cold. The breeze died away, the sun no longer reached him. He waded across to the opposite bank where the growth was more open. A low palmetto brushed him. It reminded him that his knife was snug in his pocket; that he had planned, as long ago as Christmas, to make himself a flutter-mill. Marjorie Kinnan Rawlings, *The Yearling*

2. Asiatic Elephants

Asiatic elephants presumably are descendants of early mammoths; to-day as in Pleistocene times, they inhabit southwestern Asia and the East Indies but are familiar in zoos and circuses. The skull is very short and deep and is rounded on top, often with a "bulging forehead". The tusks are directed downward and seem to be disappearing, since they never are very large. Many females, indeed, lack them, and so do some males. The molars are high and broad, and the last ones to appear have twenty-four closely folded crossplates. The back is arched behind the shoulders; the feet are short and blunt, with five toes and pads of elastic tissue that receive most of the weight, since they touch the ground before the toes do. There are five hoofs on each forefoot and four behind, though the hoof of each fifth toe may be very small. The brain, which weighs 10 to 11 pounds, seems to be superior to that of *Loxodonta*. The height of full-grown males reaches 8 to 10 feet at the shoulder, and the weight is 8,000 to 10,000 pounds. Carroll Lane Fenton and Mildred Adams Fenton, *The Fossil Book*

3. Ruby-Crowned Kinglet

The small size of the ruby-crowned kinglets, their habit of flitting about dense masses of twigs and their quiet call-notes all tend to make them among our little-known birds. It comes as a surprise to one who is learning our birds to hear this kinglet burst forth in a delightful little song. Beginning in a high, thin, whispering note, the song ripples down the scale, pausing on

118

several rich, mellow strains, so clearly uttered and of such ringing quality that the tiny singer's voice can be heard several hundred yards through the quiet spring woods. Indeed, the song would do credit to a much larger bird. Stuart L. Thompson, *Eighty Land Birds to Know*

4. Canada

Wondrous and very sweet is our name. Canada! The very word is like a boy's shout in the springtime, is like the clamour of geese going north and the roar of melting rivers and the murmur of early winds.

Can we not hear the sound of Canada? Can we not hear it in the rustle of yellow poplar leaves in October, and in the sudden trout-splash of a silent lake, the whisper of saws in the deep woods, the church bells along the river, the whistle of trains in the narrow passes of the mountains, the gurgle of irrigation ditches in the hot nights, the rustle of ripe grain under the wind, and the bite of steel runners in the snow?

Have we not felt the texture and living stuff of Canada? Have we not felt it in the damp, springy forest floor, in the caress of the new grass upon our face, in the salt spray off Fundy or Juan de Fuca, in the hot sun of the prairies, in the beat of blizzards and the fierce surge of summer growth?

And the colours of Canada, those also have we seen. We have seen them in the harsh sweep of prairie snow, in sunlight and shadow vibrant across the heavy-headed wheat, in foaming apple-orchards and in maple woods red as blood, and in bleeding sumach by the roadside, and in white sails of schooners out of Lunenburg, and in the wrinkled blue face of mountains. And we have smelled the clean, manly smell of Canada, in pine forest, and settlers' clearing fires, and in alkali lakes and autumn stubble and new sawdust and old stone. Bruce Hutchison, *The Unknown Country*

DESCRIPTION

LESSON THREE

GAINING REALISTIC EFFECTS: SENSORY DETAILS

A description will not be fully effective in achieving the impression of reality unless the writer uses descriptive details that are sensory rather than abstract.

SENSORY VERSUS ABSTRACT DETAILS

A sensory detail is one that can be apprehended through one of the five senses: seeing, hearing, smelling, tasting, feeling. *Examples*:

1. Her fear alarmed him. (abstract detail)
2. Her *face grew pale, her eyes dilated*, and *she swayed* as if overcome with dizziness. *His heart pounded*. (sensory details)

When writing description of any type, use sensory details.

119

In the following excerpt taken from an unsigned article that appeared in *The Times Literary Supplement* (London), March 4, 1926, the author contrasts the effectiveness of abstract details and sensory details. Read the article and use the questions that follow it to guide your discussion.

English Prose

. . . We shall take, in the first instance, a passage from the "Oxford Book" [a new anthology of prose]; it is a passage from a modern writer, and here we suspect that the anthologist, not being able to resort to the unanimity of time, has too readily accepted the fashionable opinions of his own age: —

When, two days previously, the news of the approaching end had been made public, astonished grief had swept over the country. It appeared as if some monstrous reversal of the course of nature was about to take place. The vast majority of her subjects had never known a time when Queen Victoria had not been reigning over them. She had become an indissoluble part of their whole scheme of things, and that they were about to lose her appeared a scarcely possible thought. She herself, as she lay, blind and silent, seemed to those who watched her to be divested of all thinking—to have glided already, unawares, into oblivion. Yet, perhaps, in the secret chambers of consciousness, she had her thoughts, too. Perhaps her fading mind called up once more the shadows of the past to float before it, and retraced, for the last time, the vanished visions of that long history—passing back and back, through the cloud of years to older and ever older memories . . .

This is not an altogether bad piece of prose: it is not sufficiently bad to avert the reader. It has, indeed, attracted a great many. But contrast the passage with the following, from the work of a contemporaneous author [James Joyce] not represented in this anthology: —

The grainy sand had gone from under his feet. His boots trod again a damp crackling mast, razorshells, squeaking pebbles, that on the unnumbered pebbles beats, wood sieved by the shipworm, lost Armada. Unwholesome sandflats waited to suck his treading soles, breathing upward sewage breath. He coasted them, walking warily. A porterbottle stood up, stogged to its waist, in the cakey sand and dough. A sentinel: isle of dreadful thirst. Broken hoops on the shore; at the land a maze of dark cunning nets; further away chalk-scrawled backdoors and on the higher beach a drying-line with two crucified shirts.

There is evidently a great difference between these two passages, which is not the difference between two kinds of goodness but between one quality

120

and its opposite. The first causes us the less surprise: we are scarcely conscious of the kind of prose we are reading—apart from a certain ironic affectation; but we are, as a matter of fact, reading a prose densely packed with images and analogies, none of which we actually visualize. "Approaching end", "astonished grief", "grief sweeping over the country", "monstrous reversal", "the course of nature", "to take place", "vast majority", "an indissoluble part", "the scheme of things", "a scarcely possible thought", "divested of all thinking", "to glide into oblivion", "the secret chambers", "fading mind", "the shadows of the past", "to float before (her mind)", "the vanished visions", "through the cloud of years"—here in eighteen lines are eighteen images or analogies, not one of which is original, not one of which is freshly felt or sincerely evoked, and consequently not one of which evokes in the mind of the reader the definite image it actually portends. Now examine the second passage; there is not a single phrase which does not evoke—which does not force the mind to evoke—the image it expresses. Art, after all, is a question of effect; and does anyone give a thought to the death of Queen Victoria as our author has described it? But merely to read of Stephen Dedalus walking on the beach is to have come into contact with the vibrating reflex of an actual experience.

Discussion Questions

1. What is the writer's thesis?
2. State and illustrate the writer's criticism of the description of Queen Victoria's death.
3. How does the second descriptive paragraph that has been quoted in this passage illustrate the writer's thesis?

A VARIETY OF SENSORY DETAILS

The use of details appealing to one or several of the five senses helps give description an effect of reality.

Although visual images usually predominate, other sensory details may be part of our impression of a scene or an incident. When thinking of a happy evening that you and a chum spent sitting near your campfire one clear August evening, you remember not only the pleasant *sights*—the leaping of the flames against the darkness, your chum's face in the flickering fire-light—but you also recall the *sounds* and *odours*: the crackling of the fire, the lapping of the water against the rocks, the spicy smell of the pines. Probably you remember, too, the smell and taste of coffee and bacon and the warmth of the fire. To give a realistic impression of this scene, therefore, you should include *all* of the sensory details that contributed to the pleasantness of the experience.

121

In this paragraph, the author describes a visit to his stable. Read the paragraph and use the questions that follow it to guide your discussion.

In the Stable

And so I stepped into the darkened stable. I could not see the outlines of the horse or the cow, but knowing the place so well I could easily get about. I heard the horse step aside with a soft expectant whinny. I smelled the smell of milk, the musty, sharp odour of dry hay, the pungent smell of manure, not unpleasant. And the stable was warm after the cool of the fields with a sort of animal warmth that struck into me soothingly. I spoke in a low voice and laid my hand on the horse's flank. The flesh quivered and shrank away from my touch—coming back confidently, warmly. I ran my hand along his back and up his hairy neck. I felt his sensitive nose in my hand. "You shall have your oats," I said, and I gave him to eat. Then I spoke as gently to the cow, and she stood aside to be milked. David Grayson, *Adventures in Contentment*

1. Show that a visit after dark to the stable is a pleasant sensory experience to Mr. Grayson.
2. As you name each detail of the experience, tell exactly why it was pleasant.

1. SENSORY DETAILS TO ESTABLISH TIME AND PLACE

When writing individualized description, a good writer will establish precisely the specific time at which the scene is viewed. Instead of stating directly the time of year, the time of day, the kind of day, he often uses sensory details, such as, the feel of the air, the sun, the rain or snow, the characteristic light and shadow effects to convey this information. He also uses sensory details to establish the point from which the scene is observed. This is referred to as the *vantage* point. It may be either fixed or moving.

CLASS DISCUSSION

1. In the following paragraph, from the novel *The Yearling,* Marjorie Kinnan Rawlings describes one of young Jody's experiences. Read the paragraph and use the questions that follow it to guide your discussion.

Jody

He turned and galloped toward home. He drew deep breaths of the pines, aromatic with wetness. The loose sand that had pulled at his feet was firmed by the rain. The return was comfortable going. The sun was not far from its setting when the long-leaf pines around the Baxter clearing came into sight. They stood tall and dark against the red-gold west. He heard the chickens clucking and quarreling and knew they had just been fed. He turned into the clearing. The weathered gray of the split-rail fence was luminous in the rich spring light. Smoke curled thickly from the stick-and-clay chimney. Supper would be ready on the hearth and hot bread baking in the Dutch oven. Marjorie Kinnan Rawlings, *The Yearling*

a) What incident is described, through whose eyes, and from what vantage point? What sensory details fix the vantage point?
b) What details fix the time?
c) What sensory details made Jody's home-coming a pleasant experience to him?

2. In the paragraph given below, the scene described is viewed by a young man, Marlow, who, with others, is standing on the deck of a little river-steamer, deep in the heart of Africa. Read the paragraph and use the questions that follow it to guide your discussion.

Heart of Darkness

Dark human shapes could be made out in the distance, flitting indistinctly against the gloomy border of the forest, and near the river two bronze figures, leaning on tall spears, stood in the sunlight under fantastic head-dresses of spotted skins, warlike and still, in statuesque repose. And from right to left along the lighted shore moved a wild and gorgeous apparition of a woman.

She walked with measured steps, draped in striped and fringed cloths, treading the earth proudly, with a slight jingle and flash of barbarous ornaments. She carried her head high; her hair was done in the shape of a helmet; she had brass leggings to the knee, brass wire gauntlets to the elbow, a crimson spot on her tawny cheek, innumerable necklaces of glass beads on her neck; bizarre things, charms, gifts of witch-men, that hung about her, glittered and trembled at every step . . . She was savage and superb, wild-eyed and magnificent, there was something ominous and stately in her deliberate progress . . .

She came abreast of the steamer, stood still, and faced us. Her long shadow fell to the water's edge . . . A whole minute passed, and then she made a step forward. There was a low jingle, a glint of yellow metal, a sway of fringed draperies, and she stopped as if her heart had failed her. Joseph Conrad, *The Heart of Darkness*

a) What effect does Conrad gain in the first paragraph by the use of sunlight?
b) In the next two paragraphs, what details *remind* the reader that the woman is walking in the sunny strip near the river's edge?
c) What effect does Conrad achieve with the detail "her long shadow fell to the water's edge"?

2. SENSORY DETAILS TO PICTURE THE SKY

Look out of the window. Unless you are in the heart of a city, you will see a great sweep of bright blue if it is a sunny day; perhaps leaden grey sky, if it is raining. Whether you are aware of it or not, *earth and sky* is the visual image you receive when you look at a landscape; *ocean and sky* if you look at a seascape. To omit the sky, then, from your description of a scene that includes it is to leave with the reader an incomplete picture. To include it is to establish a three-dimensional world—with length, breadth and height—the world we know. Watch the sky, its infinite variety of colour effects and cloud patterns; and then, when you are writing a description of the outdoors, make your reader look up and see the sky.

CLASS DISCUSSION

In the following paragraph, Donn Byrne uses only a few sensory details to give a realistic impression of a "splendid winter night".

On the Road to Dublin

Above their heads, on this splendid winter night, a huge primrose-coloured moon hung, and on the edges of sky were the faint spangles of stars. The road was black, except for here and there a patch of white hoarfrost . . . the little groves of birch-trees were silent in the windless night. Only the whistle of the snipe was heard, and the booming of the bittern from some distant bog. Donn Byrne, *Blind Raftery*

1. What is the vantage point from which the scene is described?
2. What details give you the particulars about the time?
3. What other details help create the impression of reality?

3. SENSORY DETAILS TO GIVE A SHARP PICTURE

The inclusion of a few *small* details will contribute to the impression of reality.

CLASS DISCUSSION

This paragraph is the opening one in Dylan Thomas's short story "A Prospect of the Sea". Read the paragraph and use the questions that follow it to guide your discussion.

The Boy

It was high summer, and the boy was lying in the corn. He was happy because he had no work to do and the weather was hot. He heard the corn sway from side to side above him, and the noise of the birds who whistled from the branches of the trees that hid the house. Lying flat on his back, he stared up into the unbrokenly blue sky falling over the edge of the corn. The wind, after the warm rain before noon, smelt of rabbits and cattle. He stretched himself like a cat, and put his arms over his head. Now he was riding on the sea, swimming through the golden corn waves, gliding along the heavens like a bird; in seven-league boots he was springing over the fields; he was building a nest in the sixth of the seven trees that waved their hands from a bright, green hill. Now he was a boy with tousled hair, rising lazily to his feet, wandering out of the corn to the strip of river by the hill-side. He put his fingers in the water, making a mock sea-wave to roll the stones over and shake the weeds; his fingers stood up like ten tower pillars in the magnifying water, and a fish with a wise head and a lashing tail swam in and out of the tower gates . . . The boy sent a stone skidding over the green water. He saw a rabbit scuttle, and threw a stone at its tail. A fish leaped at the gnats, and a lark darted out of the green earth. This was the best summer since the first seasons of the world . . . He could think of no words to say how wonderful the summer was, or the noise of the wood-pigeons, or the lazy corn blowing in the half wind from the sea at the river's end. There were no words for the sky and the sun and the summer country: the birds were nice, and the corn was nice. Dylan Thomas, "A Prospect of the Sea"

1. What is the boy's mood? Why?
2. Point out some of the small, sensory details Dylan Thomas has used to sharpen the picture.
3. What other details contribute to the impression of reality?

4. SENSORY DETAILS TO SUGGEST MOVEMENT

Details picturing movement contribute to the impression of reality: the movement of trees, living creatures, vehicles, rain, snow, inanimate objects moved by external forces.

CLASS DISCUSSION

In this paragraph Martha Ostenso pictures a summer scene.

On the Hill

The grass below them leaned up the hill, like the smoothly combed hair of a person's head. Lind regarded it curiously. The air was strung with humming insects, poised like little black periods in the light. Occasionally a blue-bottle sailed majestically past, the tissue of its wings gathering in the sun. A droning bee blundered into a swarm of tiny, jigging gnats, disentangled itself and soared lazily on to a distant flower, unconscious of the excitement it had caused. Below them, a few feet away, stood the gray, pocked cone of an ant hill; up and down its slope the ants twinkled, providently absorbed. A tiny world of intense life. Martha Ostenso, *Wild Geese*

1. What is the vantage point, what scene is described and through whose eyes?
2. What details establish the time element?
3. What is the dominant atmosphere?
4. How has the author established an impression of reality?

GAINING REALISTIC EFFECTS: LANGUAGE

Sensory details are fully effective only when they are expressed in words or figures of speech that convey to the reader clear impressions. For example, such details as the *sight* of a mountain seen at sunset, the *sound* of tires on pavement, the *smell* of burning leaves in the fall, the *feel* of icy lake water when you plunged into it early one morning may be clear sensory images in your memory, but unless you can find words or figures of speech that will evoke *clear* images in your reader's mind, you will not be writing effective description.

CLASS DISCUSSION

In the following excerpt, taken from an unsigned article in *The Times Literary Supplement* (London), the writer discusses the importance of word choice. Read the excerpt and use the questions that follow it to guide your discussion.

English Prose

The art of writing, whether in prose or in verse, depended, in de Gourmont's opinion on a rare union of visual and emotive memory:—

If to visual memory the writer joins emotive memory, if he has the power, in evoking a material spectacle, of putting himself precisely into the emotional state which that spectacle aroused in him, he possesses, even though he is not aware of it, the whole art of writing.

This is to say that in the creative act of writing there are two elements —the visual image and the emotions associated with this image. The good writer—the artist, if you like—sees the image clearly, and is driven by the mere emotive charge of the image to find for it a fit mating of words. The image is there, stark, visible and real; to find the right words, and only the right words, to body forth that image, becomes in the writer an actual passion. The image evokes the words; or if it fails, if to the visual memory there comes no corresponding emotive or expressive memory, then there is no art. A good writer must then be silent; and only the bad writer will accept the approximate expression—the first expression that comes into his head, which is usually a stale expression, for it is ever so much easier to remember phrases than to evoke words. These memorable phrases press invitingly round the would-be writer; they are the current coin and counters of verbal intercourse; and to refuse them, and to deal only in freshly minted coin, is possible only to a few autocrats. But these are the rulers of literature, the creators of style; and they only should find a place in an anthology of the best prose. *The Times Literary Supplement* (London), March 4, 1926

1. According to the preceding article, what three characteristics must a person develop if he is to write good description?
2. Name authors who, in your opinion, can write good description, and substantiate your opinion by referring to passages from their works.

DICTION AND IMAGERY

Below are discussed techniques that you may use to help "body forth" the images you have in your mind.

1. Use the concrete word rather than the abstract. The concrete word evokes an image.
   Abstract: John was surprised to see the *poverty*.
   Concrete: John was surprised to see the *hovels*.

2. Use the specific word rather than the general. The specific word gives a more precise meaning than the general.
   General: The siren *blew*.
   Specific: The siren *wailed*.

3. Use onomatopoeia*—making the *sound* of a word, a group of words or a sentence imitate its meaning. Here are some examples:
   a) Make the sound of a single word imitate its meaning.
      (i) To anyone outside, a speeding train is a thunderbolt of driving rods, a hot *hiss* of steam, a blurred flash of coaches, a wall of movement and of noise, a shriek, a wail, and then just emptiness and silence . . . Thomas Wolfe, *You Can't Go Home Again*
      (ii) Through the building crawled the scrubwomen, yawning, their old shoes *slapping*. Sinclair Lewis, *Babbitt*
   b) Make the sound of a group of words or a sentence imitate its meaning. For this purpose:
      (i) slow the *pace* of the group of words or the whole sentence by using words containing long vowels; for example:
      But the forest itself was silent. It slept and dreamed of something in a perpetual grey-green shadow in the summer. Hervey Allen, *The Forest and The Fort* (The use of several words containing long vowels slows the pace of the last sentence to imitate the slow passage of time.)

Onomatopoeia. Consonants may be repeated to produce interesting sound effects. *B* and *p*, because they are pronounced by compressing the lips, are called "explosives". Repeating these sounds produces the effect of straining. The *g*, *k* and hard *c*, because they are pronounced in the back of the throat, are gutteral. Repeating these produces, therefore, a harsh sound. *M* and *n* are the only resonant sounds. Pronouncing them vibrates the bones in the nose to produce a resonant, singing tone, smooth and beautiful. The liquid *l* is the most melodious consonant. Repeating it imparts a very smooth sound to a phrase or a sentence. The sibilant *s* when repeated gives a soft or a hissing sound. The consonants *t* and *d*, both pronounced with the tongue and the teeth, and *f* and *v*, both pronounced with the lips and the teeth, require more effort to say than the smooth *m*, *n*, *l*, and *s*. Repetition of *t*'s, *d*'s, *f*'s and *v*'s, as well as the *b*'s and *p*'s, therefore, produces an effect of straining against an opposing force. The aspirate *h* gives a breathy sound. Alliteration, then, is a good device with which to achieve onomatopoeia (imitative harmony), making the *sound* or the *pace* of an important word, phrase or sentence imitate its meaning.

127

(ii) hurry the *pace* of a group of words or a sentence by using words containing short vowels; for example:

The dawn mist spun away . . . Sinclair Lewis, *Babbitt* (The use of two consecutive words containing short vowels makes this sentence move more quickly than if words with long vowels had been used, as in the sentence: The dawn gloom moved away. This quick pace is imitative of the speed with which the mist cleared.)

(iii) use words containing vowels high in tone (a,e,i) or words containing vowels low in tone (o,u) to impart a tone imitative of the idea expressed; for example:

When the sun strikes aslant through driven clouds, it wakens for that moment, the light of a gaiety as swift and bright and unforgetable. Judith Robinson, "The Basin" (The repetition of vowel-sounds high in tone—ā, ă, ē, ĕ, ī, ĭ—imparts an appropriate *light* tone colour to this description of happiness remembered.)

In Flanders fields the poppies grow
Between the crosses, row on row. (The repetition of the short *o* sound in poppies and crosses, and of the long *ō* sound in blow and row imparts a sombre tone to this description. This tone subtly imitates the poet's sadness as he thinks of the young soldiers buried in Flanders fields.)

(iv) use alliteration (the repetition of the same consonant sound) to produce a sound effect that imitates the idea expressed in a group of words or in a sentence; for example:

Conrad's "the smooth, shadowless sea", because of the repetition of the soft *s,* is smoother in *sound* than *the quiet, dark ocean.* Both expressions mean the same, but the first contains a sound effect that is lacking in the second.

Up the steep hill the horses stamped and strained. (Words containing consonants that require marked effort to pronounce imitate the effort expended by the horses.)

(v) use assonance (the repetition of the same vowel sound) to produce a sound effect that imitates the idea expressed; for example:

The sun that was bright on The Bay goes down behind the pine ridge, and over The Basin, night sorrows uncomforted for the youth that will not grow old. Judith Robinson, "The Basin" (The repetition of the long *ō* sound imparts a deep and sombre tone to this description of a bay grieving for young men lost in war.)

4. Use imagery to evoke an image of size, shape, colour or texture.

(i) The towers of Zenith aspired above the morning mist; austere towers of steel and cement and limestone, *sturdy as cliffs* and *delicate as silver rods.* They were neither citadels nor churches, but frankly and beautifully office-building. Sinclair Lewis, *Babbitt* (Two similes, both evoking visual images, are used to suggest the size and the shape of modern skyscrapers.)

(ii) Between the darkness of earth and heaven she was burning fiercely upon a *disc* of purple sea shot by the *blood-red* play of gleams, upon a *disc* of water glittering and sinister. Joseph Conrad, *Youth*

CLASS DISCUSSION

From each of the following passages select words, phrases and figures of speech (imagery) that you think are particularly well chosen to make effective the sensory details in which they have been used. Explain (a) what effect has been achieved with each of your choices and (b) what techniques have been used to gain it.

1. The following excerpt is taken from *Wind, Sand and Stars* by Antoine de Saint Exupéry. In this book, the writer describes some of his exciting, strange and awesome experiences when, as a young pilot, he flew a mail route in 1926 from France to Spain.

Night Flight

Flying, in general, seemed to us easy. When the skies are filled with black vapours, when fog and sand and sea are confounded in a brew in which they become indistinguishable, when gleaming flashes wheel treacherously in these skyey swamps, the pilot purges himself of the phantoms at a single stroke. He lights his lamps. He brings sanity into his house as into a lonely cottage on a fearsome heath. And the crew travel a sort of submarine route in a lighted chamber.

2. The following passage is taken from a story appearing in The *Atlantic Monthly*, April, 1954: "The Sea Above Us" by David Cornel DeJong. It is concerned with the author's boyhood, the sea breaking over the dyke and drowning his town. In the part of the story reproduced here, DeJong, his brothers and his father are standing on the high dyke, looking back at the Dutch countryside.

The View from the Dyke

There they were, red- and blue-roofed towns hugging grey churches with slate-blue spires, scattered over a checkerboard of a landscape almost entirely made by man: prosperous golden squares of wheat, bright yellow blocks of mustard, purple rectangles of cabbage, hexagons of blue flax, latticed parcels of white and pink buckwheat, limned everywhere with canals and ditches reflecting the translucent sky. And there curved the humped bridges with their vermilion and orange railings, seemingly helping the ribbons of roads to reach all the hives of towns properly. Over everything, adding up to three-quarters of the landscape, as in all good Dutch paintings, extended the ever-varied cup of sky.

3. The following sentence is taken from Hugh Walpole's novel *Vanessa*.

Sunset

. . . Vanessa would watch the clouds hurrying like smoke to invade the serried top [of the mountains], then to spill themselves in storm or to break into pavilions snow-white or crimson with fire, or to shred and scatter into strands of gold and crimson.

129

4.   The following paragraph is taken from "A Personal Record" by Joseph Conrad. In this passage he is describing an experience he had with a company of ships' pilots at Marseilles.

Leaving Marseilles

Standing by the tiller, he [the captain] pulls out his watch from under a thick jacket and bends his head over it in the light cast into the boat. Time's up. His pleasant voice commands, in a quiet undertone, *"Larguez."* A suddenly projected arm snatches the lantern off the quay—and, warped along by a line at first, then with the regular tug of four heavy sweeps in the bow, the big half-decked boat full of men glides out of the black, breathless fort. The open water of the *avant-port* glitters under the moon as if sewn over with millions of sequins, and the long white breakwater shines like a thick bar of solid silver. With a quick rattle of blocks and one single silky swish, the sail is filled by a little breeze keen enough to have come straight down from the frozen moon, and the boat, after the clatter of the hauled-in sweeps, seems to stand at rest, surrounded by a mysterious whispering so faint and unearthly that it may be the rustling of the brilliant, overpowering moonrays breaking like a rain shower upon the hard, smooth, shadowless sea.

5.   The passage below occurs in D. H. Lawrence's *Morning in Mexico*.

The Poinsettia

Dawn was windy, shaking the leaves, and the rising sun shone under a gap of yellow cloud. But at once it touched the yellow flowers that rise above the *patio* wall, and the swaying, glowing magenta of the bougainvillea, and the fierce red outbursts of the poinsettia.

DESCRIPTION

LESSON FIVE

ANALYZING INDIVIDUALIZED DESCRIPTION

Good individualized description is unified, coherent and emphatic in structure.

It is unified when it makes one dominant impression, either of atmosphere or of mood. Atmosphere and mood are related: the atmosphere evokes the mood. For example, a writer might wish to describe a squalid street, in order to convey his pity for the children obliged to play in it. To do this, he would try to make his readers see the street (the visual image), be intensely aware of its squalor (the atmosphere of the scene), and be aware of his pity (his mood). If, instead, he wishes to establish as a dominant impression

130

an atmosphere of squalor, he will stress the squalid details of the scene rather than his own reaction.

Individualized literary description is coherent when the descriptive details have been so arranged that the scene described forms one coherent image in the reader's mind.

In order to make a description coherent, a writer uses a person to view the scene (sometimes it is the author himself), a vantage point, and a logical arrangement of the descriptive details.

Individualized literary description is emphatic *structurally* when the author has used the structure of the passage to stress the dominant impression of atmosphere or of mood. Three frequently used methods are:

climax   arranging the descriptive details that create the atmosphere or the mood in *ascending order* of *atmospheric* or *emotional* effect;

position   using the end of the paragraph or the passage to stress the dominant impression of atmosphere or of mood;

proportion   devoting more details to the effect you wish to stress than to any of the other effects.

CLASS DISCUSSION

Each of the following passages depicts a scene viewed from one place, at one time, by one person. Read each passage carefully and be ready to discuss the questions that follow it.

The River

. . . The white man rested his chin on his crossed arms and gazed at the wake of the boat. At the end of the straight avenue of forests cut by the intense glitter of the river, the sun appeared unclouded and dazzling, poised low over the water that shone smoothly like a band of metal. The forests, sombre and dull, stood motionless and silent on each side of the broad stream. At the foot of big, towering trees, trunkless nipa palms rose from the mud of the bank, in bunches of leaves, enormous and heavy, that hung unstirring over the brown swirl of eddies. In the stillness of the air every tree, every leaf, every bough, every tendril of creeper, and every petal of minute blossoms seemed to have been bewitched into an immobility perfect and final. Nothing moved on the river but the eight paddles that rose flashing regularly, dipped together with a single splash . . . Joseph Conrad, "The Lagoon"

Discussion Questions

1. What scene is described? Through whose eyes? Which detail could not be *seen* by this person from his vantage point?
2. Does this shift in point of view improve the description or not?
3. What is the dominant impression of the scene? Justify your opinion.

4. Are the details given in an order that would be natural under the circumstances?
5. Does the structure emphasize the dominant impression? Give reasons for your opinion.

In the following paragraph, taken from William Faulkner's short story "Barn Burning", the writer describes the home of a wealthy Southern planter. The two characters described in the paragraph are a young boy, Sarty, and his father, a vindictive man, who set fire to the barns of those he envied or hated.

Sarty

Presently he could see the grove of oaks and cedars and the other flowering trees and shrubs where the house would be, though not the house yet. They walked beside a fence massed with honeysuckle and Cherokee roses and came to a gate swinging open between two brick pillars, and now, beyond a sweep of drive, he saw the house for the first time and at that instant he forgot his father and the terror and despair both, and even when he remembered his father again (who had not stopped) the terror and despair did not return. Because, for all the twelve movings, they had sojourned until now in a poor country, a land of small farms and fields and houses, and he had never seen a house like this before. *Hit's big as a courthouse* he thought quietly, with a surge of peace and joy whose reason he could not have thought into words, being too young for that: *They are safe from him. People whose lives are a part of this peace and dignity are beyond his touch, he no more to them than a buzzing wasp: capable of stinging for a little moment but that's all; the spell of this peace and dignity rendering even the barns and stable and cribs which belong to it impervious to the puny flames he might contrive* . . . this, the peace and joy, ebbing for an instant as he looked again at the stiff black back, the stiff and implacable limp of the figure which was not dwarfed by the house, for the reason that it had never looked big anywhere and which now, against the serene columned back-drop, had more than ever that impervious quality of something cut ruthlessly from tin, depthless, as though, sidewise to the sun, it would cast no shadow. Watching him, the boy remarked the absolutely undeviating course which his father held and saw the stiff foot come squarely down in a pile of fresh droppings where a horse had stood in the drive and which his father could have avoided by a simple change of stride. But it ebbed only for a moment, though he could not have thought this into words either, walking on in the spell of the house, which he could even want but without envy, without sorrow, certainly never with that ravening and jealous rage which unknown to him walked in the ironlike black coat before him: *Maybe he will feel it too. Maybe it will even change him now from what maybe he couldn't help but be.* William Faulkner, "Barn Burning"

132

1. The feeling—the mood—evoked in Sarty by this experience gives the description its unity. What effect did the beautiful house have on him? Refer to the passage to support your opinion.
2. Does the description of the father, who feels very differently, spoil the unity of the description? Give reasons for your opinion.
3. What is the vantage point? Does Mr. Faulkner make the reader look at the details in some orderly way? Refer to the description to substantiate your opinion.
4. Does the description conclude by stressing the dominant mood? Give reasons for your contention.

HOME WORK ASSIGNMENT

In a paragraph of individualized description, depict some scene or experience that was interesting because it had a dominant atmosphere or because it evoked in someone a definite mood.

DIRECTIONS

1. Make the following preliminary decisions:
   a) scene or experience I shall describe:
   b) the person viewing the scene:
   c) vantage point:
   d) time of year, time of day, kind of day:
   e) dominant impression (of atmosphere or of mood).

2. Try to use *details* that will establish a sense of reality: visual details of sky, colour and colour contrasts, light and shadow, movement, living creatures; and details other than visual.

3. Be sure to let your reader know where each detail is located—either in relation to the person viewing the scene or in relation to the previously mentioned detail.

4. Try to use *words* in such a way as to suggest size, shape, bulk, texture, colour, specific movements and mood.

5. Write the description in rough. Then revise your copy: try to *improve* your diction and your sentence structure.

6. Copy the decisions and the revised description into your note-book.

Suggested Atmospheres	Suggested Moods
wildness	despair
violence	pleasure
stillness	fear
vastness	wonder
great depth	pity

Suggested Vantage Points

sitting in a canoe	standing on a large rock jutting into the sea
standing on the deck of a ship	
riding on horseback	walking along a country road
standing on a dock or a wharf	standing on the top of a high hill

IMPROVING THE STRUCTURE OF DESCRIPTION

Comparing a revised descriptive paragraph with its original version should help you improve your own descriptive writing.

CLASS DISCUSSION
Unity and Coherence

Below you will find two descriptive paragraphs written by the same person. The first paragraph, after having been graded, was returned, with critical comments designed to teach the student how to improve his paragraph. The second one is the revised version. Use the questions on page 135 to guide you in your discussion.

Repose (Original Version)

It was a mid-afternoon of a balmy July day, and an air of sweet weariness hung over all. As I lay on the soft carpet of green, beside a gently murmuring stream, I gazed dreamily with half-closed eyes at the azure dome above. It seemed close enough to touch, yet at the same time seemed to extend to eternal heights. Through the haze of bright sunlight, the arc of blue seemed to pulsate back and forth, from far to near, from near to far; and the optical illusion seemed to attract and concentrate my gaze on the apex of the sky. The place I was in formed a perfect resting place. The earth was soft and yielding to the body contours, and formed an airy cushion. A pleasant breeze fanned the hot air and subdued the fever of summer heat. From the cool grass, a slightly pungent odour emanated, tantalizing by its elusiveness. Only the lullaby of the nearby brook singing its endless song disturbed the heavy silence. The landscape was in a stupor, drugged by the warmth of the sun, and by a sense of complacency, with its flushed, yet sublime beauty. From his solitary post on the top of a towering pine close by, a mighty eagle surveyed with fearsome eye the scene below. His eyelids fell; and, for a moment, he was lost in thought. His mind determined, off he took. Up and up, round and round in ever diminishing whirls, he flew. A speck, a dot, and then he vanished into the blue. Jerome K.

Critical Comments Made by Teacher

1. You have chosen an interesting experience to describe.
2. Successful in suggesting the still heat of a summer afternoon.
3. However, description lacks unity, singleness of effect: you have not decided which of the two impressions is to be the dominant one: heat or height. Select *one* and then select details that convey this impression.
4. Paragraph also lacks coherence; you have used two vantage points: yours and the eagle's. Select *one* vantage point and describe the scene from it.
5. You have used some hackneyed expressions.

134

Repose (Revised Version)

In the mid-afternoon of a sweltering July day, I lay on my back in the centre of a secluded opening deep in the forest. It was as if some giant fist had plunged down from above and scooped out a handful of green, leaving an unnatural void. The colossal pines at the edge of the small clearing seemed braced to stem the tide of trees behind from closing in. As I gazed upwards, the cool, yielding earth seemed to sink beneath me. The towering pines, stretching high above, narrowed towards the top and leaned inwards, all pointing towards the opening of the sky directly above. The uppermost branches came together to form a small, yet perfect ring, through which an azure finger seemed to point at me. The ring appeared close enough to touch, yet, at the same time, it seemed empty, and the blue seemed to extend to eternal heights. I was forced to concentrate on the point in the centre of the ring or I failed to reach my depth. A faint odour of pine needles drifted down. Suddenly a mighty eagle hovered silently into sight. For a few minutes he circled round the rim of the ring. Then slowly he began to ascend. In ever diminishing whirls, he spiralled upwards, an invisible current of air seeming to carry him. A speck, a dot, and then he vanished in the apex of the far blue. Jerome K.

Discussion Question on Repose (Revised Version)

1. What impression—heat or height—has the writer decided to emphasize? Prove by reference to the paragraph.
2. Prove that the scene is coherent, that is, has been described from one point of view.
3. For what purpose has he used the detail about the eagle?
4. The student has removed all the trite expressions and added good imagery to create visual effects. Find these figures of speech.

WRITTEN EXERCISE

The following paragraph, A Memorable Experience, though it contains good descriptive details, is not coherent: the writer did not describe every detail of the experience from *one* point of view.

A Memorable Experience

The warm August sun smiled pleasantly down upon a sleek, red canoe gliding smoothly on the sparkling blue waters of the Petawawa River. Around the bend, however, the thundering roar of the fast-approaching rapids filled the air with tense excitement. The river rapidly became shallower; and huge, menacing boulders could be seen lining the murky riverbed. The low, wooded shoreline gradually gave way to high, rocky cliffs. A mere hundred yards away, numerous patches of white foam spread over the ever-narrowing river. Suddenly the canoe lurched forward, incited by the wild current. Dodging the invisible, dagger-like rocks, and encircled by frothy foam and turbulent waters, the canoe tossed about relentlessly throughout the set of rapids. However, as suddenly as they appeared, the rapids vanished, once again leaving the canoe in calm, unruffled waters.

135

Rewrite the paragraph, making it coherent by:
a) stating in the first sentence the vantage point and the point of view: a canoeist sitting in the bow;
b) describing every detail *as it would appear to someone sitting in the bow of that canoe.* For instance, if the canoe scrapes a rock, the canoeist will be jolted; if the canoe hits rough water, the canoeist may feel the paddle almost jerked out of his hand; if the canoe drifts near shore, the canoeist may see, *at close range,* two bear cubs playing under a pine tree. By keeping your reader constantly *aware* of the canoeist sitting in the *bow* of the canoe, and the effect each detail has *on him,* you will make the description coherent.

HOME WORK ASSIGNMENT
Writing an Individualized Description

Choose *one* of the following assignments:
1. Depict in one paragraph of individualized description some scene that has as its dominant impression one of the following: very rainy, very cold, very hot. Do not once use the words rain or rainy; cold; hot. Establish your atmosphere by *picturing the effects* of the rain, the cold or the heat on the landscape, on people, on animals. Use climax, proportion or position to emphasize the atmosphere.
2. Depict in one paragraph of individualized description a scene or an experience that evoked a strong emotional response from some person. Try to make your readers *visualize* the scene or the experience, and sense the emotional reaction that made it memorable for the person through whose eyes you are describing it. Use the structure of the paragraph to stress the dominant mood.

DIRECTIONS
1. Make the following preliminary decisions:
a) scene or experience I shall describe:
b) time of year, time of day, kind of day:
c) the person viewing the scene:
d) vantage point:
e) dominant impression of atmosphere or of mood (emotional reaction):
2. After making these preliminary decisions, choose the structure you will use, and then write the paragraph. Copy both the preliminary decisions and the finished description to hand in for criticism.

Suggested Overall Structure
a) Give the vantage point, tell who is viewing the scene or event, and acquaint your reader with the specific time you have chosen for describing the subject: the time of year, the time of day, the weather. Choose your own order for giving this information.
b) Give details to establish the dominant impression of atmosphere or of mood. Mention the details in some orderly pattern so that your reader will build up in his imagination one coherent picture.
c) Conclude by emphasizing in some imaginative way the dominant impression.

DESCRIPTION

PLANNING AND WRITING
INDIVIDUALIZED DESCRIPTION

According to *The Concise Oxford Dictionary,* original means not imitative, novel in character and style, inventive, creative, thinking or acting for oneself.

HOW TO BE ORIGINAL

How can a young and inexperienced writer compose original description? Once a person thoroughly understands the techniques of descriptive writing and has had some practice in using them, he is ready to apply his inventiveness to write description that is original. Many successful authors say that the way to write an original story, description, exposition or argument is to assemble on paper or in your head all of the facts that you wish to present. The next step is to drop all this information together with the question, "How can I present these facts effectively?" into the sub-conscious mind. At the end of two or three days—or sooner!—the sub-conscious will have solved the problem and given an answer to the question.

When writing description, you have five places in which to be original:

1. *The vantage point:* choose an unusual or an unexpected one.
2. *The point of view:* select a novel point of view. For example, describe a disaster at the Air Show from the point of view of a small child who does not understand the tragedy that has occurred.
3. *The dominant impression:* use personification or a sustained metaphor to create your desired impression.
4. *The structure:* arrange your material in some unusual yet effective way.
5. *The sensory details:* use images revealing that you have been more observant of the world and of life than have most people. You noticed things, little but significant, unobserved by the rank and file.

CLASS DISCUSSION
Analyzing Students' Individualized Descriptions

Beginning on the next page you will find four fairly long, *individualized* descriptions written by senior students. Read, and use the questions that follow each to guide your discussion of its effectiveness. This will help you plan and write the long description that will be your next assignment.

The Mink

Darkness fell suddenly, like some fantastically large stage curtain at the end of a production. However, it did not really signify the finish of a play, but rather the beginning. For the drama of night had arrived, and multitudes of actors, large and small, came onto the stage. From the marsh surrounding the lake, the familiar noises of the bullfrogs and crickets sounded like the discordant strings of an orchestra tuning up; and as I leaned against the trunk of our old elm, I could sense movement everywhere. In front of me, myriads of mayflies made little ripples on the water, smashing the reflection of the moon into thousands of particles of light, and then laboriously putting it back together again.

When I was about to turn and leave, I noticed a small, dark object on the grass, not three yards away from me. At first I thought it was inanimate; but when it moved, I realized it was the little mink that lived near our boat house. I had noticed him, at the very first of the summer, shyly peeking out at me with his sparkling, black eyes that always seemed to be smiling. As the days wore on, and I spent my time in the various, sedentary attitudes of a lazy fisherman, he had become more friendly and would play within a few feet of me, or take the occasional rock bass I threw him. Now, when I was watching him, unseen, a strange silence settled over the creatures of the marsh.

There was a reason for it, for in another second death arrived. His sound was the slight hiss of a body knifing swiftly through the air. His shape was the large and indistinct one of a great horned owl. He seized the mink, who had been too preoccupied to notice him. This, then, was the climax of the little play that had seemed to be building up, but the two dark actors in front of me made not a sound.

The mink twisted in the grasp and tried to bite into the base of his adversary's leg. The owl let go with one talon, almost dropped his prey completely, then seized the mink more securely, and began to beat his heavy wings and rise steadily. Then they went, the mink writhing, still fighting, although it was now useless, the owl balefully and inexorably ploughing on. For a moment they were silhouetted against the moon; then they completely disappeared into the blackness.

I stood there, frozen to the spot because it had happened so quickly. My little friend with the mischievous eyes was gone forever. From the silence it seemed as though all creation were motionless too. Then a frog croaked, loud and deep, and in a moment others chimed in. The tiny tragedy was over, and the chorus took the stage once more. George M.

Discussion Questions

1. Is this passage unified? Give reasons for your opinion.
2. What is the vantage point? Prove by referring to the text.
3. How has the writer conveyed the impression that he was witnessing a drama?
4. Is every paragraph unified, coherent and emphatic? Give reasons for your opinion.

5. How has the writer made his description original?
6. Point out parts of this description that you consider effective. If you think parts of it might be improved, explain how.

The Outcast

A supernatural being lurks in the depths of the northern lake, as the clear, late-summer dusk holds its breath and succumbs softly to the night. As if drawn by the spirit's invisible hand, the small green boat slips slowly sideways, leaving a path of tiny, black swirls on the motionless water. With a gentle grating of wood on wood, and a snapping of brittle twigs, the boat comes to rest against a half-submerged spruce log, a grizzled, scraggly monster in the deepening gloom.

Nudged out of a reverie, I turn my gaze across the darkening lake towards the south-east, where the dying sun's last rays crown the distant hills in a fiery glow. I am awed by the wildness and loneliness of this place; by its fierce yet delicate beauty. Surrounding the entrance of a small river on the eastern shore stretches a large area of marsh grass and drowned land. It is close enough that I can almost discern each individual bush and tree, yet there is a feeling of endless expanse, for behind the deep swamp bay, long bush-covered slopes sweep back for mile after mile, far into the distance. High above the fantastic, sombre tangle of drowned land, a pair of ospreys wheel in slow, wide circles. A little to the left of the winding river channel, a huge pine tree rises, majestic and aloof, above the horizon, a gaunt silhouette against the pale, green-blue sky.

A dark, steep slope looms high above me like a gigantic wall. Shooting up almost vertically from the water, it is blanketed by a dense forest of hemlock, interspersed with stately white columns of birches. Somewhere in the great, shadowy tangle, a branch slides crashing to the ground. The faint, almost inaudible peeps of tiny, unknown birds whisper in the tree-tops far above. A cedar bough, with its sweet, heavy fragrance, brushes softly over my face. From just out of sight around a small point comes an intermittent sound, like the rippling of a tiny stream. It stops, splashes again, then is still—a school of fish, jumping.

As the farthest hill-top fades into darkness, the hermit thrush begins an arpeggio of clear, flute-like notes. The liquid, fleeting melody seems to echo from everywhere at the same time, singing of the forest and all its elusive beauties that are hidden forever from human eyes. I suddenly feel that in this place I am a stranger, an outcast. Yet, for one second, a spell is cast over me . . .

Once, ever so long ago, I belonged here. The beauty, the peace, the loneliness are like a haunting memory, flooding back for this one magic, trance-like interval. An incredible yearning overwhelms me, . . . I hear a voice . . . calling . . . calling . . . an irresistible longing fills me—I want to yield, to follow the voice . . . I cry out in answer, passionately, eagerly . . . my cry flies out into the gloom to echo from the shores of an empty lake, to race with the wind through silken pine boughs, to mingle with the piercing whistle of a broad-winged hawk, riding high over the dark forest—but

139

my language is a strange, unknown language; and my cry goes unheard, and out there, in the gloom, it dies.

A chill breeze springs up from the lake; dark wavelets slap gently against the boat and the shore. The water rises and falls in a crevice in the rocks, making an eerie, sucking sound. Night, creeping forth stealthily from its hiding-place in the mysterious depths of the thickets, slowly, relentlessly, envelops the world in darkness. Somewhere, far down the lake, the mournful wail of a loon swells and fades. For an instant, a bat flits swiftly, erratically before my eyes, and then is gone. The weird, ghostly skeletons of the drowned land, just faintly visible across the water, are now strangely frightening. My bare arms begin to shiver, for it is cold. As if wakened from a dream, I seize the oars; and the loud creaking and splashing seal me off from the strange whispering of the night. Like a tiny world floating in space, I speed along the shore towards the trail.

A little way up the path, I stop for one last look. The full moon, a gigantic red ball, rising behind that huge pine tree, has transformed the black water into glittering golden sand, enticing me to come and walk on it. But I turn my back, and run instead towards the cosy glow of lighted windows, the murmur of happy voices, the smell of hot cocoa on the kitchen stove, and the drowsy warmth of a soft bed.

And behind me as I run there suddenly echoes from across the still water the haunting laughter of three loons calling to one another . . . taunting, mocking me. Bettina S.

Discussion Questions

1. Why was this an interesting experience for the writer?
2. Is this description unified? Give reasons for your opinion.
3. Would the description have been improved if the writer had omitted the last paragraph?
4. What is the vantage point? Has the writer described the experience always from her chosen position? Give reasons for your opinion.
5. Has the writer kept her reader aware of the time of day? Justify your opinion.
6. For what purpose has the writer used each of her paragraphs?
7. What are some of the distinctive qualities of this description? Read aloud passages that illustrate your opinion.
8. If you find flaws in this description, offer suggestions for eliminating them.

Groundhog Hunting

The roosters were crowing at the Johnson's farm as Tommy diligently began his chores. After he had fed the chickens and hastily cleaned the stalls in the barn, he happily set off to the south pasture to see Mac, a big, red roan, which Tommy swore was the finest piece of horseflesh in the country. When he had swung around a freshly planted oat field and skipped over the creek, he heard a loud report echo, then re-echo from the south. He began running up the hill that overlooked Mac's pasture. His

140

father's familiar, lanky frame blocked his view at the crown of the hill.

"Have you seen Mac?" Tom urgently enquired.

"Yes," Mr. Johnson quietly replied as he led his son back down the hill. Mr. Johnson then explained to Tom that although it seemed cruel to shoot Mac, no horse would have been able to recover with a leg as badly broken as the roan's.

Unfortunately Mac had stumbled into a woodchuck hole.

Woodchucks, or groundhogs, as they are commonly called, have become a popular target for sportsmen. In spite of the fact that timid women, moralists and some farmers who value their livestock detest hunting, I know groundhogging is a thrilling, invigorating sport.

You start out early in the morning across the rolling hills, broken terrain, then over lush, green fields. The silence, sweet smell of the woods and freshly tilled soil are all enjoyable features of a jaunt in the country. You are filled with the exhilarating feeling that the next few hours are yours to spend on an exciting day of hunting.

There were four of us. Peter and I headed west, leaving Jim and Len to scour the east section of the concession. When we silently started from a lightly wooded valley towards a prospective groundhog hill, Peter noticed the trilliums to our left: hundreds of white trilliums surrounding a brown mound of earth—which supported an inquisitive groundhog! After casually looking us over, the sleek, plump marmot plopped into his hole, leaving two surprised hunters gaping.

Determined to spot the next woodchuck before it spied us, we continued to advance on our hill. Manoeuvering to the south, we approached downwind and under the cover of a maple grove. We saw him! To the novice's eyes, he was just a brown blob blended into a background of a rotting rail fence and strewn boulders. Both rifles sounded in unison; the chuck flopped on his side. Although who hit the marmot still remains a mystery, we dispatched him with an accurate head shot.

Since the morning was still chilly, we established ourselves on a lofty hill. Below, a farmer methodically ploughed his field. Above us, Peter spotted a red-tailed hawk searching for breakfast. Across the valley a strident, squeaky 'yip, yip' floated up to us. After scanning the terrain in that direction with binoculars, we saw a lively, reddish, furry tail, partially hidden by undergrowth. Patient waiting solved the enigma. A fox kit, the owner of the tail, finally disclosed himself. Nearby, Peter discovered the den and the rest of the family. The wary vixen, however, presently chased the frolicking kits into the den.

The fox episode appeared to be the highlight that morning, because the chucks in our district were hunter-wise. Regardless of how carefully we stalked the varmints, the closest we crept to them was about 300 yards. That is a long shot.

Later, sprawled on the shore of a small lake, your hunters were inventing novel plans of attack. A brown speck on the clover field before us had interested me several times in the last few minutes. One glance through the trusty binoculars identified the speck as a daring woodchuck at a mere 175 yards. What an opportunity for a marksman!

Peter meticulously readied his .270 Winchester; sighted on the scope; gradually squeezed the trigger. After the explosion, the woodchuck remained inert. Elated, two proud hunters marched up to their prey. The woodchuck dived into his burrow!

Two unnerved hunters circled back home for lunch. David S.

Discussion Questions

1. Why was this hunting expedition an interesting experience for the writer? Give reasons for your opinion.
2. Is this description unified? Justify your opinion.
3. Why did the writer include the shooting of the roan?
4. The writer uses a moving vantage point. Does he keep the reader aware of the change and describe only what he can see and hear from each new vantage point? Refer to the description to justify your opinion.
5. By direct reference to the text, show that this student has learned to be specific rather than general.
6. What are some of the characteristics of this student's style?

A Memorable Experience

There must have been a time when the Island bore the proud look of prosperity, but when I came to know it as a small boy, it was all but deserted and emanated already its soft atmosphere of decay. We would come occasionally on Sundays for a family outing, in later years even in winter, to explore the mysteries of its windswept boardwalk, and long willow-lined avenues. It was on one such winter Sunday that, as a boy of ten, whose imagination was already stirred by the strange atmosphere, I gained my strongest impression of the Island.

I had set out alone that afternoon to walk the length of the old boardwalk by the lake up to the Eastern Gap and back. The strip of beach still lay under the dusty brown cloak of fall; but from behind me, cold and wet from the lake's purple swells, came a wind that numbed my bare ears and made me walk rapidly, my hands seeking refuge deep in the warmth of my coat pockets. The sky was wintry—at the zenith a round patch of blue that faded and dulled to a hazy mixture of blue and brown at the south horizon, where it met the legions of purple waves. The weak light of the December sun stretched out my shadow before me on the resounding boardwalk and washed with its pale orange-red light the forlorn line of rotting wooden mansions that receded endlessly eastward on my left. The wind swept up the slanting beach, driving before it the last stained papers from the summer; it slipped through sagging gates and tumbling fences to investigate the varied forms of old verandahs and roofs, and finally expired with a gentle moan in the tall willows behind.

The promenade was bare but for the distant figure I was gradually overtaking—a man with a cane and a top hat. His walk was that of an

142

elegant gentleman, but seemed wavering and unsteady. Twice I thought I saw him kneel and carefully place something heavy from the frozen sand into his coat pockets. I could see his coat now, fastidiously tailored in black cloth, but even in that rose light it appeared threadbare and frayed. His high silk hat looked faded with age as if it were covered with the fine dust of passing years. His whole being had for me the air of something refined, yet something frail and dusty, like old cob-webs.

Meanwhile from a shadowy walk between the staring facades of two old houses, the shapes of three old ladies arm in arm loomed up. Three blanched and whitened faces under outdated, black chapeaux turned into the walk before me; three bulks, in black coats that hinted of accumulated layers of cloth beneath, moved ahead of me; and in their wake I caught the smell of alcohol.

Having by this time reached the unfamiliar half of the Island, and fearing to pass these awesome creatures before me, I held back and began again to take notice of my surroundings.

By the water's edge cold waves were rolling pebbles to the hollow beat of heels advancing on the wooden walk; or, where the walk had long been washed away, the dry clicking of heels on concrete would mix with the swirling sound of waves about old pilings; and all about would rise the sharp, cold odour of dead fish and refuse lying in the water. At intervals by the walk there hung on slanting concrete posts elaborate old street lamps, now all broken and blind. Here and there, from the sand, arose the gaunt skeletons of dying poplars, which glowed luridly in the slanting light. Sedately looking on all this ruin, stood the grand old forms of the houses— ornamental woodwork, rotting foundations, sagging gardens, washed-out walks, unpainted gable roofs collapsing, windows broken, ornate shutters hanging—indeed, with every sign of decrepitude; yet in that moment their dignity was not shaken but rather deepened by sadness as they looked on their own demise.

My three old ladies had passed through a wooden gate and were swallowed by the brooding shadows of a house. Before me stretched out my goal, the long concrete pier of the eastern channel; and on it, bathed in the soft rose light of the setting sun, I imagined I saw the gentleman walk. But now, as I recall, his step was firm and sure, his bearing dignified. His top hat sat proudly on his head; his black coat seemed fine and new. He reached the end, his cane swinging gently; and did not stop, but stepped in, and sank, erect and elegant, into the purple swells. Laurence S.

Discussion Questions

1. What is the dominant impression of this description? How is it created?
2. The place described, Toronto Island, was formerly a favourite summer resort for Torontonians. The writer has used a moving vantage point. Explain how he has made his description coherent.
3. By what means has he achieved an impression of reality?
4. a) Who is the old gentleman? Give reasons for your opinion.
   b) Evaluate the effectiveness of the concluding detail.

5. One of the ways to make description interesting is to include people. Discuss the dramatic purposes for which the student used the old gentleman and the three ladies.
6. Point out some of the original features of this description.
7. This description reveals the character of the writer. What are some of his characteristics? Where in the description does he reveal the ones you mention?

HOME WORK ASSIGNMENT

Write a fairly long individualized description in which you depict some scene, occasion or incident that is interesting for one of the following reasons:
a) it possesses a dominant atmosphere;
b) it evokes in you or in some fictitious person a definite mood;
c) it will, if well described, evoke from your reader a sigh because of its pathos;
d) it will, if well described, evoke from your reader a smile because of its humour or its irony;
e) if will, if well described, compel your reader "to glance for a moment at the surrounding vision of form and colour, of sunshine and shadow".

DIRECTIONS

1. Using as a guide the model given below, make a plan for your description.
2. Write the description in rough. Revise it carefully until you have:
a) kept your reader aware of the vantage point;
b) composed unified, coherent and emphatic paragraphs;
c) used a variety of sensory details;
d) kept your reader aware of the time of year, the time of day and the kind of day.
3. Revise it again, trying to improve your choice of words.
4. Copy both the plan and the revised description into your note-book.

Example of a Plan for a Long Description

Preliminary Decisions to be Made

a) *Scene*: the opening baseball game in a big city
b) *Purpose of description*: the passage is to be used in an article entitled: "American Manners and Customs" and is addressed to readers in England
c) *Person viewing the scene*: a young Englishman who has never before attended a big ball game
d) *Vantage point*: a seat high in the bleachers of the stadium
e) *Time*: three o'clock on a sunny and windy day in May
f) *Dominant impression*: atmosphere of unbelievable excitement (reason scene is interesting to person viewing it)
g) *Organization of material into paragraphs*:
  (i) throngs of young and old pouring into the stadium (opposite me)—dominant impression, throngs

144

(ii) young boys in holiday mood and free from school (sitting behind me)—dominant impression, noise
(iii) middle-aged business men betting excitedly with their neighbours (sitting ahead of me)—dominant impression, excitement
(iv) vendors noisily hawking their wares (below me)—dominant impression, tantalizing smells: coffee, hot-dogs, peanuts
(v) entrance of the teams in bright new uniforms; shouts of crowd—dominant impression, movement
(vi) entrance of mayor on field: tense silence in bleachers as he raises his arm to pitch the ball—dominant atmosphere, silence
(vii) "Play ball!"—dominant impression, unbelievable roar

Suggested Overall Structure for a Long Description

The Opening Paragraph: gives the vantage point, the point of view, the time of year, the time of day, the kind of day.

The Body of the Description: contains the paragraphs that create the desired impression of atmosphere or of mood. Every paragraph should be one clear-cut picture that contributes to this impression.

The Conclusion: stresses, in some imaginative way, the impression of atmosphere or of mood you are trying to establish.

Suggested Subjects

The Ski-jumper	Subway Rush
The End of the Race	A Forest Drama
The City at Night	The Flood
The Country at Night	A Thrilling Moment
Early Morning on the River	A Solemn Moment
The Portage	An Amusing Scene
The Old Dock	A Breath-taking Experience
A Flight Over Mountains	An Unforgettable Experience
A Flight Over City at Night	The Last Lap of the Race
The Garden in November	The Swimming Hole
The First Snowfall on Our Street	The Storm
Fisherman's Paradise	The Forest Fire
Coming Into Harbour	Catching That Fish!
The Swamp	The Eighteenth Hole
The Fight	Three Minutes To Go!
The Campfire	Thirty Below Zero

CRITERIA BY WHICH INDIVIDUALIZED DESCRIPTION MAY BE JUDGED

1. *Credit*

Merits: To be worth a credit, a description must have merit in structure and in content. The description, as a whole, must be unified, coherent and emphatic. Every paragraph of the description must be unified. The student must use details and must keep the reader aware of the time of day, time of year and kind of day.

Flaws: The flaws that prevent this description from receiving a higher grade are:

    a) *paragraph structure*: paragraphs lack coherence and emphasis;

    b) *lack of pictorial power*: the details tend to be general rather than specific; or abstract rather than sensory;

    c) *immature style*: diction and sentence structure are still poor.

2. Third-Class Honours

Merits: To be worth third-class honours, a description must possess the above merits of structure and content and, in addition:

    a) *well-constructed paragraphs*: coherent and emphatic as well as unified;

    b) *pictorial power*: the details are sensory and specific.

Flaws: This student has mastered the techniques of descriptive writing but has not yet learned to write a pleasing style. He shows little sensitivity to words and sentence structure.

3. Second-Class Honours

Merits: This description has all of the merits possessed by the third-class essay and, in addition, sensitive use of words.

Flaws: A student receiving this grade has not yet mastered the technique of writing good sentences.

4. First-Class Honours

Merits: The first-class description has merit in structure, content and style. It differs from the second-class description in one respect: sentence structure. A student receiving this grade has learned to compose unified, coherent and emphatic sentences; to vary sentence structure in order to avoid monotony; to use rhetorical devices for specific effects.

DESCRIPTION

LESSON EIGHT

CHOOSING THE BEST INDIVIDUALIZED DESCRIPTIONS WRITTEN BY STUDENTS

Using the procedure given on page 56 for group evaluation of expositions, choose the best descriptions that have been written for the preceding home work assignment.

At the conclusion of the period in which the best descriptions are read aloud to the class, discuss this question: *What characteristics of good descriptive writing do you find in these individualized descriptions? Refer to specific descriptions to illustrate your opinions.*

DESCRIPTION

PLANNING AND WRITING
GENERALIZED DESCRIPTION

Generalized description depicts the typical, not the individual. For example, *Canoe trips are usually exciting experiences* could serve as the thesis for a generalized description, in which the writer might describe some of the most exciting experiences he had ever had on canoe trips. An individualized description of a canoe trip, on the other hand, would depict *one* specific trip.

ANALYZING THE OVERALL STRUCTURE
OF GENERALIZED DESCRIPTION

Generalized description can have an overall structure like that used in exposition: a lead that will attract the reader's interest in the subject; a statement of the thesis; an orderly development of this thesis by means of topic sentences expanded by descriptive details; and a conclusion that stresses the thesis. However, you may use any overall structure that will enable you to convey your desired effect to your reader, and impress it on him. You might, for instance, omit the lead and the statement of the thesis, and suggest an impression of city streets at five o'clock rush hour by means of several vignettes arranged in climactic order.

Good generalized description is unified, coherent and emphatic. The establishment of *one* dominant impression (of atmosphere or of mood) or the development of *one* thesis gives it unity. The orderly development of the aimed-at impression or of the thesis imparts coherence. The use of position, proportion and/or climactic arrangement of material to stress the dominant impression or the thesis gives structural emphasis.

CLASS DISCUSSION
Analyzing a Description Written by a Student

1. The following descriptive passage was written by a student. Is the description generalized, or individualized? Give reasons for your opinion.
2. How has the writer achieved unity?
3. Is the description structurally emphatic? Refer to the passage to support your opinion.

City at Night

Night lends dignity to a city. Buildings cease to be grey, grimy mountains of steel and glass and concrete; they take on a softness by night, and seem to blend into each other in shades of velvet gray, spangled by the small, shining squares of windows. The traffic's roar is hushed to a faint echo, a whisper of rubber on concrete, without the impatient blare of horns, and clang of streetcar bells. The people, themselves, seem to be more dignified. There are no hurrying crowds; only a few people walk leisurely along the strangely silent sidewalks, taking time to look into the gaily decorated store-windows. Even the air is different: cooler, fresher, without the choking fumes of exhaust smoke, or city smog. From the bright streets, up past the silent buildings to the inky sky there is, in the hours from dusk to dawn, an enchantment that hides a city's flaws, and accents its beauty, solemnity and dignity. Margot H.

WRITTEN EXERCISE I

Read the following piece of generalized description. Answer in writing the questions that you will find at the end of the selection. The paragraphs are numbered for convenience in discussing.

The Fraser

1. The character of the Fraser has changed. Its direction is still south but it has collided for the first time with the Coast Range, which runs from the southeast to the northwest sideways along the edge of the continent. Seeking a pass to the sea, the current moves in a quickened pace but yet parallel to the coast. It is now squeezed tight within the mountains and turns furious at its imprisonment. Its channel here is cut out of the living rock, its trench dug ever deeper to accommodate its distended body, its water convulsed in whirlpool, back eddy and hidden cavern.

2. This is the black canyon of the Fraser, where even the salmon is often hurled bodily from the current, where the first explorers crawled on hands and knees along the edges of the precipice, where the Indians traveled on dangling ladders, where the gold rush hauled its freight by a road built on stilts, where the engineers blasted their railway grades out of the naked cliff.

3. The canyon has been called beautiful. If this be beauty, it is the beauty of nightmare. It has been called magnificent, but this is the magnificence of destruction. It has been called sublime, and so it is, with the sublimity of blind and senseless force.

4. From the road, high up the mountains, the river appears as a twisted line of brown, solid and motionless, no wider than a clothesline. The Coast Range around it, unlike the more orderly defiles of the Rockies, sprawls in chaos as if its builders had mislaid their plans—a jumble of ragged peaks, dim gorges, smears of green forest, shadows miles wide in ceaseless shift of pattern.

5. Hour by hour this jumble of rock, earth, timber and water changes its aspect and almost seems to change its substance in man's sight. At dawn the surface of the mountains thrusts itself out, acquires body and shape

and seems to lurch toward the river. At noon, as the shadows move down them, the slopes retreat, fading into dull grays and greens. In the twilight the canyon is hung with ragged curtains of blue and purple, haze streams out of every crevice and the mountains stand solid against the stars, almost within touch of your hand. Always, in daylight or dark, the canyon is clamorous with the voice of its passenger.

6. In such a closed and wrinkled pocket man and his works are lost. The two railways and the single road have left only a nick on the cliffs, a few feet of level space across the slides. A freight train a mile long is a toiling worm, at night a glow worm, whose spark flickers for a moment and is snuffed out. Only a wink of light from some railway town on the canyon's lip proclaims the presence of any life but the river's.

7. To observe the dimensions and power of this larger life you must crawl down the rock slides to the riverbank. There the smooth line of water as seen from the mountains turns into a paroxysm of dirty foam, rising and falling in steady pulse. The perpetual mist has coated the canyon walls with slime and the water has worn them smooth, squared them off like old masonry so that in places they might have been built by human hands. A few islands still stand in the channel, whittled down to narrow splinters and already doomed. The final product of this erosion, the white sand pulverized out of the mountainsides, is laid in glistening bars by every back eddy. The dust of gold lies in these bars from the undiscovered mother lode.

8. All other sounds, the human voice, the whistle of the locomotive a few yards off, are obliterated by the din of this caldron. The motion of the river seems to set the entire canyon in motion. Before this spectacle of flux, the beholder turns dizzy and, looking up, finds the cliffs closing over his head.
Bruce Hutchison, *The Fraser*

Discussion Questions

1. What is the thesis of this generalized description?
2. For what purpose has Mr. Hutchison used each of the eight paragraphs?
3. In which paragraphs has the author chosen a fixed vantage point from which to give his impression? State the vantage point.
4. In what paragraphs has he used a topic sentence? Copy the topic sentences into your note-book.
5. In which paragraph do you think the author is most successful in creating his desired impression? State the impression and explain how he gained it.
6. Is the arrangement of the paragraphs a logical one? Give reasons for your opinion.
7. Does this description end emphatically; that is, does it stress the thesis? Give reasons for your opinion.

WRITTEN EXERCISE II

Read the following description, which was used by Hervey Allen as the opening section of his novel *The Forest and the Fort*, and answer in writing the questions that follow it.

The Forest

In the beginning was the forest. God made it and no man knew the end of it. It was not new; it was old; ancient as the hills it covered. Those who first saw it saw it had been there since the beginning of habitable time. There were rivers in it and distant mountains; birds, beasts, and the mysterious villages of red men. The trees were vast, round, and countless; columns of the roof of heaven. There were green glades where the deer fed and looked at the buffalo; trails that went back into the animal time. There were valleys where the clouds lay and no man came there; caves where the wolves mated; peaks where the panther screamed . . .

But the forest itself was silent. It slept and dreamed of something in a perpetual grey-green shadow in the summer. The lightning flashed at evening and the thunder echo rolled. In the fall the leaves fell and the stars looked down through the roof of sticks. The snow sifted and glittered. Winds heavy with the silver breath of winter smoked on the mountains. The trees burgeoned. Red flashed into the green flame of spring. The grey-green shadow brooded in the forest again, gestating sunlight.

Birds, those free spirits of the weather, were the only beings who saw the spectacle entire. As the earth rocked, every spring and autumn their blood burned. They rose, trillions of them, feathered nations with innumerable tongues and various languages, and took to the air. Their nests and their love songs followed the tilting ecliptic like a paean of time. They also sang the praises of the Almighty One with innocent, unthinking hearts. High in cold atmospheres, they beheld the grandeur and beauty of His thought.

Northward a necklace of great lakes glittered across the breast of the continent. Eastward the tabled plains of the Atlantic flashed lonely to the unbroken water rim. Not a sail gleamed. Only the steam clouds over the warm river in the ocean cliffed towering into heaven. The moon rose out of them at the full and looked at the sun setting beyond the Appalachians into a sea of western grass. Between lay the forest, green, gladed, unbroken, beautiful; riding the still waves of the long mountains, stretching from ice blink to palms.

The fingers of innumerable days trailed across the roof of the forest, while spring and autumn ran up and down it countless thousands of times. The stars shifted in their houses. Eastward over the waters the wings of gulls wheeled; gleamed and vanished; vanished and gleamed—prophetically. Until in the fullness of time something whiter glinted there; held the sunlight steadily; discovered the tracery of sails. Man-made thunder saluted the land. Hervey Allen, *The Forest and the Fort*

Discussion Questions

1. What dominant impression, of atmosphere or of mood, is Mr. Allen trying to establish? Give reasons for your opinion.
2. For what purpose has he used each paragraph?
3. Is the description emphatic in structure? Give reasons for your opinion.

BLOCK PLANS FOR GENERALIZED DESCRIPTION

When organizing material for a generalized description, you may find it helpful to make an outline plan in diagrammatic form, as shown below. Such a diagram has the advantage of spreading out before you the component parts of the proposed description. What is to be included in each part is thus seen at a glance, and necessary revisions can be made before the writing of the description is undertaken. Such a diagrammatic plan is referred to as a *block* plan.

1. BLOCK PLAN — WITH STATED THESIS

Para. 1: *Introduction*   *Para.* 2: *Body*   *Para.* 3: *Body*

Thesis	What I shall describe?	What I shall describe?
How can I state it imaginatively?	a) dominant impression b) vantage point (if any) c) point of view (if any) d) time of year, time of day, kind of day (if you plan to use these facts)	a) dominant impression b) vantage point (if any) c) point of view (if any) d) time of year, time of day, kind of day (if you plan to use these facts)

Para. 4: *Body*   *Para.* 5: *Conclusion*

What I shall describe?	How I shall stress the dominant impression of my thesis.
a) dominant impression b) time element c) vantage point	

2. BLOCK PLAN — WITHOUT STATED THESIS

Subject: The North Country   *Dominant Impression*: wild beauty

Para. 1: *Introduction*   *Para.* 2: *Body*   *Para.* 3: *Body*

Scene or incident I shall describe?	Scene or incident I shall describe?	Scene or incident I shall describe?
a) vantage point b) time of year c) atmosphere	a) vantage point b) time of year c) atmosphere	a) vantage point b) time of year c) atmosphere

Para. 4: *Body*   *Para.* 5: *Conclusion*

Scene or incident I shall describe?	Scene or incident I shall describe?
a) vantage point b) time of year c) atmosphere	a) vantage point b) time of year c) atmosphere

Using one of the suggested subjects, or one of your own choice, write a generalized description, in which you use suitable sensory details to develop your thesis or establish your dominant impression. Your description should be at least five paragraphs in length.

DIRECTIONS

1. *Make the following preliminary decisions:*
   a) Subject:
   b) Thesis or dominant impression of atmosphere or of mood:
   c) To whom will I address my generalized description?
   d) My purpose (Keep in mind a chosen group.)
2. The incidents or the details I shall use to develop the thesis or to establish the dominant impression of atmosphere or of mood. (Make a block plan.)

Suggested Subjects

(Choose your Atmosphere, Mood or Thesis.)

Skiing	The Farm in Winter
Sailing	The City Awakes
Windows	Our Street in Spring
The City at Night	

Suggested Impressions

Atmosphere	*Mood*
The *excitement* of football games	*dislike* of picnics
The *pleasantness* of summer holidays	*dislike* of camping trips
The *beauty* of the ocean (or mountains or prairies)	*enjoyment* of canoe trips
	enjoyment of air travel
The *beauty* of a certain river	*enjoyment of skiing* (sailing, hiking, fishing, riding)
The *wildness* of a certain lake	

Suggested Theses

Watching others go skiing is my favourite sport.
Football games amuse me!
Golfers are queer people.
Don't go fishing!

LITERARY CRITICISM OF DESCRIPTION

LOOKING AT PROFESSIONAL CRITICISM

A literary criticism of description is a special kind of exposition in which the critic evaluates one or more of the following: the author's success in achieving a desired effect and in writing a unified, coherent and emphatic description; the use of descriptive details; the originality of thought; the style: diction, imagery, sentence structure and any other elements that characterize the author's writing.

CLASS DISCUSSION

Read carefully each of the following descriptive passages and the criticisms that have been composed by professional writers. Use the questions that follow the criticisms to guide you in your discussion. (Note that passages 4 and 5 are considered comparatively, and hence have one set of questions.)

Descriptive Passage 1

The sky is peacefully untroubled white through the bare brown branches; in parts, on the limes, hang the last golden leaves. The damp earth is elastic under your feet; the high dry blades of grass do not stir; the long threads lie shining on the blanched turf, white with dew. Ivan Turgenev, *A Sportsman's Sketches*

Criticism

This passage is not only of remarkable beauty; it has ceased, in Turgenev's hands, to be the ordinary "description of nature". It has a quality of porousness; it has absorbed the colour, fragrance, and hushed tranquillity of an autumn day; so that at last it no longer indicates but *is* the thing itself. H. E. Bates, *The Modern Short Story*

a) What has Ivan Turgenev described in the short passage taken from *A Sportsman's Sketches*?

b) What aspect of Turgenev's description is Bates evaluating: its unity, its coherence, its impression of reality, its diction? Give reasons for your opinion.

c) Name and illustrate three qualities of Mr. Bates's appreciation.

Descriptive Passage 2

The horror, the confusion, and the separation of the murdered from his comrades were all over before I came. There remained only on the barrack-square the blood of man calling from the ground. The hot sun had dried it to a dusky goldbeater-skin film, cracked lozenge-wise by the heat; and as the wind rose, each lozenge, rising a little, curled up at the edges as if it were a dumb tongue. Then a heavier gust blew all away down wind in grains of dark-coloured dust. Rudyard Kipling, "Love-O'-Women"

Criticism

In this short passage Kipling's qualities are well seen. The projection of the scene by a series of flamboyant images, all showy and theatrical in tone, is an excellent example of the journalistic "eye" for a dramatic and bloody moment. "Dusky goldbeater-skin film", "dumb tongues", "the blood of man calling from the ground" are all vivid, stagey, and spurious effects which are combined to create a main effect of disturbance, violence, and great tropical heat. "The blood of man" is a typical example of Kipling's use of Biblical English, common to almost every page he wrote, and behind every line lies a certain impression of arrogance, of an aggressive mind speaking without reticence, consistently under-estimating the receptive qualities of the reader. H. E. Bates, *The Modern Short Story*

a) What scene has Kipling described in this passage?
b) What qualities in Kipling's passage does Mr. Bates dislike?
c) From reading this criticism, what impressions do you get of Mr. Bates's personality?

Descriptive Passage 3

A few light taps upon the pane made him turn to the window. It had begun to snow again. He watched sleepily the flakes, silver and dark, falling obliquely against the lamplight. The time had come to set out on his journey westward. Yes, the newspapers were right: snow was general all over Ireland. It was falling on every part of the dark central plain, on the treeless hills, falling softly upon the Bog of Allen and, farther westward, softly falling into the dark mutinous Shannon waves. James Joyce, "The Dead"

Criticism

There is no word in this passage that a child of ten could not understand, no picture that it could not at once assimilate. Its prevailing tone is one of poetic naturalness. Without trick or metaphor, but simply by using words as a musical notation which in turn transmits, as music will, a pictorial and emotional effect, Joyce weaves the spell of great beauty that hangs over the final pages of "The Dead" . . . H. E. Bates, *The Modern Short Story*

a) What scene has James Joyce described?
b) What qualities does Mr. Bates admire in this descriptive writing?
c) Do you agree with Mr. Bates's opinions?
d) What other qualities do you find in the passage by James Joyce?

Descriptive Passage 4

There was a row of jars upon the top of this desk. For the most part they were silent amid this rioting, but there was one which seemed to hold a scintillant and rioting serpent.

Suddenly the glass splintered, and a ruby-red snake-like thing poured

154

its thick length out upon the top of the old desk. It coiled and hesitated, and then began to swim a languorous way down the mahogany slant. At the angle it waved its sizzling molten head to and fro over the closed eyes of the man beneath it. Then, in a moment, with a mystic impulse, it moved again, and the red snake flowed directly down into Johnson's upturned face.

Afterwards the trail of this creature seemed to reek, and amid flames and low explosions drops like red-hot jewels pattered softly down it at leisurely intervals. Stephen Crane, "The Monster"

Descriptive Passage 5

There was just enough light to see. Henrietta, though dazed after her night journey, sat up straight in the taxi, looking out of the window. She had not left England before. She said to herself: This is Paris. The same streets, with implacably shut shops running into each other at odd angles, seemed to unreel past again and again. She thought she saw the same kiosks. Cafés were lit inside, chairs stacked on the tables: they were swabbing the floors. Men stood at a steamy counter drinking coffee. A woman came out with a tray of mimosa and the raw daylight fell on the yellow pollen: but for that there might have been no sky. These indifferent streets and early morning faces oppressed Henrietta, who was expecting to find Paris gay and kind. Elizabeth Bowen, *The House in Paris*

Criticism

This incident [passage 4] is from a story called "The Monster", and describes how, during a fire, the acid on a laboratory bench topples over and drips on the face of an unconscious man lying on the floor. Note the slow style, as well as the accumulation of detail. . . A novelist employing so carefully incised an English as this would produce but few books; their movement would be of the slowest; and the effect would probably become intolerable after a time. . .

Compare this slow meticulous style with that of a novelist who does load every rift with ore, who does caress her details, who makes every word work: the first page of Elizabeth Bowen's *The House in Paris* [passage 5]. Note that there is no lack of detail, but note, too, that . . . the entire chunk is working towards the observation of the final sentence of the paragraph. . .

. . . Note the information conveyed—the sweep of the pure fact: that Henrietta has been travelling all night, is English, has not been in Paris before, and is touched by foreboding. Note, especially that . . . the paragraph moves quicker and quicker, and finally debouches, like an estuary, into the large expectation, or expansive delta of the novel. . . Sean O'Faolain, *The Short Story*

a) What is Mr. O'Faolain's opinion of the passage taken from "The Monster"?
b) In what respect does Mr. O'Faolain consider passages 4 and 5 similar?
c) According to this critic, which description is better and why?
d) Do you agree with the critic's comparison of these passages? Be prepared to justify your opinion.

LITERARY CRITICISM OF DESCRIPTION

PLANNING AND WRITING CRITICISM

Before attempting to write an evaluation of a descriptive passage, read the passage carefully and ask yourself these questions about it:

1. a) What scene or experience is the author describing?
   b) What is the time of day, the kind of day, the time of year?
   c) What is the point of view, the vantage point?
2. What is the effect aimed at in the passage?
3. Is the passage unified? If so, what details have been used to establish a dominant impression?
4. Is the passage coherent? If so, how has the author achieved this quality?
5. Is structural emphasis achieved in the passage? If so, by what means?
6. Do the diction and the imagery contribute to the effects the author wishes to gain? If so, how? If not, why not?
7. Is the sentence structure effective? (Think of specific sentences that will justify your opinion.)

Then use the answers to these questions as the content of your criticism. The following structure is a satisfactory one for criticism of description.

THE OVERALL STRUCTURE OF CRITICISM

1. A brief summary of the scene that the author has described, and a statement of the effect he is trying to achieve
2. A statement of the critic's thesis
3. A development—in several paragraphs—of this thesis
4. A conclusion that stresses the critic's thesis

CLASS DISCUSSION
Analyzing Criticisms Written by Students

1. Below you will find a student's criticism of Joseph Conrad's description entitled "The River". The student attempted to evaluate the paragraph structure, the diction, the imagery and the sentence structure. Use the questions that follow the criticism to discuss its effectiveness.

The River

. . . The white man rested his chin on his crossed arms and gazed at the wake of the boat. At the end of the straight avenue of forests cut by the

156

intense glitter of the river, the sun appeared unclouded and dazzling, poised low over the water that shone smoothly like a band of metal. The forests, sombre and dull, stood motionless and silent on each side of the broad stream. At the foot of big, towering trees, trunkless nipa palms rose from the mud of the bank, in bunches of leaves, enormous and heavy, that hung unstirring over the brown swirl of eddies. In the stillness of the air every tree, every leaf, every bough, every tendril of creeper, and every petal of minute blossoms seemed to have been bewitched into an immobility perfect and final. Nothing moved on the river but the eight paddles that rose flashing regularly, dipped together with a single splash . . . Joseph Conrad, "The Lagoon"

Student's Criticism of The River

In this paragraph, Joseph Conrad is describing a tropical scene as it is viewed by a white man sitting in a canoe that is being paddled up a river. From his vantage point in the canoe, the man gazes at the river stretching before him, the sun low in the sky above it, and the forests flanking it on either side. The dominant atmosphere is the utter stillness of intense tropical heat. The author succeeds in creating this atmosphere by means of his paragraph structure, and by his use of diction, imagery and sentence structure.

Through his choice of descriptive details, the author establishes unity of impression in the paragraph. The white man is in an attitude of repose, sitting with his chin resting on his crossed arms. The sun shines with intense brightness from a cloudless sky, a detail that gives the impression of a hot, still day. This impression is sustained by the description of the sombre, dull forests standing, quiet and motionless, on either side of the stream. At the feet of the trees are nipa palms, whose large leaves hang unstirring over the water. The air is still; there is no movement of leaf, bough, or petal; all are bewitched into "perfect immobility". No detail destroys the dominant atmosphere of the paragraph; each aids in building and maintaining it.

The structure of the paragraph contributes to its coherence. First, the general picture of the forest, river and sun is given. Then, these composite elements of the scene are each described in greater detail. There is a logical sequence to these details—those farthest from the white man, the sun, forests, and river—are noticed first—and those closest to him—the palms, leaves, boughs, tendrils and blossoms—are examined last. This arrangement of details strengthens the coherence of the passage.

The dominant impression of stillness is made yet more emphatic through climactic arrangement of details and a forceful conclusion. The paragraph begins with a description of the largest details of the scene— the "motionless and silent" forests—and ends with the smallest—the perfectly immobile leaves, boughs, tendrils, and blossoms. The effect of this descending order of details is that of a stillness so pervading that it "bewitches" even the tiniest flower petal into "immobility". The stillness and quietness are complete save for the slow, sure passage of the canoe over the river, and the rhythmic splash of the paddles in the water. This single sound serves to accentuate the predominant silence, and the sole

157

movement gives an emphatic contrast to the immobility of the rest of the scene.

The author's use of words and phrases helps him to gain his effects. The powerful heat and brilliance of the sun are suggested by the adjectives "unclouded" and "dazzling", and further emphasized by the description of its reflection by the river as an "intense glitter". The "sombre and dull" forests, and the "big, towering" trees are particularly good visual images. The static state of these trees and palm leaves is brought out by the adjectives "unstirring", "motionless" and "silent". The use of the verb "bewitched" gives the stillness of the scene an almost supernatural quality. The immobility is "perfect and final".

Conrad uses sentence structure to help him gain his effects. By using the devices of position and parallelism, he impresses on the reader important details in the description. In sentences 2 and 4, he places at the first of each sentence, and in parallel structure, the details that tell *where* the white man is looking: "at the end of the straight avenue of forests cut by the intense glitter of the river" and "at the foot of the big, towering trees". In sentence 5, by putting the phrase "in the stillness of the air" at the beginning and out of its natural place, he impresses on the reader the dominant atmosphere of the scene. The two pairs of adjectives, both placed out of their natural positions—"sombre and dull" and "enormous and heavy"—attract attention to these two effective visual details. In sentence 5, that contains, perhaps, the best details in the passage, Conrad uses both repetition and climax. The repetition of *every* in "every tree, every leaf, every bough, every tendril of creeper and every petal of minute blossoms", and the arrangement of these details (with the exception of "every bough") in the order of size, from the great trees to the tiny petals, help establish an atmosphere of almost incredible calm. Terry A.

Discussion Questions

a) What is the thesis of this student's criticism?
b) For what purpose has the student used each paragraph of her criticism?
c) Has she discussed every point she proposed (according to her thesis) to discuss?
d) What are some of the merits of this criticism?
e) What suggestions can you offer for improving it?

2. Below you will find a descriptive passage followed by a student's criticism written in answer to the following: *Evaluate the overall structure, the diction, the imagery and the sentence structure of Mr. Gibbs's description of a jazz band.* Use the questions that follow the criticism to guide your discussion of it.

The Band

The saxophone reared its brazen head in the air, swayed like some sort of gleaming python intoxicated by the charmer's pipe, sent an excruciating whinny reeling across the room, and squirted a little spout of sucking chuckles to gibber in its wake. A very fat man, with his plump cheeks creased by the thin end of this infernal machine, sent an inspired blast of carbon dioxide roaring through its sweating innards, which, being wrought on by his pudgy fingers, issued forth in the form of weird moans, choking coughs, dyspeptic sighs, and the bleating of lambs.

"It haddabe yew," tittered the violinist through the megaphone.

And the banjos thrummed eternally, and a lean man with india-rubber fingers hurled himself at the piano until it squeaked at the violence of his onslaught, or rippled over its placid surface in a rush of twitterings, as if all the sparrows in London had gone suddenly mad, and the saxophone hoicked, and the drum throbbed its insinuating rhythm, and the violin shrieked like a soul in pain, and all the demons in hell swayed to this diabolical syncopation of demented monsters lumbering through fetid swamps; and the pulsing agony became more and more insistent with the last verse, and the music mounted up and up, modulating through penetrating quarter tones that have no place in a printed score, and the time became more and more fantastically distorted, and the cornet lifted up his voice to heaven and let forth a cry of vengeance, until, with a crash of cymbals, and a last howling discord, the band laid down their instruments with every appearance of haste, and disappeared through a small door in the back. Anthony Gibbs, *Little Peter Vacuum*

Student's Criticism of The Band

1. In this passage, Anthony Gibbs has described an unpleasant personal experience—listening to the agonizing music of a jazz band. By means of good structure, skilful choice of words, imaginative figures of speech and effective sentence structure, he has succeeded in establishing an atmosphere of howling discord, and conveying his reaction to it.

2. The description is unified. The author has, by means of well-chosen details, created an atmosphere of howling discord. He has described the excruciating whinny and the insane chuckles of the saxophone; the unbearable and continuous thrumming of the banjos; the squeaking of the violins and the inane twitterings of the piano; the painful shrieks of the violin. Then, as the music mounts to its climax, the cornet's wild cry coupled with the crash of cymbals nearly deafens the booming ears of the author; and the unholy din ceases. The band disappears through a small back door. Because Mr. Gibbs has used descriptive details that establish an overall impression of howling discord, he has written a unified passage.

3. Coherence is achieved by using a logical arrangement of details. We *see* and *hear* each instrument in turn as it plays and are always conscious of the author's point of view, that of a pained listener to the jazz band.

4. Mr. Gibbs has used a climactic arrangement of details to give structural emphasis to his passage. He begins with a description of each instrument in turn contributing its particular tone of barbarity; then he describes each one again, but this time the tone of each is wilder, shriller, more unbearably insistent; then he concludes with the description of the music mounting to a frenzy, wild and distorted in tone and rhythm, until finally the cornet lets out a cry of vengeance, the cymbals crash, and with a last howl of discord, the band lays down its diabolic instruments.

159

5. Mr. Gibbs has used imagery and diction skilfully to help him achieve his effects: to make his readers visualize the band and the instruments, to hear the infernal music, and to sense his deep distaste for it. For these effects, he has used figurative language, specific adjectives, nouns and verbs, and onomatopoeic words. The simile "The saxophone reared its *brazen head* in the air and swayed *like some sort of gleaming python*" makes the reader visualize the shape and the movement of the saxophone as well as sense the author's dislike of it. In the "violin shrieked *like a soul in pain*" and "the cornet *lifted up its voice to heaven and let forth a cry of vengeance*", Mr. Gibbs has used a simile and a personification to suggest the dreadful sounds emitted by these instruments. He has used specific words to evoke images in the reader's mind: *pudgy* fingers, *india-rubber* fingers, *plump* cheeks, *hurled* himself at the piano, *lumbering* through *fetid* swamps; and onomatopoeic words to make the sounds almost leap from the printed page: an excruciating *whinny*, the banjos *thrummed*, the saxophone *hoicked* and the cymbals *crashed*. Perhaps the most distinctive feature of the language is Mr. Gibbs's use of specific words to suggest that to him the music is insane, diabolical and well nigh unbearable; to *gibber* in its wake, *weird* moans, its *insinuating* rhythm, *diabolical syncopation*, *demented* monsters, *pulsing agony*.

6. Mr. Gibbs uses rhetorical devices in sentence structure to help establish the impression of an unbearable din. He begins his description with a climactic sentence. Each of the four predicates describes an unpleasant action of that monster, the saxophone; and these actions are arranged in ascending order of unpleasantness. This climactic arrangement establishes at once the author's desired effect. In the second sentence, the author uses position to stress the din: he has placed at the end of his sentence an accumulation of four sounds, all strangely out of place in music. He next uses a very short sentence to provide a lull before the mounting frenzy of sound described in the last, extraordinarily long, compound-complex sentence. In this last sentence, Mr. Gibbs has linked together *ten* independent clauses to create his desired effect: each instrument adds its peculiarly painful notes to produce an intolerable accumulation of barbaric sounds. The main part of this mighty sentence is climactic: the first nine clauses give the impression of frantic, pulsating music increasing in tempo and discord until the final howling din; the last clause provides a superb anti-climax that stresses the preceding frenzy. Mr. Gibbs has used sentence structure to help him give the reader the impression of agonizing music.

7. Thus, by means of good structure, clever use of imagery and diction, imaginative use of sentence structure, Mr. Gibbs has successfully conveyed to his readers the intense revulsion he experienced when he listened to the "pulsing agony" of the jazz band. Leonard R.

Discussion Questions

1. What is the thesis of this criticism, and where is it stated?
2. For what purpose has this student used each of the paragraphs in his criticism?

3. Is each of the paragraphs on-topic; that is, does it contribute to the development of the thesis? Give reasons for your opinion.
4. Is paragraph 2 unified? Give reasons for your opinion.
5. Is paragraph 5 unified, coherent and emphatic? Give reasons for your opinion. What characteristics of Mr. Gibbs's language have been exemplified?
6. What ideas in paragraph 6 have been exemplified?
7. In which paragraph has the student made an illogical shift in the tense of some of the verbs he uses? Read the paragraph aloud, changing the tenses where necessary.
8. In what ways are the students' criticisms similar to the professional criticisms? In what ways are they different? Suggest reasons for these differences.

"BRANCHING OUT" IN CRITICISM

In the two lessons on Criticism of a Descriptive Passage, you examined critical passages, some composed by professional writers, others composed by students.

You may have noticed that the professional writers' criticisms were intuitive and individual, whereas the students' criticisms were concerned primarily with the mechanics of structure and the various writing techniques.

To be a good critic, a person must have an exact and working knowledge of the mechanics of writing and an awareness of the effects that can be gained by the use of writing techniques. An experienced critic, however, usually does not comment on mechanical devices that are common to competent writing. Instead, he tries to make the reader aware of the impression the passage (or short story, poem or novel) made on him, and suggests (although not by pedestrian reference) how the writer set about creating this impression.

H. E. Bates and Sean O'Faolain are not only able critics but accomplished creative writers, capable of making structure, diction and imagery serve their specific needs. In the brief critical passages by which they are represented in this book they were content to mention some of the effects that writers, such as Turgenev, Kipling and Joyce, gained by means of structure, diction and imagery. Neither of these critics allowed himself to become engrossed with describing mechanical "props".

Literary Criticism of a Descriptive Paragraph

1. Write a criticism of the paragraph structure, the diction, the imagery and the sentence structure of the first paragraph in the following excerpt taken from the novel *Babbitt*.

As he appproached the office he walked faster and faster, muttering, "Guess better hustle." All about him the city was hustling, for hustling's sake. Men in motors were hustling to pass one another in the hustling traffic. Men were hustling to catch trolleys, with another trolly a minute behind, and to leap from the trolleys, to gallop across the sidewalk, to hurl themselves into buildings, into hustling express elevators. Men in dairy lunches were hustling to gulp down the food which cooks had hustled to fry. Men in barber shops were snapping, "Jus' shave me once over. Gotta hustle." Men were feverishly getting rid of visitors in offices adorned with the signs, "This Is My Busy Day" and "The Lord Created the World in Six Days—You Can Spiel All You Got to Say in Six Minutes." Men who had made five thousand, year before last, and ten thousand last year, were urging on nerve-yelping bodies and parched brains so that they might make twenty thousand this year; and the men who had broken down immediately after making their twenty thousand dollars were hustling to catch trains, to hustle through the vacations which the hustling doctors had

Among them Babbitt hustled back to his office, to sit down with nothing much to do except see that the staff looked as though they were hustling. Sinclair Lewis, *Babbitt*

2. Write an appreciation of the merits of the following description.

The wind by now was more than redoubled. The shutters were bulging as if tired elephants were leaning against them, and Father was trying to tie the fastening with his handkerchief. But to push against this wind was like pushing against rock. The handkerchief, shutters, everything burst. The rain poured in like the sea into a sinking ship; the wind occupied the room, snatching pictures from the wall, sweeping the table bare. Through the gaping frames the lightning-lit scene without was visible. The creepers, which before had looked like cobwebs, now streamed up into the sky like new-combed hair. Bushes were lying flat, laid back on the ground as close as a rabbit lays back his ears. Branches were leaping about loose in the sky. The negro huts were clean gone, and the negroes crawling on their stomachs across the compound to gain the shelter of the house. The bouncing rain seemed to cover the ground with a white smoke, a sort of sea in which the blacks wallowed like porpoises. One little boy began to roll away. His mother, forgetting caution, rose to her feet; and immediately the fat old beldam was blown clean away, bowling along across fields and hedgerows like someone in a funny fairy-story, till she fetched up against a wall and was pinned there, unable to move. But the others managed to reach the house, and soon could be heard in the cellar underneath. Richard Hughes, *A High Wind in Jamaica*

3. Markheim, the man mentioned in the following descriptive paragraph, has just killed an old shop-keeper, and is now on his way upstairs to steal the old man's money. Write a criticism of the paragraph structure, the diction, the imagery and the sentence structure of this description.

The faint, foggy daylight glimmered dimly on the bare floor and stairs; on the bright suit of armour posted, halbert in hand, upon the landing; and on the dark wood-carvings, and framed pictures that hung against the yellow panels of the wainscot. So loud was the beating of the rain through all the house that, in Markheim's ears, it began to be distinguished into many different sounds. Footsteps and sighs, the tread of regiments marching in the distance, the chink of money in the counting, and the creaking of doors held stealthily ajar, appeared to mingle with the patter of the drops upon the cupola and the gushing of the water in the pipes. The sense that he was not alone grew upon him to the verge of madness. On every side he was haunted and begirt by presences. He heard them moving in the upper chambers; from the shop, he heard the dead man getting to his legs; and as he began with a great effort to mount the stairs, feet fled quietly before him and followed stealthily behind. If he were but deaf, he thought, how tranquilly he would possess his soul! And then again, and hearkening with ever fresh attention, he blessed himself for that unresting sense which held the outposts and stood a trusty sentinel upon his life. His head turned continually on his neck; his eyes, which seemed starting from their orbits, scouted on every side, and on every side were half-rewarded as with the tail of something nameless vanishing. The four-and-twenty steps to the first floor were four-and-twenty agonies. R. L. Stevenson, "Markheim"

4. Write a criticism of each of the following descriptive passages. In your criticisms evaluate the overall structure and also the paragraph structure, the sentence structure, the diction and the imagery of any *two* paragraphs.

a) The Sea Above Us

"Count them," Father said. It was a brilliant Sunday afternoon, and we were standing on top of the two-storey-high dike and looking landward, with the rolling North Sea behind us. Father was encouraging my younger brothers to count the towers and spires, and the villages and towns that clustered tightly around them. It might be a lesson in applied geography— though that was not very likely on this day of the Lord—but it was certainly one in human endeavour and patience. Twenty-four spires and towns we could count on ordinary days, twenty-nine when the light was good, but on a clear afternoon like today, as many as thirty-three.

"Now you name them, Rem and David," Father ordered us two oldest boys. We started on the western horizon where the dike shut off the sea, on toward the east where the dike met the sky once more. We named all the towns in their proper order, the near score of names ending in "um" and all those that had "wier" in them, like our own town, the oldest, gravest, and perhaps bleakest of them all, Wierum. All those names evoked age, and many of them suggested aspects of the sea and man's endless battle with that sea. . . .

There they were—red- and blue-roofed towns hugging gray churches with slate-blue spires, scattered over a checker-board of a landscape almost entirely made by man; prosperous golden squares of wheat, bright yellow blocks of mustard, purple rectangles of cabbage, hexagons of blue flax, latticed parcels of white and pink buckwheat, limned everywhere with canals and ditches reflecting the translucent sky. And there curved the humped bridges with their vermilion and orange railings, seemingly helping the ribbons of roads to reach all the hives of towns properly. Over everything, adding up to three-quarters of the landscape, as in all good Dutch paintings, extended the ever-varied cup of sky.

We named all the towns, and Father was proud of us. The vision we saw seemed eternal in peace and prosperity, like a perfect greeting card. From the beginning we had been taught to be proud of the land. There was not a square yard of waste upon it.

But behind our backs, to the north of us, was the sea. Father had not yet asked us to turn around and look seaward. That would be the second step, like appraising an enemy, after we had evaluated our own bounty. My youngest brother would be asked to name the row of sandy islands ten miles away, which once upon a time had been part of our fixed shore line. Now between us and the islands stretched the gray sea, which nearly everyone in our town still called "the lost land", even though it had been lost as long as eight hundred years ago. On an afternoon like this the sea looked friendly, but there were the wrecks of old ships, broken piers, smashed-up palisades, and the faraway gaps between the islands to warn us that it was merely slumbering.

The dike stretched west and east, and lost itself against the horizon. It looked secure. Black-and-white cattle stood upon it in solemn conclave, immensely statuesque and enlarged, and looked out to sea while chewing their cud. The sheep, newly shorn and white, together with their half-grown lambs, lay huddled among the ox-eye daisies and buttercups against its slopes. Gulls and terns, rooks and magpies, busy musseling, screamed and skirled over us. Practically with its foot on the dike stood the old tower of our town, its grim gray church saddled behind it. That tower, the most ancient in our province, was more than a thousand years old, and had been built miles from the sea. Now it hugged the elbow of the dike, and was both our sentinel and our comfort. . . .

On sparkling Sunday afternoons in summer it was easy to be confident. In winter we had permissible fears. There behind the heavy dike, with its brick steps leading up to the scudding skies, ten, fifteen, twenty or more feet above us thundered the waves, when the tides were high and when the winds came hurling across the North Sea. David Cornel DeJong, from The *Atlantic Monthly,* April, 1954

b) Journey Through the Night

And now his brother and he were given to this earth, this dark, this loneliness again. And as they rushed on into the darkness, held, save for the throbbing motor of the little car, in the immutable silence of the earth and darkness, the flickering headlights of the car would suddenly pierce into the huge surrounding mystery of night, lunging for an instant the flashing finger of their light upon some fugitive and secret presence in the vault of night, where all the million lives of men were held. Sometimes, the flashing light would blaze upon the boarding of a little house at the bend of the road, and then the house would flash behind and be engulfed in darkness.

Sometimes, it would reveal the brown and dusty stubble of the cotton fields, a stretch of ragged pine, a lonely little wooden church, a shack, a cabin, the swift and sinuous forking of another road that spoked into their own, flashed past, and curved away—was gone forever—leaving an instant and intolerable pain and memory—a searing recognition and discovery—a road once seen but never followed and now forever lost with all its promises of a life that they had never known or explored, of faces they had never seen.

And again, out of this huge and mournful earth, out of the limitless mystery of this continent of night, the lights upon his brother's car would for an instant pick out faces, shapes, and people, and they, too, would blaze there for a moment in our vision with an intolerable and lonely briefness, and then be lost forever—and in that moment of instant parting and farewell was written the history of man's destiny—his brother's life, and that of all men living on the earth around him.

Once their lights picked out the figure of a country negro: his weary plodding figure loomed up for an instant dustily—a mournful image of bowed back, shapeless garments stained with red field earth, and clumsy brogans coated with the red dust of the road, plodding along against a terrific and desolate landscape of brown cotton fields, clay, and lonely pine, as much a part of it as the earth he walked upon, fixed instantly into it in a vision of labour, sorrow, and destiny, that was eternal.

And again they passed by negroes coming from a country church, and for a moment saw their white eyes and their black and mournful faces staring towards the light, and lost these, too, forever, and passed into a little town and out again, and saw far-off, and at its edges, a pollen of bright light above a little travelling carnival, and heard the sad wheeling music of the carousel, the mixed and woven clamor of the barker's cries, the shouts, the people's voices, and all far-faint and lost and mournful as a dream; and then the earth again—the two back wheels, claycaked and rattling, of an ancient buggy, the lifting hooves of an old boneyard nag, that slowly turned away from the road's centre to make way for them, the slow, staring, stupid looks of wonder and astonishment of a young country fellow and his girl as they went by them and finally, always and forever, nothing but the earth—that mournful, desolate, and lonely earth of cotton fields, and raw red clay and lonely pine, wheeling past forever in rude and formless undulations, immemorable, everlasting, and terrific, above which the great stars blazed their imperturbable and inscrutable messages of deathless calm. Thomas Wolfe, *Of Time and the River*

c) Picking Cherries

There was a great crop of cherries at the farm. The trees at the back of the house, very large and tall, hung thick with scarlet and crimson drops, under the dark leaves. Paul and Edgar were gathering in the fruit one evening. It had been a hot day, and now the clouds were rolling in the sky, dark and warm. Paul climbed high in the tree, above the scarlet roofs of the buildings. The wind, moaning steadily, made the whole tree rock with a subtle, thrilling motion that stirred the blood. The young man, perched insecurely in the slender branches, rocked till he felt slightly drunk, reached down the boughs, where the scarlet beady cherries hung thick underneath, and tore handful after handful of the sleek, cool-fleshed fruit. Cherries touched his ears and his neck as he stretched forward, their chill fingertips sending a flash down his blood. All shades of red, from golden vermilion to a rich crimson, glowed and met his eyes under a darkness of leaves.

The sun, going down, suddenly caught the broken clouds. Immense piles of gold flared out in the southeast, heaped in soft, glowing yellow right up the sky. The world, till now dusk and grey, reflected the gold glow, astonished. Everywhere the trees, and the grass, and the far-off water, seemed roused from the twilight, and shining.

Miriam came out wondering.

"Oh!" Paul heard her mellow voice call, "isn't it wonderful?"

He looked down. There was a faint gold glimmer on her face, that looked very soft, turned up to him.

"How high you are!" she said.

"Clouds are on fire," he said.

"Beautiful!" she cried.

She seemed so small, so soft, so tender, down there. He threw a handful of cherries at her. She was startled and frightened. He laughed with a low, chuckling sound, and pelted her. She ran for shelter, picking up some cherries. Two fine red pairs she hung over her ears; then she looked up again.

"Haven't you got enough?" she asked.

"Nearly. It is like being on a ship up here."

"And how long will you stay?"

"While the sunset lasts."

She went to the fence and sat there, watching the gold clouds fall to pieces, and go in immense, rose-coloured ruin towards the darkness. Gold flamed to scarlet, like pain in its intense brightness. Then the scarlet sank to rose, and rose to crimson, and quickly the passion went out of the sky. All the world was dark grey. Paul scrambled quickly down with his basket, tearing his shirt-sleeve as he did so. D. H. Lawrence, *Sons and Lovers*

LITERARY CRITICISM OF THE NOVEL

PLANNING AND WRITING A CRITICAL ESSAY

Literary criticism of novels is of two types, the book review and the critical essay. Both kinds are found in our newspapers and periodicals. The aim of the book review is to present a new novel to the public. The reviewer usually summarizes the book, perhaps interprets it and then evaluates it. The aim of the critical essay is to present to the reader the critic's estimate of the total worth of a novel, either a new one or an old one. The critical essay is the more difficult to write but probably the more interesting to read.

CLASS DISCUSSION I
The Aims of Criticism

Below you will find part of an article that appeared in *The Times Literary Supplement* (London). Use as a guide for your discussion the questions that follow the excerpt.

The Critical Mind

The study of literature has three main branches: literary theory; literary history; and literary criticism in a fairly narrow sense—the sense of direct appreciation of, and the attempt to assign a precise degree of importance to, a given body of work. . .

Literary criticism is concerned with the permanent value of chosen examples of the form. . . What are the qualities in any work of literature that we should specially attend to, before attempting to decide whether it has permanent value, and how much value? Are they, for instance, broad formal qualities (like structure), qualities of detailed workmanship (like texture), qualities having to do with the moral content or perhaps the moral tone of a work of literature (like Arnold's "high seriousness"), qualities of depth of wisdom or visionary insight (so that at least the greatest works of literature ought to be discussed rather as the devout discuss sacred texts), qualities of broad or deep relevance to everyday living (so that we should prefer loose vitality to dead perfection), or qualities that can best be defined in terms of our own responses: or what? There does not seem to be any basic agreement on what the broader criteria of literary judgment are; and in fact no good critic ever applies such criteria in an abstract way, like yardsticks, from the outside. He trusts his responses to order themselves: he trusts his habits as a reader, and, if he is a mature man, what he thinks of as a certain depth or sanity in his basic attitudes of life. . .

The literary critic is very often concerned . . . with what can be preserved, recognized, esteemed, fostered towards continuing value, in a context which might be thought of as broadly disastrous. Good practical criticism is often concerned to say, for instance, that in spite of melodrama, sentimentality, caricature, great areas of overwriting or of hasty writing, perhaps in spite of some fundamental conceptual flaw, some novel, say by Dickens or Dostoevsky has major qualities; or that a lot of Mark Twain is literature in spite of being journalism; or that when you come really to like Wordsworth there is a sense in which you enjoy him even when he is dull and clumsy; or that the haphazardness of *Hamlet,* the desultory process of its plot, the apparent incoherences or inconsistencies of Hamlet's character, the lack of anything that one can crisply call a thematic centre in the play —that all these are, in fact, part of its perennial fascination. Literary perfection exists, but not on anything like the same scale as examples of things perfect in their kind exist in music or the visual arts; and the hunger for perfection, for what Jane Austen, or Turgenev, or Thomas Campion, or Racine can offer us is never, or very rarely, a main motive for studying literature; engrossment with literature is more like engrossment with life, like the vice or virtue of curiosity, than it is like engrossment with any of the other arts. . . . *The Times Literary Supplement,* March, 1960

Discussion Questions

1. According to this writer, what is the general aim of the literary critic?
2. What, according to this article, are some of the criteria a critic might consider before attempting to decide whether a piece of writing has permanent value, and how much value? State these qualities in your own words.
3. a) Explain the meaning of the following statement: "The literary critic is very often concerned . . . with what can be preserved, recognized, esteemed, fostered towards continuing value, in a context which might be thought of as broadly disastrous".
   b) Do you agree with the above statement? Refer to a specific novel or play to illustrate your ideas.

CLASS DISCUSSION II

Analyzing a Critical Essay Written by a Professional Critic

Below is Robert Lynd's criticism of Mary Webb's novel *Seven for a Secret.* Read aloud the essay and then discuss the critic's opinions, using as a guide the discussion questions that follow the criticism.

Mary Webb had that always fascinating quality of genius—imaginative energy. It is a quality so precious that, when an author possesses it, the waves of criticism beat against his work in vain. It appears in a hundred different forms, and is the immortal soul alike of the romances of Dumas, the seventy-times-seven-to-be-forgiven, as Henley called him, and of the novels of Victor Hugo, who needs our forgiveness even more often. Dickens, possessing it, made us believe in the existence of a vast population of men and women in whom we should have believed under no other compulsion, and Hans Andersen, possessing it, endowed a tin soldier with greater reality for us than the thirty tyrants of Athens. Spellbound by it, we accept Emily Brontë's vision of life in *Wuthering Heights.* There are other qualities as enchanting in literature—wisdom, humour, and observation without fear or favour—but there is no other quality that, by itself, exercises such power over us.

I do not suppose that many of the admirers of the work of Mary Webb —and they were a larger multitude during her lifetime than is generally realized—if asked to express an opinion as to which is the best of her books, would name *Seven for a Secret*. Yet in its pages what a tempestuous energy storms through that landscape 'between the dimpled lands of England and the gaunt purple steeps of Wales—half in Faery and half out of it!' Gillian Lovekin, the farmer's daughter, may be a fool from the beginning—a greater fool, indeed than Mary Webb supposed her to be— but at least she is a fool to whom we can no more be indifferent than we can be indifferent to a gale that blows a house down. Not that Gillian is magnificently ruinous: she is no Helen of Troy. She is petty even in the magnitude of her ambition—as petty as a parish Hedda Gabler. She has, when we meet her first, no real ambition, except to be a greater Gillian Lovekin and to escape from the farm that is too small a stage for her. If she is intent on learning to sing or to play the harp, it is not because she wishes to succeed as an artist so much as because she wishes to triumph over her fellow-creatures. 'I want,' she confesses frankly to her cowman worshipper, 'to draw tears out of their eyes and money out of their pockets.' 'She wanted,' we are told, 'to make men and women hear her, love her, rue her'. It is probably a common enough daydream of egoists of both sexes, and with most of them it remains a daydream. But Gillian put her egotism into practice, and began by causing the death of the elderly gentle- man who wooed her aunt with readings from Crabbe and by the end of the story had caused a murder.

The story would have been a sordid one if Mary Webb, with her imaginative and fantastic gifts, had not exalted it into a tale of the conflict between light and the powers of darkness in a setting in which Gillian's lover's house is like a refuge of the sun, and the house to which her husband takes her is a predestined habitation of evil spirits. Mr. W. B. Yeats once declared, when defending Synge's 'Playboy,' that art is 'exaggeration à propos', and *Seven for a Secret* is written in a vein of noble and appropriate exaggeration. Here men are stronger than common men: they are nature's giants, as they woo Gillian to the thunder of hoofs, galloping bareback past her house in a breakneck fury. The atmosphere of 'The Mermaid's Rest', Gillian's home after marriage, again, is like that of an ogre's castle, with the beautiful dumb woman-servant as an imprisoned princess, and the monkey-like, toothless, hilarious Fringal as a gnome abetting his master in evil. In the dumb girl and in Fringal it is as though a beautiful and a hideous grotesque had stepped out of the pages of Hugo into an English landscape. Mary Webb has in this book created her characters in a high fervour of the romantic spirit.

This in a novelist is possibly more important than psychology. At least, when it is present, we are less likely to be critical of an author's psychology. We may wonder whether Gillian, at an hour when she was deep in love with Robert Rideout, would have yielded so easily to Elmer on the night of the fair at Weeping Cross, but our doubts are lost in the romance of her subsequent sufferings and salvation—salvation that comes only after she has drawn the secret of her husband's past, letter by letter, from Rwth, the dumb woman, and the secret has cost Rwth her life. We may not quite believe that Gillian, the egotist, when she finally found safety in Robert Rideout's arms, whispered to him: 'Oh, Robert! Robert! The powers of darkness have lost their hold, and I'm not a child of sin any more'; but because of the vehement good faith with which the fable has been told, we do not quarrel with the author for putting into Gillian's mouth a sentence that rounds it off like a moral.

If it is necessary to classify novelists—and we all attempt to do it—Mary Webb must be put in a class that contains writers so different as Emily Brontë and Thomas Hardy, for whom the earth is predominantly a mystery-haunted landscape inhabited by mortals who suffer. To class her with these writers is not to claim that she is their equal: all that we need claim is that her work is alive with the fiery genius of sympathy, pity and awe. There is scarcely a scene in *Seven for a Secret* that some touch of poetic observation does not keep alive in the memory. The characters, as I have suggested, may seem at times a little fabulous, but with what a poetic intensity of emotion she compels us to believe in the scenes in which they take part! It is not too much, indeed, to say that in her writings fiction became a branch of poetry—a flowering branch that will still give pleasure for many years to come. Robert Lynd, "Introduction" to *Seven for a Secret*

Discussion Questions

1. What is Mr. Lynd's opinion of the permanent value of this novel? What reasons does he give for holding this opinion?
2. What weaknesses does the critic find in the novel?
3. For what purposes has he used the opening paragraph? the concluding paragraph?
4. Is Mr. Lynd's criticism of *Seven for a Secret* a fair estimate of the novel? (Answer only if you have read the novel.) If you have not read it, would you be encouraged to do so by reading Mr. Lynd's criticism?

HOME WORK ASSIGNMENT

Write a criticism of a novel that you have read recently. Make the aim of your criticism an "attempt to assign a precise degree of importance" to the novel you select.

DIRECTIONS

1. Select the group to whom you will address your criticism: either those who have read the novel or those who have not.
2. Compose the thesis of your criticism. The thesis is *your* evaluation of the novel. Use the questions on page 168 to guide you in forming your opinion.
3. Compose a lead that will interest your readers in the novel you discuss.
4. Develop the thesis by giving reasons for your opinion. Make specific references to the text of the novel to illustrate your ideas.
5. Compose an arresting conclusion that will stress your thesis.

NARRATIVE TO REVEAL CHARACTER

LESSON ONE

ANALYZING NARRATIVE

A narrative is a recital of events, or a tale.*
Description and narrative are often interwoven. When an author recounts something that *happened,* such as *the burglars crept into the house,* he is narrating. Usually, however, he also gives his readers visual images of the people in the narrative and of the setting in which the action occurs. He is then interweaving description and narrative.

Narrative, whether written or related orally, usually has a specific purpose. For example, the writer may wish to amuse his readers, to surprise them, to evoke their pity or their wonder, to characterize a person, or to suggest some universal truth about people or life.

A good narrative is unified, coherent and emphatic. To make narrative unified, a writer establishes a singleness of effect; to make it coherent, he tells his events in some logical order; to make it emphatic, he stresses, in its conclusion, the effect he has been trying to achieve.

In these lessons you will learn how to use narrative to characterize a person or persons.

To depict a person's character, a writer may recount one or more of the following:

1. his behaviour;
2. his speech;
3. his thoughts;
4. another person's opinion of him.

CLASS DISCUSSION
Using Narrative to Reveal Character

1. The following narrative, one of Christ's parables, is related in the Bible, Luke X: 30-35. Read the passage and use the questions that follow to guide your discussion of it.

The Good Samaritan

A certain man was going down from Jerusalem to Jericho, and fell among robbers, who both stripped him and beat him, and departed, leaving him half dead.

And by chance a certain priest was going down on that road, and see-ing him, he passed by on the other side.

---

*In these two lessons on narrative, the short story proper, that is, a deliberately fashioned work of art and not just a straightforward tale of one or more events, is not dealt with.

And likewise, a Levite also, coming to the place, and seeing him, passed by on the other side.

But a certain Samaritan, as he journeyed, came where he was: and seeing him, had pity, and came to him, and bound up his wounds, pouring on oil and wine; and he set him on his own beast, and brought him to an inn, and took care of him.

And on the morrow he took out two shillings, and gave to the inn-keeper, and said, Take care of him; and whatever thou spendest more, I, when I come back again, will repay thee. Luke X: 30-35

Discussion Questions

1. What incident is narrated?
2. a) What aspects of character have been revealed in this incident?
   b) By what means are these traits revealed?

2. The following narrative constitutes the preface of Judith Robinson's biography *Tom Cullen of Baltimore*. Miss Robinson has selected an incident that occurred when Dr. Cullen, a Canadian-born gynecologist at Johns Hopkins Hospital, was nearing the end of his long teaching career.

Resuming in the Green Room

Dr. Cullen's operative clinic in Fourth Year Gynecology adjourned to the green room. The young men jostled and joked in the glass-walled gallery behind the operating theatre, waiting their turn to hang surgical gowns on pegs and drop caps and masks in the basket set for them. But all were in place in the chairs along the walls when the round man in white came to sit behind the lecturer's table.

The lecturer's table in the gynecological department lecture room at Johns Hopkins hospital is an old-fashioned short operating table with a cracked glass top.

The other walls are hung with photographs, some brown with age, some as fresh as last year's diplomas; the likenesses of successive senior residents in gynecology from the beginning at Hopkins. All of them — *or just about all* — bear the stamp of the man at the old-fashioned table: teacher to them and to their fellows since the first class graduated from Johns Hopkins Medical School in 1897. Still the teacher, he sat down to discuss with the graduating class of '47 the operation they had watched.

The chin was a degree less challenging than the chin pictured in the portrait, the mouth under the white moustache smiled more tolerantly, but the eyes were no less bright and the curve of the nose no less arresting than when the artist noted them on canvas. It was the same man and, having completed an operative clinic, he went on to the next thing in his accustomed way:

"All right, Mr. Brown, in just a minute you can tell us what we did. . ."

(I don't teach 'em. I never have. I just try to show them what there is to learn. It's all anybody can do.)

172

Sitting behind the books piled on the scratched table-top, forearms bare, small thin hands clasping upper arms or moving in quick curved gestures from the elbow, black eyebrows, red face and white chin-whisker set against a blackboard for contrast, battered sneakers neatly crossed on the bronze table-foot, the man fitted the room like a part of it; easy and accustomed as the big study table, the sag-cushioned lounge, the cool air from the open gallery door . . .

". . .Now, Mr. Brown. . ."

An unhappy Mr. Brown stood, giving wrong answers with dreadful facility, smothering right ones in hoarse uncertainty. Remote behind his table, mild-voiced and questioning, Professor Cullen sat out Mr. Brown's disaster. Only the right eyebrow lifted higher and the blue eyes beamed brighter interest as the answers grew more wild. At last, appraisal warmed to kindliness and the inquisition ended.

"That's a mean question, Mr. Brown," the inquisitor said. "Never mind about it. Sit down and I'll tell you how I became interested in finding an answer."

Then to the young men before him, the old man spoke, unfolding the riches of his remembrance; of things learned and how they were learned, of men long dead whose lives had widened knowledge, of the work they had done and why; of how, doing it, they had served their generation . . .

When he had ended, his class crowded around to get his name in the books he had given them, and a boy from China . . . climbed on the big table to snap a candid camera shot. Fifty years ago taking a photograph was a more difficult business. That faded group, for example, on the wall to the left of the lecturer; that was the reward of effort.

They are all young in the faded picture, and they look with awful confidence straight ahead. They stand, immutably poised, about a metal-footed table draped in white; the same table the class of 1947 crowds around, waiting a word with the old man sitting behind it. Beneath each figure in the pictured group a name is printed: *Dr. Kelly*—out in front, his boy's face wearing its long moustache like an imperfect disguise. *Miss Beckwith*— in nurse's white at the foot of the table, young, intense, under rein . . . and, between them, behind the table *Dr. T. S. Cullen* . . .

The Hopkins Resident in Gynecology in 1896 was slim, thin-faced, beak-nosed, black-haired, with a jaw all stubborn angles, a wide and friendly mouth and eyes as dark as caves under their dark bushes of brow. . . The last book was autographed, the last hand clasped. The man in white got up from behind his table and turned to look again at the picture out of the past. Judith Robinson, *Tom Cullen of Baltimore*

Discussion Questions

1. What incident does Miss Robinson narrate?
2. a) What aspects of Dr. Cullen's character does it reveal?
   b) By what means have these traits been revealed? Refer to specific passages to substantiate your opinion.

3. What is Miss Robinson's attitude towards Dr. Cullen? Why?
4. For what purposes has Miss Robinson used description?
5. Has this narrative singleness of effect? Give reasons for your opinion.

3. William Faulkner in his short story "Barn Burning", uses the following incident to characterize a young boy, Sarty, and his father. The traits revealed here are the ones that precipitate the events of this unusual story. Read the passage aloud and use the questions that follow to guide your discussion.

Barn Burning

The store in which the Justice of the Peace's court was sitting smelled of cheese. The boy, crouched on his nail keg at the back of the crowded room, knew he smelled cheese, and more: from where he sat he could see the ranked shelves close-packed with the solid, squat, dynamic shapes of tin cans whose labels his stomach read, not from the lettering which meant nothing to his mind but from the scarlet devils and the silver curve of fish— this, the cheese which he knew he smelled and the hermetic meat which his intestines believed he smelled coming in intermittent gusts momentary and brief between the other constant one, the smell and sense just a little of fear because mostly of despair and grief, the old fierce pull of blood. He could not see the table where the Justice sat and before which his father and his father's enemy (*our enemy* he thought in that despair; *ourn! mine and hisn both! He's my father!*) stood, but he could hear them, the two of them that is, because his father had said no word yet:

"But what proof have you, Mr. Harris?"

"I told you. The hog got into my corn. I caught it and sent it back to him. He had no fence that would hold it. I told him so, warned him. The next time I put the hog in my pen. When he came to get it I gave him enough wire to patch up his pen. The next time I put the hog up and kept it. I rode down to his house and saw the wire I gave him still rolled onto the spool in his yard. I told him he could have the hog when he paid me a dollar pound fee. That evening a man came with the dollar and got the hog. He was a strange man. He said, 'He say to tell you wood and hay kin burn.' I said, 'What?' 'That whut he say to tell you,' the man said 'Wood and hay kin burn.' That night my barn burned. I got the stock out but I lost the barn."

"Where is the man? Have you got him?"

"He was a strange man, I tell you. I don't know what became of him."

"But that's not proof. Don't you see that's not proof?"

"Get that boy up here. He knows." For a moment the boy thought too that the man meant his older brother until Harris said, "Not him. The little one. The boy," and, crouching, small for his age, small and wiry like his father, in patched and faded jeans even too small for him, with straight, un-

174

combed brown hair and eyes gray and wild as storm scud, he saw the men between himself and the table part and become a lane of grim faces, at the end of which he saw the Justice, a shabby, collarless, graying man in spectacles, beckoning him. He felt no floor under his bare feet; he seemed to walk beneath the palpable weight of the grim turning faces. His father, stiff in his black Sunday coat donned not for the trial but for the moving, did not even look at him. *He aims for me to lie,* he thought, again with that frantic grief and despair. *And I will have to do hit."*

"What's your name, boy?" the Justice said.

"Colonel Sartoris Snopes," the boy whispered.

"Hey?" the Justice said. "Talk louder. Colonel Sartoris? I reckon anybody named for Colonel Sartoris in this country can't help but tell the truth, can they?" The boy said nothing. *Enemy! Enemy!* he thought; for a moment he could not even see, could not see that the Justice's face was kindly nor discern that his voice was troubled when he spoke to the man named Harris: "Do you want me to question this boy?" But he could hear, and during those subsequent long seconds while there was absolutely no sound in the crowded little room save that of quiet and intent breathing it was as if he had swung outward at the end of a grape vine, over a ravine, and at the top of the swing had been caught in a prolonged instant of mesmerized gravity, weightless in time.

"No!" Harris said violently, explosively. "Damnation! Send him out of here!" Now time, the fluid world, rushed beneath him again, the voices coming to him again through the smell of cheese and sealed meat, the fear and despair and the old grief of blood:

"This case is closed. I can't find anything against you, Snopes, but I can give you advice. Leave this country and don't come back to it."

His father spoke for the first time, his voice cold and harsh, level, without emphasis: "I aim to. I don't figure to stay in a country among people who . . ." he said something unprintable and vile, addressed to no one.

"That'll do," the Justice said. "Take your wagon and get out of this country before dark. Case dismissed." William Faulkner, "Barn Burning"

Discussion Questions

1. What incident is Mr. Faulkner narrating? From whose point of view and from what vantage point does he relate it?
2. The boy's mood gives the incident its singleness of effect, its unity. What are his feelings, and by what means has Mr. Faulkner revealed them to the reader?
3. a) What character traits, of (i) Sarty and (ii) his father, are revealed?
   b) By what means have these traits been revealed?
4. For what purposes has Mr. Faulkner used description?

NARRATIVE TO REVEAL CHARACTER

LESSON TWO

PLANNING AND WRITING A CHARACTER-REVEALING NARRATIVE

To be effective, a narrative must depict people, animals and settings that will seem real to the reader. Even a narrative poem such as *The Ancient Mariner,* that recounts a series of supernatural incidents, contains characters and settings that establish an impression of reality. The Mariner and the sea that "burnt an awful red" are not like any person or any ocean we have seen, yet Coleridge creates for us, while we are reading, the impression that this strange man and this strange setting could have existed.

In order to compose a character-revealing narrative that creates the impression of reality, you must, in addition to characterizing each person:

1. individualize each person;
2. provide a definite setting and handle it well.

INDIVIDUALIZATION

The aim of individualization is to differentiate the people in a narrative, so that each character will seem distinct to the reader.

Use one or more of the following methods to individualize each person in a story:

1. *a suitable name.* The name should not be so obvious as to suggest caricature. By present-day standards, Dickens's "Veneerings" and Fielding's "Lady Booby" are not good choices. On the other hand, Galsworthy's "Soames Forsyte" is a suitable name for a dignified, reserved, unimaginative, upper-middle-class Englishman. Sometimes an inappropriate name is chosen to suggest pathos and irony. In William Faulkner's novel *As I Lay Dying,* an underprivileged child of "poor white" parents is given the pretentious name of "Vardaman", after James K. Vardaman, one-time Governor of the State of Mississippi.

2. *description of the physical appearance of each person:* a detailed description in a single paragraph, or a few details that will focus the reader's attention on the most conspicuous feature or features of a person, or dispersed description, i.e., the details interwoven with the narrative;

3. *description of an habitual gesture;*

4. *style of speech*—speech mannerisms, use of dialect, idiom, vocabulary.

176

In each of the following passages, by what means has the author individualized the person or the persons portrayed?

1. The Captain

In the evening, all the decks of the *Atlantis* yawned in the darkness, shone with their innumerable fiery eyes, and a multitude of servants worked with increased feverishness in the kitchens, dish-washing compartments and wine-cellars. The ocean, which heaved about the sides of the ship, was dreadful, but no one thought of it. All had faith in the controlling power of the captain, a red-headed giant, heavy and very sleepy, who, clad in a uniform with broad golden stripes, looked like a huge idol, and but rarely emerged for the benefit of the public from his mysterious retreat . . . Ivan Bunin, "The Gentleman from San Francisco"

2. Paul

It was Paul's afternoon to appear before the faculty of the Pittsburgh High School to account for his various misdemeanors. He had been suspended a week ago, and his father had called at the Principal's office and confessed his perplexity about his son. Paul entered the faculty room suave and smiling. His clothes were a trifle outgrown, and the tan velvet on the collar of his open overcoat was frayed and worn; but for all that there was something of the dandy about him, and he wore an opal pin in his neatly knotted black four-in-hand, and a red carnation in his buttonhole. This latter adornment the faculty somehow felt was not properly significant of the contrite spirit befitting a boy under the ban of suspension.

Paul was tall for his age and very thin, with high, cramped shoulders and a narrow chest. His eyes were remarkable for a certain hysterical brilliancy, and he continually used them in a conscious, theatrical sort of way, peculiarly offensive in a boy. The pupils were abnormally large, as though he were addicted to belladonna, but there was a glassy glitter about them which that drug does not produce. Willa Cather, "Paul's Case"

3. The Dinner Guests

Bill and Dennis ate enormously. And Isabel filled glasses, and changed plates, and found matches, smiling blissfully. At one moment she said, "I do wish, Bill, you'd paint it."

"Paint what?" said Bill loudly, stuffing his mouth with bread.

"Us," said Isabel, "round the table. It would be so fascinating in twenty years' time."

Bill screwed up his eyes and chewed. "Light's wrong," he said rudely, "far too yellow"; and went on eating. And that seemed to charm Isabel, too. Katherine Mansfield, "Marriage à La Mode"

4. Mr. Micawber and Uriah Heep

I was excessively anxious to get Mr. Micawber away; and replied, with my hat in my hand, and a very red face, I have no doubt, that I was a pupil at Doctor Strong's.

"A pupil?" said Mr. Micawber, raising his eyebrows. "I am extremely happy to hear it. Although a mind like my friend Copperfield's" — to Uriah and Mrs. Heep — "does not require that cultivation which, without his knowledge of men and things, it would require, still it is a rich soil teeming with latent vegetation — in short," said Mr. Micawber, smiling, in another burst of confidence, "it is an intellect capable of getting up the classics to any extent."

Uriah, with his long hands slowly twining over one another, made a ghastly writhe from the waist upwards, to express his concurrence in this estimation of me.

"Shall we go and see Mrs. Micawber, sir?" I said, to get Mr. Micawber away.

"If you will do her that favour, Copperfield," replied Mr. Micawber, rising. "I have no scruple in saying, in the presence of our friends here, that I am a man who has, for some years, contended against the pressure of pecuniary difficulties." Charles Dickens, *David Copperfield*

SETTING

Handling the setting well contributes to the impression of reality. In order to gain this effect, follow these suggestions.

1. Apply your knowledge of the techniques used for writing individualized description: inclusion of a vantage point, a point of view, the time element, sensory details, logically arranged details.
2. Decide when in the narrative to establish the setting. You have your choice of three positions:
    a) at the beginning of the narrative;
    b) after the action has started;
    c) interwoven with the action.
3. Include, *every so often* in the story, *a detail* that will force the reader to visualize the setting you have previously described, and a *detail* that will keep the reader aware of the time of year, time of day, and kind of day. If you do not use such details, the incident may seem to be occurring in a vacuum.

CLASS DISCUSSION II

Handling Setting

In each of the following excerpts, the author acquaints the reader with the setting of an incident. Read aloud each excerpt and then, for each one, answer the questions below:

a) What is the setting—place and time?
b) What is the position of the setting?
c) For what purposes has the author used descriptive details?

DEFINITION OF WORDS

THE TECHNIQUES OF DEFINING

Practice in defining words is useful for those who wish to write clearly. When writing an exposition or an argument, a person often considers it necessary to define an important word so that his readers will understand in exactly what sense he is using it. Sometimes it is a technical word; sometimes, a word that is frequently used loosely or inaccurately. Defining the word exactly often makes a person so conscious of its precise meaning that he writes more lucidly than he otherwise might have written. Skill in defining, then, is worth mastering.

To "define" means to *limit,* or *set the boundaries of.*

1. To define a word, put it into its general class and then state the characteristics that distinguish it from others in that class. Here are some examples:

WORD	GENERAL CLASS	DISTINGUISHING CHARACTERISTIC
canoe	boat	propelled with paddles
yacht	boat	propelled by wind, steam, electricity, or motive power other than oars, and used for private pleasure excursions
insinuate	to hint	subtly
ingenious	clever	at contriving
democracy	government	by the people

2. Two terms used in biology may be employed in defining words: *genus* and *differentiae.* The general class to which a word belongs is sometimes called its *genus;* the characteristic or characteristics that distinguish it from all others in its class, the *differentia* or *differentiae.*

3. A very simple way of explaining the meaning of a word is the use of a synonym. Sometimes, however, you cannot think of a synonym. Then you must define the word by stating its *genus* and noting the *differentiae.*

Examples of both kinds of definition of the adjective *eccentric* and the verb *thwart* are given on page 184.

a) eccentric — odd (synonym)

b) eccentric — used to describe a person or an action that is so different from the ordinary that he or it is considered odd or queer. (The *genus* is *unusual* or *different*. The *differentia* is to *the point of oddity*.)

a) thwart—frustrate (synonym) (The *genus* and *differentia* are implied in this synonym.)

b) thwart—to prevent a purpose or a desire (The *genus* here is *to prevent Thwart* differs from other verbs meaning to prevent because the preventing is limited to *purposes* and *desires*, which are the *differentiae*.)

CLASS DISCUSSION I

Practising the Techniques of Definition

1. Without using a dictionary, put each of the following words into its proper *genus*:

a) autocracy
b) immigrate
c) soliloquize
d) platitude
e) gesture

2. Give the correct *differentia* for each of the above words.

CLASS DISCUSSION II

Finding Mistakes in Definitions

Below you will find:

a) the dictionary meaning of several words;
b) students' definitions of the same words.

Each student's definition is wrong. State clearly why. (Is the *genus* incorrect? Is the *differentia* inaccurate? Too limited? Too broad? Is the word defined as the wrong part of speech? Has one wrong meaning been included? Is the word defined in terms of itself?)

1. a) *The Concise Oxford Dictionary*:

gesture, n. Significant movement of limb or body;
use of such movements as expression of feeling or rhetorical device;
step or move calculated to evoke response from another or to convey (esp. friendly) intention.

b) Students' Definitions:

(i) gesture — an action or a motion made by some person
(ii) gesture — a form of expression usually by means of a movement of the hand for the purpose of emphasis
(iii) gesture — a movement of the hand to convey one's feeling

2. a) *The Concise Oxford Dictionary*:
    democracy, n. (State practising) government by the people, direct or
    representative; etc.
  b) Students' Definitions:
    (i) democracy — a particular way of life in a country. Such a country
        has a government elected by the people, which
        strives for peace and the obliteration of all types
        of discrimination.
    (ii) democracy — a policy by which an individual has freedom of
        religion, freedom of speech, freedom of the press
        and freedom to choose his own government
    (iii) democracy — a type of government in which all parts of the
        government are under the control of the vote of
        the people

3. a) *The Concise Oxford Dictionary*:
    eccentric, a., odd, whimsical; etc.
  b) Students' Definitions:
    (i) eccentric — different to the extreme as far as living habits are
        concerned
    (ii) eccentric — odd; not easily understood

4. a) *The Concise Oxford Dictionary*:
    propaganda, n. Organized scheme for the propagation of a doctrine
    or practice; efforts; schemes; etc.
  b) Students' Definitions:
    (i) propaganda — information that is biased
    (ii) propaganda — information, not wholly accurate, used by a body
        either for its own benefit or for intentional harm
        to another party
    (iii) propaganda — opinions disseminated by a government and its
        supporters to convince neutral observers that the
        government is doing the best thing and is good for
        the people
    (iv) propaganda — to spread ideas in order to influence opinion

5. a) *The Concise Oxford Dictionary*:
    fabulous, a. Given to legend; celebrated in fable; unhistorical, legend-
    ary, incredible, absurd, exaggerated.
  b) Students' Definitions:
    (i) fabulous — like a fable
    (ii) fabulous — a person who is rich beyond the imagination
    (iii) fabulous — exciting

185

Using a Sentence to Reveal the Meaning of a Word

In each of the following sentences, the student attempted to reveal through the context of the sentence the meaning of the italicized word. Has he succeeded? Give reasons for your opinion. (The first sentence has been worked out for you.)

1. *dilemma*
   a) The boy's *dilemma* aroused my pity. (Wrong. Though the student used the word *dilemma* correctly, he did not reveal its meaning. Many things might arouse pity for the boy: illness, disappointment or humiliation.)
   b) The boy, caught between a precipitous cliff that dropped three hundred feet to the sea and a maddened bear, broke into a cold sweat at the thought of his *dilemma*. (Right. The context of the sentence reveals that a dilemma is a predicament in which one is forced to choose between two unpleasant alternatives.)

2. *opulence*
   a) The fabled *opulence* of the king was found to be a reality when, hundreds of years later, his treasure of jewels and fine paintings was discovered.
   b) The *opulence* of the great actor facilitated his purchase of a $100,000 home.
   c) The rank and file envied his *opulence*.

3. *eccentric*
   a) The children stared at the *eccentric* old man.
   b) Old man Brown, who lives in a cave by himself, is considered *eccentric*.

4. *lurid*
   a) What a *lurid* story!
   b) He told *lurid* tales of the horrible event.
   c) Jack the Ripper is said to have committed some of the most *lurid* crimes in history.

WRITTEN EXERCISE
Defining Words

1. Without reference to the dictionary, try to make an accurate definition of each of the following words. First try to think of a synonym. Then, if none comes to mind, put the word into its correct *genus;* and then state the characteristics that differentiate it from all other words ir ` class.

   a) unique   c) subsidize   e) livid
   b) decisive   d) diffidence   f) disinterested

2. Without using a dictionary, define each of the words given in the lists that follow. If you can think of a synonym, use it instead of a definition. If not, try to put the word into its *genus,* and then determine the *differentia* or the *differentiae.* Then write a definition of the word.

   a) credible, credulous, creditable, incredible
   b) luxuriant, eminent, trite, paradox

3. After you have defined each word in 2, use it in a sentence that will make clear by its context the meaning of the word.

THE PRÉCIS

ANALYZING THE CONTENT OF A PASSAGE

A précis is a summary that contains in the words of its writer the essential ideas of a written passage. Students and many people in business and in the professions frequently need condensed versions of reports, documents, chapters in text-books, etc. Often these people require not only a condensation of the original but also a simplification of it. For this reason, many précis are simpler than the original.

CLASS DISCUSSION

1. Suggest occasions when each of the following might need to write a précis of a report or a series of reports:
   - a) the head of a department in a large business;
   - b) a lawyer;
   - c) a doctor;
   - d) an engineer.
2. What, in your opinion, are the characteristics of a good précis?
3. Practice in précis writing should develop certain skills. What are they?
4. In order to summarize a passage, you should read it carefully and then analyze its content. The purpose of this analysis is to find the author's central idea and the ideas and/or details he has used to develop it.

Read carefully Dean Inge's discussion of "Civilised Man". Then use the questions and directions that follow the passage to analyze its content.

Civilised Man

There is something to be said for the man who would prefer to be a savage rather than a member of a 'civilised' race. What exactly has civilisation done for us? For one thing, it has deprived us of the ability to be self-sufficing 'men of our hands'. The labourer, nowadays, understands one thing only—perhaps how to punch out biscuits from a slab of pulp without making the circles intersect. It has made us mentally lazy. Actual reading in early times, even in the seventeenth century, demanded real mental exercise on the part of the reader. Modern prose, even the most ephemeral, is generally clear, both in expression and in print. In consequence, reading is now purely receptive—it is not work at all— a mild anodyne, or a stimulus to day-dreaming. Newspaper-reading seems to be largely the result of interest in vicarious athletics and betting, topics which make no demand on the intellect whatever. There is a wide desire for general knowledge, it is true, but only the results are of interest, not the method by which they are arrived at. Science must be presented in easily assimilated snippets, tabloid form — this in a 'scientific' age. People even prefer that photographs or cartoons should replace reading matter altogether. They require less mental effort to absorb.

Even education is mainly spoon-feeding. Fifty years ago the student had to puzzle out difficulties by himself, but to-day he sits luxuriously before a crib, two commentaries and a book of lecture notes. He need not use his brains at all.

All this may be right, or it may only be inevitable. But do not let us deceive ourselves. Nature will make us pay for it. Nature takes away any faculty that is not used. She is taking away our natural defences, and has probably added nothing, since the beginning of the historical period, to our mental powers. The power of grappling with difficulties and finding our way out of labyrinths will soon be lost if we no longer need it, and after any derangement of our social order we might come to need it very badly. The Very Rev. W. R. Inge, *Lay Thoughts of a Dean*

a) To whom is Dean Inge speaking, in general what is he saying, and why is he interested in saying this particular thing to this particular group?

b) For what purpose has he used paragraph 1? Paragraph 2?

c) In each paragraph of the above passage:
   (i) bracket the topic sentence(s);
   (ii) divide the rest of the paragraph into its natural units of thought; bracket each unit; and be able to justify your divisions;
   (iii) give a title to each of your divisions.

d) Below is an excerpt from the above passage by Dean Inge. Read it aloud and then answer the questions that follow it.
   Actual reading in early times, even in the seventeenth century, demanded real mental exercise on the part of the reader. Modern prose, even the most ephemeral, is generally clear, both in expression and in print. In consequence, reading is now purely receptive — it is not work at all — a mild anodyne, or a stimulus to day-dreaming.
   (i) What is the central idea?
   (ii) What idea stated previously in the passage does this excerpt exemplify?
   (iii) What is the relationship in idea between sentence one and sentence two of the excerpt?
   (iv) What is the relationship in idea between sentence two and sentence three?

e) Below is another excerpt from the same passage.
   Newspaper reading seems to be largely the result of interest in vicarious athletics and betting, topics which make no demand on the intellect whatever.
   (i) What is the central idea?
   (ii) What idea previously mentioned does it exemplify?
   (iii) What is the relationship between this excerpt and the previous one?

f) Which of the following words best indicates the relationship between the first excerpt and the second: *however, therefore, furthermore?* Give a reason for your choice.

AIDS IN CONDENSING

To help you condense a passage, keep the following points in mind:

1. *Repetition*: In order to emphasize an idea, a writer sometimes repeats it. Such repetition should be omitted from a précis.

> *Example*: Equality improves manners, for it strengthens the basis of all good manners, respect for other men and women, *simply as men and women, irrespective of their station in life.* (The two italicized phrases mean the same.)

2. *Words or Phrases in Series*:

   a) Condense a series of common nouns by substituting for it the general class to which all the nouns belong. Sometimes this class is mentioned in the sentence or in the preceding or the following one.

   > *Example*: People who idolize victory and aggressiveness ... often lose, in their attempt to win a contest, *their soul, their critical judgment, their open mind, and their generous heart.* (The nouns in this series belong in the general class of *good qualities.*)

   b) Condense a series of proper nouns belonging to the same class by using one or two of them to illustrate their class or by substituting for the proper nouns the general class to which they all belong.

   > *Example*: In the nineteenth century, England gave birth to a large group of brilliant poets, *Keats, Shelley, Wordsworth, Browning, Tennyson, Coleridge and Byron,* whose poetry stirred the imaginations of their fellow Englishmen. (In a précis, the underlined series is condensed to: *such as Keats and Browning.)*

   c) Condense descriptive details by eliminating all but the significant ones.

   > *Example*: From the roadway they saw a small house, its paint peeling off, and its roof and verandah sagging badly; an enormous barn, its shapely roof and its large door obviously newly painted; and a long, narrow paddock enclosed by a wrought-iron fence, as intricately and beautifully

189

designed as if it had been intended to surround the park of some great nobleman.

Précis of the Preceding Sentence: They saw from the road a shabby and dilapidated little house, a large and well-kept barn, and a long paddock surrounded by a beautiful wrought-iron fence. (The significant details are: that the house is *shabby, small, dilapidated,* but the barn is *large* and *well-kept;* and the paddock is enclosed by a *beautiful wrought-iron fence.)*

3. *A Group of Words*: Sometimes a group of words may be replaced in a précis by a synonym.

Example: At the end of your essay, attach *a list of books that you have used as the source of your material.* (The italicized group of words may be replaced by the one word *bibliography.)*

4. *Parenthetic Expressions*: Omit parenthetic expressions.

Example: Years ago — it seems ages ago — I have seen the crew of a ship fight the fire in the cargo for a whole sleepless week. (Omit *it seems ages ago.)*

5. *Condense Two Sentences Closely Related in Thought*: Often in a paragraph two or more sentences are closely linked in thought. In a précis indicate this relationship of ideas.

Example: What appals him [Macbeth] is . . . always the image of his own guilty heart or bloody deed, or some image which derives from them its terror or gloom. These, when they arise, hold him spellbound and possess him wholly . . . A. C. Bradley, *Shakespearean Tragedy*

Correct Précis: When Macbeth thinks of his guilt, images arise that obsess him. (Here the relationship between the two experiences is indicated by means of a complex sentence.)

Incorrect Précis of the Passage: Macbeth is always obsessed by his guilt. (This précis is inaccurate. The student has not noticed that Macbeth is spellbound *only* when the image of his own guilty heart or bloody deed arises.)

6. *Summarize Illustrative Material*: When making a précis of a paragraph in which the author has used more than one example to illustrate the *same* idea, retain and condense only the example that seems to be the best illustration.

The Beauty of Grecian Objects

Example: In the first place, it is not a beauty of ornament; it is a beauty of structure, a beauty of rightness and simplicity. Compare an athlete in flannels playing tennis and a stout dignitary smothered in gold robes. Or compare a good modern yacht, swift, lithe, and plain, with a lumbering heavily gilded sixteenth-century galleon or even with a Chinese state junk; the yacht is far more beautiful though she has not a hundredth part of the ornament. It is she herself that is beautiful, because her lines and structure are right. The others are essentially clumsy, and, therefore, ugly things, dabbed over with gold and paint. Now ancient Greek things for the most part have the beauty of the yacht . . . Gilbert Murray, *The Legacy of Greece*

Précis of the Above: Grecian objects are beautiful, not because of ornamentation, but because of structure. Compare a good modern yacht and a sixteenth century galleon. The yacht is beautiful because its structure is good; the galleon, though richly ornamented, is ugly because it is clumsy. Most ancient Grecian objects are beautiful because, like the yacht, they are shapely.

7. *Figurative Language*: Since the purpose of a précis is usually to simplify, as well as to condense, the thought contained in a written passage, figurative language should be changed into literal language. Often such a change will shorten the passage as well.

Example: Crowning Caesar will give him power that he may abuse. Therefore think of him as a serpent's egg which, when hatched will, like its kind, grow mischievous; and kill him in the shell.

Précis: Crowning Caesar will give him power to do evil. Therefore, kill him before he becomes king.

8. *Direct Discourse*: When writing a précis, turn direct discourse into indirect, because if you change a statement enclosed in quotation marks, it is no longer what was said, and hence must not be quoted.

Example: The vice-principal made the following announcement: "In view of the fact that the Easter examinations begin next week, the office is cancelling all detentions that students have incurred this week."

Précis: The vice-principal announced that detentions incurred this week will be cancelled because of the forthcoming Easter examinations.

WRITTEN EXERCISE
Writing a Précis of One Sentence

Using the rules given in this lesson, write a précis for each of the following sentences. Do not exceed the word-limit given in brackets.

1. Equality improves manners, for it strengthens the basis of all good manners, respect for other men and women simply as men and women, irrespective of their station in life. James Bryce (15)

2. The history of the world consists mostly in the memory of those ages, quite few in number, in which some part of the world has risen above itself and burst into flower or fruit. Gilbert Murray (15)
3. In Montreal, in Winnipeg, in Vancouver and other centres the great stores of the Hudson's Bay Company are as ready to supply to urban populations delicate fabrics in silk as to equip a distant post with kettles and blankets . . . George M. Wrong, *The Rise and Fall of New France* (16)
4. Those who have travelled year after year to countries beyond the borders of their native land often develop an accurate understanding of the economic problems that now beset the world. (10)

ORAL EXERCISE

Below you will find four sentences and two précis of each sentence. For each sentence, which of the two précis is better? Give reasons for your opinion.

1. There you may see him [the rigger] working like a tiger at some piece of construction work, with steel or wood or cable, hanging by one hand and a foot while he pulls, pushes, and pries with the other . . . Henry Noyes Otis.

Précis a) The Rigger hangs precariously as he works.
b) The Rigger, hanging precariously, works fiercely.

2. Our civilization is decadent and our language — so the argument runs — must inevitably share in the general collapse. George Orwell, *Politics and the English Language*

Précis a) Our language will surely deteriorate.
b) Some say that the decadence of our civilization will be reflected in our language.

3. Modern English, especially written English, is full of bad habits which spread by imitation, and which can be avoided if one is willing to take the necessary trouble. George Orwell, *Politics and the English Language*

Précis a) The bad habits exhibited by modern written English can be avoided.
b) Modern English, especially written English, exhibits bad habits that are easily copied; however, if one tries, one can avoid them.

4. Most people who bother with the matter at all would admit that the English language is in a bad way, but it is generally assumed that we cannot by conscious action do anything about it. George Orwell, *Politics and the English Language*

Précis a) Most people interested in English recognize that the language is being debased but think that conscious action will not prevent this trend.

192

b) Most people recognize that the language is being debased but think the trend cannot be prevented.

Write a précis of each of the following selections. Try to assimilate the ideas given in each selection, and then *simply* and *briefly* express them in your own words. Each précis should contain not more than two sentences. Do not exceed the word limit given in the brackets.

1. Kent is one of the best loved characters in Shakespeare. He is loved for his own sake and also for the sake of Cordelia and of Lear. A. C. Bradley, *Shakespearean Tragedy* (9)

2. The trend of our epoch up to this time has been consistently towards specialism and professionalism. We tend to have trained soldiers because they fight better, trained singers because they sing better, trained dancers because they dance better, specially instructed laughers because they laugh better, and so on and so on. G. K. Chesterton, *The Twelve Men* (18)

3. Until 1858 his [Lincoln's] outer life ran much in the same groove as that of hundreds of other Western politicians and lawyers. Beginning as a poor and ignorant boy, even less provided with props and stepping stones than were his associates. he had worked his way to a position of ordinary professional and political distinction. Herbert Croly, *The Promise of American Life* (18)

4. But more difficult problems lie ahead — above all the problem of aggression, the basic problem before our race and the future of civilised society. It is the last obstacle to be overcome in our long climb from our primeval savagery. Field-Marshall Smuts, Speech, Oct. 19, 1943 (14)

5. Was he [Napoleon] a great man?... If by "great" be intended the combination of moral qualities with those of intellect, great he certainly was not. Lord Rosebery, *Napoleon: The Last Phase* (9)

6. The immediate task when the war ends will be the salvaging of Europe from the wreck of the war. The scorched-earth policy, the inevitable war destruction, the unspeakable devastation which accompanies the retreat of the enemy in Russia, Italy and other liberated countries will confront the Allies with a problem almost as great as the war itself. Field-Marshall Smuts, Speech, Oct. 19, 1943 (21)

PLANNING AND WRITING A PRÉCIS

One of the merits of a good précis is coherence. Coherent prose is prose in which the relationship between each idea and the following one is clearly apparent to the reader.

To make a précis coherent, you must present the ideas in the same order as they have been presented in the original; and you must use, where needed, transitional sentences, words and/or phrases.

Adverbs, adverbial phrases, subordinating and co-ordinating conjunctions may be used to function as transitional words and phrases:

1. to prepare the reader for a contrast: *however, nevertheless, on the contrary, but;*
2. to prepare the reader for an idea that will reinforce the previous one: *moreover, furthermore, in addition, and, also;*
3. to prepare the reader for a result: *therefore, consequently, thus, as a result;*
4. to prepare the reader for a reason: *because, for;*
5. to prepare the reader for a concession: *although, even though.*

A demonstrative pronominal adjective, followed by a noun that refers to an idea contained in the previous sentence, provides a precise transition. Examples are:

a) The European's outlook, his standards, his point of view are quite unlike the American's. *These differences* make it hard for America and Europe to understand each other's problems.

b) Lincoln was respected by his neighbours as an honest man and a competent lawyer. *This reputation* was deserved.

CLASS DISCUSSION

1. In the following paragraph, what is the central idea?
2. Divide the paragraph into its natural units of thought. Justify your divisions.
3. Has the author presented his ideas in an orderly way? Give reasons for your opinion.
4. Find every transitional word or phrase the author has used. Explain, as specifically as you can, the function of each.

Lincoln's Contemporaries

The average Western American of Lincoln's generation was fundamentally a man who subordinated his intelligence to certain dominant practical interests and purposes. He was far from being a stupid or slow-witted man. On the contrary, his wits had been sharpened by the traffic of American politics and business, and his mind was shrewd, flexible, and alert. But he was wholly incapable either of disinterested or of concentrated intellectual exertion. His energies were bent in the conquest of certain stubborn external forces, and he used his intelligence almost exclusively to this end. The struggles, the hardships, and the necessary self-denial of pioneer life constituted an admirable training of the will. It developed a body of men with great resolution of purpose and with great ingenuity and fertility in adapting their insufficient means to the realization of their important business affairs. But their most exclusive preoccupation with practical tasks and their failure to grant their intelligence any room for independent exercise bent them into exceedingly warped and one-sided human beings. Herbert Croly, *The Promise of American Life*

PRECIS TECHNIQUES

The following eight steps may be used as a guide in making a précis of a passage.

1. Read the passage thoroughly three times, and then answer *in writing* these questions:
    a) To whom is the author speaking?
    b) In general, what is he saying?
    c) Why is he interested in saying this particular thing to this particular group?
2. Underline the transition sentence (if the author has used one to remind readers of what he discussed in the previous paragraph) and the topic sentence (if the author has used one) of each paragraph. Also underline any transitional words and/or phrases the author has used.
3. Using brackets, divide the paragraph into its units of thought, and give a title to each unit.
4. Using these titles to help you keep in mind the author's sequence of ideas, write in rough a précis of the passage.
5. Condense, if necessary, this rough draft.
6. Add to this rough draft any transitional words or phrases that you think will make your précis coherent.
7. Before making the final copy of your précis, check your sentence structure to see that you have written unified, coherent and emphatic sentences; and that you have used variety in your sentence structure. Your précis is marked for style as well as for content.
8. Copy in your best handwriting the précis that you have written in **rough.**

Applying Précis Techniques to a Passage

Passage of Three Paragraphs Divided into Units of Thought by Brackets

(Topic Sentences and Transitional Words Underlined) · *Titles of Units*

1. The first principle on which the theory of a science of history can be plausibly argued is that all actions whatsoever arise from self-interest. — **self-interest man's motive**

(It may be enlightened self-interest, it may be unenlightened but it is assumed as an axiom that every man, in whatever he does, is aiming at something which he considers will promote his happiness. His conduct is not determined by his will; it is determined by the object of his desire.) — **expansion of above idea**

2. (Now, that which especially distinguishes a high order of man from a low order of man —that which constitutes human goodness, human greatness, human nobleness—is surely not the degree of enlightenment with which men pursue their own advantage:) — **difference between a low order of men**

(but it is self-forgetfulness; it is self-sacrifice; it is the disregard of personal pleasure, personal indulgence, personal advantages remote or present, because some other line of conduct is more right.) — **and a high order of men**

3. (We are sometimes told that this is but another way of expressing the same thing: that, when a man prefers doing what is right, it is only because to do right gives him a higher satisfaction.) — **frequent explanation of unselfishness**

(It appears to me, on the contrary, to be a difference in the very heart and nature of things.) — **not the true explanation**

(The martyr goes to the stake, the patriot to the scaffold, not with a view to any future reward to themselves, but because it is a glory to fling away their lives for truth and freedom. And so through all phases of existence, to the smallest details of common life, the beautiful character is the unselfish character. Those whom we most love and admire are those to whom the thought of self seems never to occur; who do simply and with no ulterior aim — with no thought whether it will be pleasant to themselves or unpleasant—that which is good and right and generous.) Taken from Grade Thirteen examination paper, Ontario, 1949. — **the true explanation**

Read the following précis of the passage on page 196, and omit the underlined transitional words. Then read it and include these words. Notice that the use of transitional words has improved the coherence of the précis.

History can be explained as a science by assuming that all actions are the result of self-interest. Whether conscious or instinctive, man's selfishness leads him to seek primarily his own well-being. His conduct is controlled, not by reason, but by desire. Now that which distinguishes the noble individual from the average is not the intelligence with which he seeks happiness, but the selflessness with which he pursues the right. However, the author believes that man acts selflessly because unselfishness gives him pleasure. This is not true: the martyr suffers, not for reward, but for high principles. Indeed in all phases of life, the beautiful character and the one most beloved is the person who is unselfish. (Written by a student on the Grade Thirteen examination, Ontario, 1949)

HOME WORK ASSIGNMENT

Using not more than 90 words, write a coherent précis of the paragraph on page 195. Try to assimilate the ideas contained in each unit and then put them into your own words. Though you may use words from the original, avoid using the author's *phraseology*. Since a précis is intended, among other things, to test a student's fluency, examiners usually require that the précis be written, for the most part, in a student's own words.

TEN ADDITIONAL PASSAGES FOR PRÉCIS WRITING

(Final précis not to exceed the word limit in brackets at the end of each passage.)

1. Values in Life

Now, I do not ask you not to be carried away by the first rush of the great game of life. That is expecting you to be more than human. But I do ask you, after the first heat of the game, that you draw breath, and watch your fellows for a while. Sooner or later, you will see some man to whom the idea of wealth as mere wealth does not appeal, whom the methods of amassing that wealth do not interest, and who will not accept money if you offer it to him at a certain price.

At first you will be inclined to laugh at this man and to think that he is not "smart" in his ideas. I suggest that you watch him closely, for he will presently demonstrate to you that money dominates everybody except the man who does not want money. You may meet that man on your farm, in your village, or in your legislature. But be sure that, whenever or where-ever you meet him, as soon as it comes to a direct issue between you, his little finger will be thicker than your loins. You will go in fear of him: he will not do what you want. You will find that you have no weapon in your armoury with which you can attack him; no argument with which you can appeal to him. Whatever you gain, he will gain more. (85) Kipling

2. Energy From Earth to Man

Man's bodily energy can reach him only through the slender channels of millions of green plants. Despite his growing comprehension of natural laws and command of natural forces, he has not learned to take the raw materials of the earth and air — carbon, nitrogen, hydrogen, phosphorus, etc. — and synthesize them into the foods he needs to build his bone and muscle. This can be done only through the alchemy of the chlorophyll that paints our landscape green. Like the amoeba, the starfish, the crocodile, the hummingbird, and the tiger, man is a biological creature subject to biological laws, and the first of these is that he cannot live without plants. The carnivorous animal, such as the lion and the short-eared owl, secures its food second-hand through the bodies of herbivores; the lion feeds on the herbivorous zebra, the owl on herbivorous field mice, which serve in this food chain as a means of passing on the energy stored in plants.

Unless we realize this fact, there is no possibility of approaching a full understanding of man. The end of the Babylonian Empire is usually written in terms of wars with the Persians. Little or no weight is given to the fact that Ur, the great city of Abraham and once a thriving seaport, now lies 150 miles within a sterile desert. The goat and the ax, driving the sands down to the coast, were far more destructive weapons than the horses and javelins of the conqueror Cyrus. Hannibal had an empire worth fighting for, and the means of supporting a powerful army. Today the very habitat of the elephants that were his tanks and half-tracks has been overwhelmed by desert sand, and even the elephants are no more. Cato, in his bitterest brooding, could not have foreseen such utter destruction. The history of Babylon, Assyria, Carthage, China, Spain, Britain — and of the United States — is meaningless unless it is related to the way the peoples of these countries have treated the plants on which they depend. Indeed, most of the history that has been written of these areas gives a picture as distorted as a Picasso drawing, because it blindly ignores the part that plants and their habitats have played in man's story. (140) William Vogt, *Road to Survival*

3. Abraham Lincoln

To all appearance nobody could have been more than Abraham Lincoln a man of his own time and place. Until 1858 his outer life ran much in the same groove as that of hundreds of other Western politicians and lawyers. Beginning as a poor and ignorant boy, even less provided with props and stepping-stones than were his associates, he had worked his way to a position of ordinary professional and political distinction. He was not, like Douglas, a brilliant success. He was not, like Grant, an apparently hopeless failure. He had achieved as much and as little as hundreds of others had achieved. He was respected by his neighbours as an honest man and as a competent lawyer. They credited him with ability, but not to any extraordinary extent. No one would have pointed him out as a remarkable and distinguished man. He had shown himself to be desirous of recognition and influence; but ambition had not been the compelling motive of his life.

198

In most respects his ideas, interests, and standards were precisely the same as those of his associates. He accepted with them the fabric of traditional American political thought and the ordinary standards of contemporary political morality. He had none of the moral strenuousness of the reformer, none of the exclusiveness of a man whose purposes and ideas were consciously perched higher than those of his neighbours. Probably the majority of his more successful associates classed him as a good and able man who was somewhat lacking in ambition and had too much of a disposition to loaf. He was most at home, not in his own house, but in the corner grocery store, where he could sit with his feet on the stove swapping stories with his friends; and if an English traveller of 1850 had happened in on the group, he would most assuredly have discovered another instance of distressing vulgarity to which the absence of an hereditary aristocracy and an established church condemned the American democracy. Thus, no man could apparently have been more the average product of his day and generation. Nevertheless, at bottom Abraham Lincoln differed as essentially from the ordinary Western American of the Middle Period as St. Francis of Assisi differed from the ordinary Benedictine monk of the thirteenth century. (130) Herbert Croly, *The Promise of American Life*

4. Abraham Lincoln

Lincoln, on the contrary, much as he was a man of his own time and people, was precisely an example of high and disinterested intellectual culture. During all the formative years in which his life did not superficially differ from that of his associates, he was in point of fact using every chance which the material of Western life afforded to discipline and inform his mind. These materials were not very abundant; and in the use which he proceeded to make of them Lincoln had no assistance, either from a sound tradition or from a better educated master. On the contrary, as the history of the times shows, there was every temptation for a man with a strong intellectual bent to be betrayed into mere extravagance and aberration. But with the sound instinct of a well-balanced intelligence Lincoln seized upon the three available books, the earnest study of which might best help to develop harmoniously a strong and many-sided intelligence. He seized, that is, upon the Bible, Shakespeare, and Euclid. To his contemporaries the Bible was for the most part a fountain of fanatic revivalism, and Shakespeare, if anything, a mine of quotations. But in the case of Lincoln, Shakespeare and the Bible served, not merely to awaken his taste and fashion his style, but also to liberate his literary and moral imagination. At the same time he was training his powers of thought by an assiduous study of algebra and geometry. The absorbing hours he spent over his Euclid were apparently of no use to him in his profession; but Lincoln was in his way an intellectual gymnast and enjoyed the exertion for its own sake. Such a use of his leisure must have seemed a sheer waste of time to his more practical friends, and they might well have accounted for his comparative lack of success by his indulgence in such secret and useless pastimes. Neither would this criticism have been beside the mark, for if Lincoln's great energy and powers of work had been devoted exclusively to practical ends, he might well have become in the early days a more prominent lawyer and politician than he actually was. But he preferred the satisfaction of his own intellectual and social instincts, and so qualified himself for achievements beyond the power of a Douglas. (140) Herbert Croly, *The Promise of American Life*

5. Mediocrity

In sober truth, whatever homage may be professed, or even paid, to real or supposed mental superiority, the general tendency of things throughout the world is to render mediocrity the ascendant power among mankind. In ancient history, in the Middle Ages, and in a diminishing degree through the long transition from feudality to the present time, the individual was a power in himself; and if he had either great talents or high social position, he was a considerable power. At present individuals are lost in the crowd. In politics it is almost a triviality to say that public opinion now rules the world. The only power deserving the name is that of masses, and of governments while they make themselves the organ of the tendencies and instincts of masses. This is as true in the moral and social relations of private life as in public transactions. Those whose opinions go by the name of public opinion are not always the same sort of public; in America they are the whole white population; in England, chiefly the middle class. But they are always a mass, that is to say, collective mediocrity. And what is a still greater novelty, the mass do not now take their opinions from dignitaries in Church or State, from ostensible leaders, or from books. Their thinking is done for them by men much like themselves, addressing them or speaking in their name, on the spur of the moment, through the newspapers. I am not complaining of all this. I do not assert that anything better is compatible, as a general rule, with the present low state of the human mind. But that does not hinder the government of mediocrity from being mediocre government. No government by a democracy or a numerous aristocracy, either in its political acts or in the opinions, qualities, and tone of mind which it fosters, ever did or could rise above mediocrity, except in so far as the sovereign. Many have let themselves be guided (which in their best times they always have done) by the counsels and influence of a more highly gifted and instructed One or Few. The initiation of all wise or noble things comes and must come from individuals; generally at first from some one individual . . . (130) John Stuart Mill, *On Liberty*

6. The Value of the Classics

"All that is of value from the past," they will say, "has surely been incorporated in our current practice. We do not go back to study Archimedes in the physics laboratory nor do we take our botany from Theophrastus. For political oratory let us consider Churchill and Roosevelt, rather than Demosthenes or Cicero. We of the present are the cambium-layer, the growing frontier of civilization. 'Let the dead past bury its dead'.

Our problems are the only vital ones for our time. Therefore, 'let us act, act in the living present' !"

Two fallacies are inherent in such a position. One is that there is any particular virtue in action, regardless of the amount of intelligence involved. Activity, unaccompanied by thought, is commonly termed a 'conditioned reflex'; and the eager advocate of action is in constant danger of becoming a mere robot . . .

The other fallacy is that all that is worth while in the Mind of the Past has, like Greek science or Roman architecture, been sifted out and accumulated for modern use, and requires no studious effort to acquire it. The trouble here is partly that of confounding memory with mental development. It can never be too emphatically declared that the mere gathering of facts in the mind is not education. A man might commit the entire *Encyclopedia Britannica* to memory and still lack the essentials of intellectual competence. Unless he can, as it were, rise above his knowledge and from some superior point of vantage reduce it to perspective and unity, his mind will be no better than the loaded shelves of a bookseller's shop — of some practical advantage to the minds of others, but certainly of little to his own. The higher educational value of mathematics does not lie in the ability to remember formulae, but in the capacity to think mathematically, one of the highest functions of abstract reasoning. The end of literary study is not to have by heart all the data of biography, history, criticism, and philology, but through and beyond these to extend our imaginative comprehension of life. Still more pertinent to the fallacy of disregarding the classical past is the existence of a fundamental difference between science and art. Science proceeds from century to century by the accumulation of tested facts, concepts, and inventions; in literature, each great work of art is the living embodiment of imaginative experience, self-justifying in all times. The latest good textbook on astronomy includes all that is of value from the past and renders Babylonian and Greek astronomics obsolete, discredited, and unnecessary; but the latest novel on a theme comparable to that of *Macbeth* or of *Antony and Cleopatra* does not make Shakespeare's art obsolete and negligible. Locked away in each written masterpiece of the Past is the experience of a great mind in its contact with human existence; and by the method of intelligent and loving study we can relive something of that experience for ourselves. In these higher ranges of education, the chief need is not for memory, precious as that capacity may be. It is rather for judgment and imagination, which are faculties indisputably higher; and it is on these as the absolute essentials of liberal education that emphasis should be laid. (190) Watson Kirkconnell, *The Twilight of Liberty*

7. Browning's Philosophy

Browning nowhere shows his native strength more clearly than in his treatment of love. He has touched this world-old-theme — which almost every poet has handled, and handled in his highest manner — with that freshness and insight, which is possible only to the inborn originality of

201

genius. Other poets have, in some ways, given to love a more exquisite utterance, and rendered its sweetness, and tenderness, and charm with a lighter grace. It may even be admitted that there are poets whose verses have echoed more faithfully the fervour and intoxication of passion, and who have shown greater power of interpreting it in the light of a mystic idealism. But, in one thing, Browning stands alone. He has given to love a moral significance, a place and power amongst those substantial elements on which rest the dignity of man's being and the greatness of his destiny, in a way which is, I believe, without example in any other poet . . . To love, he repeatedly tells us, is the sole and supreme object of man's life; it is the one lesson which he has to learn on earth; and love once learnt, in what way matters little, "it leaves completion in the soul". Love we dare not, and, indeed, cannot absolutely miss. No man can be absolutely selfish and be man. (80) Henry Jones, *Browning as a Philosophical and Religious Teacher*

8. What is Genius?

I have already mentioned that there is confusion about the word genius. It is sometimes taken to mean talent which is prodigious and altogether exceptional, such as the talent of mathematical prodigies, or of great virtuosi. Although men of genius sometimes have exceptional gifts of virtuosity, creative genius in itself does not consist in exercising that which is inaccessible to the rest of humanity. On the contrary, it lies in the deepest understanding of that which is common to all human beings. The great creative geniuses tower above the rest of humanity as do mountainous volcanoes which, seemingly most high, reach down far below into depths where all the surrounding landscape, and the valleys even, are melted into one unity. The writer of genius is not isolated, drawing force from idiosyncrasies which divide him from other people. He is exceptional in having the deepest understanding of situations in life which are shared by many people, and in being able to give voice to the unexpressed needs and feelings of the people around him. He releases, not his own genius only but the genius of all men, who, for the most part, are gagged and silenced, unable to express themselves, to know even what they feel. (75) Stephen Spender, *Life and the Poet*

9. Free Speech

Free speech is an idea which has at present all the unpopularity of a truism; so that we tend to forget that it was not so very long ago that it had the more practical unpopularity which attaches to a new truth. Ingratitude is surely the chief of the intellectual sins of man. He takes his political benefits for granted, just as he takes the skies and the seasons for granted. He considers the calm of a city street a thing as inevitable as the calm of a forest clearing, whereas it is only kept in peace by a sustained stretch and effort similar to that which keeps up a battle or a fencing match. Just as we forget where we stand in relation to natural phenomena, so we forget it in relation to social phenomena. We forget that the earth is a star, and we forget that free speech is a paradox.

202

It is not by any means self-evident upon the face of it that an institution like the liberty of speech is right or just. It is not natural or obvious to let a man utter follies and abominations which you believe to be bad for mankind any more than it is natural or obvious to let a man dig up a part of the public road, or infect half a town with typhoid fever. The theory of free speech, that truth is so much larger and stranger and more many-sided than we know of, that it is very much better at all costs to hear everyone's account of it, is a theory which has been justified upon the whole by experiment, but which remains a very daring and even a very surprising theory. (105) G. K. Chesterton, *Robert Browning*

10. Great Literature

We cannot have too much science, technology, economics, but they lose their usefulness unless we see clearly the ends for which we intend to use them, and unless those ends are worthy of man. They deal with means and not with ends, and the more we have of them the more we need to strengthen, in both education and life, those studies whose subject is the 'knowledge of good and evil'. Education, we are often told, should be related to a social background. But a social background includes a spiritual element as well as economics, technology, and political machinery; and these exist for the sake of the spiritual element and not for their own. To ignore that element is to make life material and mechanical, and — what is not always realized — to deprive the machine of its chief motive power. In the modern world it is too often ignored; and part of the greatness of Plato and Aristotle as political and social thinkers is that they never forget it. There are truths of economics and science: but there are even more important truths in which the mind needs to be dipped so deeply that it never wholly loses the dye — such, for instance, as Aristotle's words, "The state originates for the sake of life; it continues in existence for the sake of the good life". "The chief task of politics is to produce a certain character in the citizens and to make them good and capable of noble actions". "Man, when perfected, is the best of animals, but when divorced from justice he is the worst of all. . . . Justice is the principle which brings order into political societies". "The study of what man should be and what he should pursue is the noblest of all studies". It is also the most important. That study fascinated the Greeks and pervades their thought on politics and life. Their success in it may be judged from Goethe's saying that of all men they have dreamed the dream of life best. Their literature is the record of that dream. That is why the world has continually recurred to it, and that, for any age and above all for our own, is the greatest argument for reading it. (130) Sir Richard Livingstone, "Address to the Classical Association"

THE TECHNIQUES OF DRAMA

THE ELEMENTS OF DRAMA

(With Special Reference to Shakespearean Tragedy*)

A drama is a play. It usually contains four elements: setting, characters, plot and theme.

Writing a drama is difficult, because, in a short space of time, the dramatist must introduce a conflict in the life of the principal character, acquaint the audience with any antecedent events that affect this conflict, and then develop it through suspense-creating incidents to a critical scene. Finally, the dramatist must resolve this conflict in a way that is consistent with the characters of all who are involved in it.

The Concise Oxford Dictionary defines *tragedy* as a "drama, in prose or verse, of elevated theme and diction and with an unhappy ending".

SETTING

Setting includes the time, place and accompanying circumstances. In modern plays, the producer usually suggests the setting by means of flats, backdrops and/or curtains and stage properties appropriate for the play. In Shakespeare's time, no such elaborate setting was provided. This limitation of the Elizabethan stage made it necessary for the dramatist to use dialogue to evoke in the audience's mind an impression of the setting.

Some modern dramatists also favour dispensing with the setting and relying on the dialogue to evoke in the audience's mind an impression of time and place.

CHARACTERS

A drama usually consists of two *main* characters (*protagonist* and *antagonist*), *secondary* characters and *minor* characters.

The protagonist is the person in whose conflict the dramatist is primarily concerned. To arouse and maintain the audience's interest in this conflict, the dramatist must present the protagonist so completely that the audience understands the reasons for his behaviour and his decisions. If the dramatist fails in his delineation of the protagonist, the play will be lacking in emotional appeal.

---

* For a scholarly discussion of four great tragedies, *Hamlet, Othello, Macbeth* and *King Lear*, read the late Andrew Cecil Bradley's series of lectures entitled *Shakespearean Tragedy*. This book would be a valuable addition to the library of every senior student who is studying Shakespeare.

The end of a well-written and well-acted tragedy pictures such a tremendous reversal of fortune for its protagonist that the audience is filled not only with pity, but also with awe, at the realization that man can suffer so greatly.

The antagonist is the person who directly opposes the protagonist. The protagonist versus the antagonist(s) forms the main external conflict in the drama. The secondary characters are all the other people whose actions have some bearing on the advancement of the main conflict. They, therefore, contribute to plot development. The minor characters are those whose actions have no bearing on the advancement of the main conflict. They are included in the drama for purposes other than plot development.

PLOT

The sequence of incidents in the conflict of the protagonist, who is struggling consciously (as Macbeth or Hamlet) or unconsciously (as Othello) to gain an important objective, constitutes the plot. The incident that starts the conflict is referred to as the *inciting force;* the crucial incident, the *climax,* and the resolution of the conflict, the *dénouement.*

Dramatic conflicts are of three types: the protagonist versus nature, the protagonist versus another character or characters, the protagonist versus himself. The first two are called *external* conflicts; the third is referred to as an *internal* conflict. Usually an incident early in the play sets in motion an external conflict, which, in turn, precipitates an internal conflict in the mind of the protagonist. This inner conflict and its resolution are the significant features of the play.

Unity of Action

In a well-constructed plot, the incidents that constitute the protagonist's struggle to gain his objective are inter-dependent; that is, the principle of cause and effect is present. The inciting force precipitates an incident; this incident precipitates another, and so on. If this sequence of events is not broken by coincidence, the plot has unity of action.

Macbeth is an example of a drama that, with the exception of one coincidence, has unity of action. The inciting force of Macbeth's external conflict—his attempt to gain the throne of Scotland and to keep it for himself and his heirs—is the incident in which the witches make their strange prophecies. This incident precipitates a sequence of events: Macbeth writes to Lady Macbeth; she encourages him to murder Duncan; Macbeth does so. As a result of this dreadful deed, he loses his peace of mind and is unwilling for

Banquo's descendants to profit from the murder. Macbeth, therefore, has Banquo killed. This incident, in turn, precipitates a sequence of events: at the banquet Macbeth sees the ghost of the man he has murdered; distraught, he decides to visit the witches; when he hears their last prophecy, he is filled with frustration and fury because he cannot destroy Banquo's unborn descendants.

Shakespeare now breaks the unity of action by introducing coincidence as a plot incident—the arrival, *at this inopportune time,* of a messenger who reports that Macduff has fled to England. This report precipitates an important decision: Macbeth's order to have Macduff and his family killed. This decision precipitates the remaining events in the plot-sequence: the return of Macduff, the fight between Macduff and Macbeth, and Macbeth's death.

As a general rule, a plot is more credible and more effective in establishing an impression of inevitability if unity of action is maintained. However, since coincidence often occurs in life, many good writers do not hesitate to make use of it. Shakespeare used it in his tragedies *after* he had developed, from the inciting force, a tragic sequence of events. He did not, however, allow coincidence to play such an important part in the drama that fate, rather than the law of cause and effect, became the determining factor in the destiny of the protagonist. On the other hand, Thomas Hardy, the novelist, used coincidence frequently, often at key points in the protagonist's conflict. He did this, not because he was unable to construct a plot having unity of action, but because he believed that coincidence played an important part in determining man's fate. Hardy, therefore, used coincidence in the plot to develop his theme.

Graph of the Plot Structure of Shakespearean Tragedy

Below is a graph that shows the progress of the plot action in a Shakespearean tragedy. From the beginning of the play to the middle of Act III, the protagonist is winning his struggle; from then on he is losing it. Before Shakespeare begins his plot, he gives the audience necessary background information. When the plot is completed, he gives the audience information that foreshadows future events.

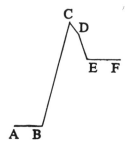

A-B: preliminary exposition
B: inciting force of the conflict that constitutes the plot
B-C: protagonist is winning
C: the climax
C-E: protagonist is losing
D: inciting force of the action from D-E
E: dénouement
E-F: final exposition

Explanation of Terms Pertaining to Plot Structure

A-B: *preliminary exposition* — an explanation of antecedent events. Shakespeare uses part of the first act to give the audience whatever background information it needs in order to understand the conflict that will constitute the plot.

B: *inciting force* — the incident that starts the conflict: the protagonist's attempt to gain an objective

B-C: *rising action* — the term often given to that part of the play between the inciting force and the climax. In this section of a Shakespearean tragedy the protagonist is winning his struggle, in spite of the opposition he is encountering.

C: *climax* (sometimes called the crisis) — the turning point in the plot: in a Shakespearean tragedy, the scene in which the protagonist suffers his first *major* reverse. This is so great that it strongly foreshadows to the audience his ultimate downfall. In *Macbeth,* the banquet scene, in which the ghost of Banquo so horrifies Macbeth that he reveals to a group of influential nobles his guilty secret, is the climax or turning point of the play. The audience now realizes that he cannot win his struggle.

The climax of a Shakespearean tragedy differs in dramatic purpose from that of a modern play. In a modern play the climax does not foreshadow the outcome of the conflict. Instead, it suggests that the end of the conflict is *imminent*. For example, the climax in Robert Ardrey's *Thunder Rock* occurs in Act III when Dr. Kurtz tries to persuade Charleston that "men may lose, but mankind never". The audience realizes that this incident is the crucial one in Charleston's attempt to find an answer to his intellectual problem, but still does not know what his decision will be.

C-E: *falling action* — that part of the play between the climax and the dénouement.

D: *inciting force of the falling action* — an incident that hastens the downfall of the protagonist

E: *dénouement* — the incident in which the protagonist loses his struggle

E-F: *final exposition* — Shakespeare does not end his tragedies with the death of the protagonist. In *Macbeth,* he adds a short scene in which he foreshadows the events that will restore order to a stricken country.

THEME

The theme of a novel, a short story or a play is the comment that the author is making on life and people. Shakespeare in his tragedies was dramatizing his belief that character is destiny: that what a man is determines his behaviour; his behaviour determines his fate. In addition to this general theme that runs through all of the tragedies, each play has its own specific theme. In *Macbeth,* for example, the dramatist reminds his audience that evil, once admitted into a man's life, has the power to destroy him.

CLASS DISCUSSION

Start your discussion of each of the following problems with a definition of the term you are using. Your thinking will then be precise.

Discussion Questions

1. Who is the protagonist in the Shakespearean play you are studying? What is his objective? Why is it hard to achieve?

2. a) Why did the protagonist fail to gain his objective?
   b) How does Shakespeare impart tragic force to the last scene, that is, evoke the audience's pity for the protagonist, and awe at the realization that man can bring great suffering on himself?

3. Who is the antagonist?

4. Name the secondary characters and point out the part each plays in the main conflict.

5. Who are the minor characters? For what dramatic purpose or purposes has each been used by the playwright?

6. What is the theme of the play?

7. What is: a) the inciting force of the plot, b) the climax, c) the dénouement?

8. Find, and read aloud, two passages that Shakespeare uses to acquaint the audience with the setting of the scene.

THE TECHNIQUES OF DRAMA

LESSON TWO

SUSPENSE

Suspense is a quality—in a situation, in an incident, or in behaviour—that causes anxious uncertainty. In a well-planned play, the suspense keeps the audience anxious concerning the out-come of the protagonist's conflict. This anxiety should increase as the plot develops.

TYPES OF SUSPENSE

Suspense can be of two types: one type provokes intellectual curiosity; the other, emotional involvement.

1. Sometimes situations, behaviour or incidents pose an intellectual "teaser". For example, when the audience hears the witches' strange prophecies, it is intrigued by the intellectual riddle: how can Banquo be "lesser than Macbeth, yet greater"; "not so happy, yet much happier"?
2. Emotional suspense occurs when a situation, an incident, a series of incidents or behaviour is so tense with feeling or imminent danger that the audience, too, experiences the emotions felt by the characters.

THE DEGREE OF SUSPENSE

The suspense in a drama can produce varying degrees of anxiety. The type of suspense that presents an intellectual poser can engender a state of anxiety ranging from mild curiosity to fascinated absorption. For example, the audience experiences mild curiosity when Macbeth and Banquo meet the witches. Will Macbeth become king? If so, how will Banquo be "greater than Macbeth"? In the second meeting with the witches, however, the third prophecy—that no man born of woman will harm Macbeth—keeps the minds of the audience absorbed with the apparently insoluble riddle: Macbeth is obviously headed for destruction, but *who* will kill him? Until Shakespeare solves this riddle, he continually reminds his audience of it.

The type of suspense that produces an emotional involvement of the audience can also range in degree from mild to intense anxiety. When Lady Macbeth is waiting for her husband to return from Duncan's chamber, the audience seems to share her tense anxiety. However, the suspense engendered by Macbeth's hysterical behaviour after the murder is much more intense, since the audience shares Lady Macbeth's fearful apprehension that her husband's dazed horror will trap them both.

METHODS USED TO CREATE SUSPENSE

Skilful dramatists vary the type and the degree of suspense in order to prevent the suspense-pattern from becoming monotonous. Here are some of the methods used.

1. *Conflict*: The audience wonders how each conflict will end.
2. *A precarious situation*: How can the person involved extricate himself?

209

3. *An apparently insoluble problem*: How can the person concerned solve it?
4. *Foreshadowing*: suggesting subsequent actions and events. The audience wonders whether these will materialize; and if so, what effect they will have on the conflict.
5. *Delay*: postponing an anticipated event
6. *See-saw*: of victories and defeats for the protagonist
7. *A vigil*: a conscious waiting for the outcome of some important event (an example: Portia's waiting for news of the assassination)

MAINTAINING SUSPENSE IN THE LAST PART OF THE TRAGEDY

Because Shakespeare usually placed the climax of his tragedies in the middle of Act III and used it to foreshadow disaster, he set himself a difficult problem—that of maintaining suspense during the rest of the play.* Here are some of the methods he used:

1. the inclusion of a scene so startling that the audience wonders what effect it will have on the fortunes of the protagonist; for example, Hamlet's killing of Polonius;
2. the inclusion of an unexpected conflict between the protagonist and some other character in the play; for example, in *Julius Caesar,* the violent quarrel between Brutus and Cassius;
3. placing the climax and the dénouement of the sub-plot in the last part of the play; for example, in *Hamlet,* the scene of Ophelia's madness (climax); her death (dénouement);
4. the inclusion of small victories for the protagonist.

CLASS DISCUSSION
Suspense
1. From the Shakespearean play that you have studied most recently, select three incidents or scenes that engender suspense. For each one chosen, answer the following questions:
    a) What questions would come to the minds of those watching the scene? b) What type of suspense is it?
    c) What method did Shakespeare use to create this suspense?
2. Compare the degree of the suspense engendered in any two of these three scenes.

---
* The modern dramatist is not confronted with this problem of maintaining suspense. He so constructs his play that the suspense mounts to a climax (at which point it suddenly increases in intensity), and the play then terminates with the (usually short) dénouement.

THE TECHNIQUES OF DRAMA

METHODS OF CHARACTERIZATION

One of the most important, yet most difficult, problems that a writer faces is that of delineating his characters in such a way that they appear real to the reader or to the audience. A skilful writer of fiction can, by the use of exposition, description, narration, conversation and monologue, create "well-rounded" characters. Although the dramatist is limited to the use of conversation, monologue and action, he can, if he understands human nature and is skilled in his craft, achieve effective and sometimes memorable characterizations.* In order to depict a character "A", a dramatist may make use of these three methods:

1. *Conversation*
   a) What A says to and about the other characters
   b) What the other characters say to and about A
2. *Monologue*
   a) A's soliloquies (in which he frequently reveals his inner conflicts his moods, and suggests the choices he will make)
   b) soliloquies of other characters in which A may be described
3. *Action*   What A does.

CLASS DISCUSSION

Characterization in a Shakespearean Play

1. Using the Shakespearean play you have studied most recently, choose a speech or an incident that reveals an internal conflict in the mind of the protagonist. What conflicting emotions or ideas produce the turmoil? Does this conflict reveal the character of the speaker? Give reasons for your opinion.
2. What traits of the protagonist are revealed in Act One? What methods does Shakespeare use to acquaint the audience with these characteristics?
3. a) From Act II, choose a scene or an incident in which the nature of the antagonist is revealed to the audience. What traits of character are revealed?
   b) By what means has Shakespeare revealed these traits?
4. Select one secondary character that interests you and find two incidents in which he reveals his nature to the audience. Name the traits revealed.
5. Choose a scene or a part of a scene in which the character-revelation contributes to plot development by strongly foreshadowing the protagonist's loss of his struggle.
   a) What trait or traits are revealed?
   b) What situation or event is foreshadowed?
6. Choose a scene or an incident in which the character-revelation makes you sympathetic with the protagonist. Account for this.

*The modern dramatist often includes descriptions of settings and characters.

7. Select an incident in which the protagonist is in conflict with someone else. What causes this external conflict? What does it reveal about the protagonist's character?
8. Select an incident in which the protagonist's attitude towards some person is evident.
   a) What is his attitude?
   b) What characteristics account for this attitude?
9. Select an incident in which the protagonist's emotions are evident.
   a) What emotions is he expressing?
   b) What characteristic(s) account for these emotions?
10. Who are the minor characters? For what dramatic purpose(s) has each been used?

THE TECHNIQUES OF DRAMA

LESSON FOUR

DRAMATIC PURPOSES

In order to depict in a short space of time* a conflict that will hold the attention of the audience and evoke a progressively strong emotional response, a dramatist must plan the structure and the dialogue of his play with great care. Every conversation, soliloquy and action must have a definite purpose in the drama that unfolds. This purpose is termed a *dramatic purpose.*

Below is a list of the dramatic purposes for which a writer may use a speech, a conversation, an incident or a whole scene in a play.

1. *to develop the plot*: to start the conflict, depict the victories and the defeats of the protagonist; depict some incident or decision that will precipitate further events in the conflict;
2. *to characterize*: to reveal the nature of a person;
3. *to create suspense;*
4. *to create atmosphere;*
5. *to impart mood;*
6. *to provide dramatic relief*: to include after a tense scene an incident that will break the tension;
7. *to provide comic relief*: to include after a tense or serious scene an incident that will provoke laughter from the audience;
8. *to give information*:
   a) to give background facts that the audience needs to know in order to understand the conflict;
   b) to give information about events that, during the play, were supposed to occur off-stage.
9. *to arouse the emotions of the people who comprise the audience*: to make their sympathies lie where the dramatist wants them to lie.

---

* From two and a half to three and a half hours is the usual playing time of a Shakespearean drama. Frequently, in modern productions, scenes that are less important or less interesting than others are shortened or eliminated.

1. a) What is the dominant atmosphere in the Shakespearean play you have most recently studied?

   b) In what scene did the dramatist introduce this atmosphere?

   c) Find one other scene that accentuates this atmosphere. Explain how the effect is achieved.

2. Select a scene or an incident that Shakespeare used to create an atmosphere in contrast to the prevailing atmosphere of the play; and: a) name this new atmosphere; b) explain how it is created; c) point out the dramatic purpose or purposes of this contrast.

3. Find two scenes or incidents used to give the audience the background facts it needs to know in order to understand the conflict. What information is given? Explain how Shakespeare makes it seem natural for this information to be given at this time.

4. Find two scenes that give the audience information about events that, during the play, were supposed to occur off-stage. What information is given? What method does Shakespeare use to give this information to the audience?

THE TECHNIQUES OF DRAMA

LESSON FIVE

DRAMATIC DEVICES

Playwrights use many devices to help them gain their desired effects. Among these are the soliloquy, dramatic irony and contrast.

THE SOLILOQUY

In dramatic terms, a soliloquy is a speech. It is made by a character when he is on stage alone (or thinks he is out of earshot). In Shakespearean drama, the soliloquy is often a lyric poem, highly emotional or philosophic in content and poetic in expression.

Usually, Shakespeare had the protagonist soliloquize several times during the course of the conflict; the antagonist or some secondary character, once. These soliloquies serve one or several dramatic purposes. They may:

1. reveal the mood of the speaker and the reason for it;
2. reveal the character of the speaker;
3. reveal his opinion of some other important person in the play;
4. create suspense, often by foreshadowing events;
5. reveal the motives of the speaker;
6. advance the plot.

213

The Soliloquy

1. What occasioned the first soliloquy in the Shakespearean play that you have studied most recently?
2. In general, what is the speaker talking about? Why?
3. What is his mood? Explain fully. What induced this mood?
4. Does this soliloquy reveal the character of the speaker? If so, what trait or traits are revealed? How does the soliloquy reveal these traits?
5. For what other dramatic purposes does Shakespeare use this soliloquy?
6. What qualities make this soliloquy a lyric poem? Illustrate.
7. What emotion(s) does the speaker express by means of: a) images and b) figurative language?

DRAMATIC IRONY

Thrall and Hibbard in *A Handbook of Literature* say of dramatic irony:

The words or acts of a character in a play may carry a meaning unperceived by himself but understood by the audience. Usually the character's own interests are involved in a way he cannot understand. The irony resides in the contrast between the meaning intended by the speaker and the added significance seen by others. Thrall and Hibbard, *A Handbook of Literature*

CLASS DISCUSSION
Dramatic Irony

Select from the Shakespearean play that you have studied most recently two incidents in which the playwright has used dramatic irony.
1. Explain clearly the source of the irony.
2. Who are aware of the irony?
3. What is the purpose of the dramatic irony?

CONTRAST

In *A Handbook of Literature* contrast is defined as:

A device by which one element (idea or object) is thrown into opposition to another for the sake of emphasis or clearness. The effect of the device is to make both contrasted ideas clearer than either would have been if described by itself. The principle of contrast, however, is useful for other purposes than to make definitions or to secure clearness. Skilfully used by an artist, contrast may become, like colours to the painter or chords to the musician, a means of arousing emotional impressions of deep artistic significance. Thrall and Hibbard, *A Handbook of Literature*

CLASS DISCUSSION
Contrast

Select from the Shakespearean play that you have studied most recently one effective use of contrast.
1. Who or what are contrasted?
2. What is the dramatic significance of this contrast?

WRITING ESSAYS ON DRAMA

FORMULATING THE THESIS

An important part of any course in literature is the writing of essays in which you discuss the prescribed novels, poems, plays or short stories. During the school year and at examination time, the teacher assigns such essays in order to test your insight into the reading you have done and your ability to interpret a question and to organize your ideas. Often students with mature insight do poorly on such assignments because they misinterpret the question, and have little skill in writing lucid exposition.

THE OVERALL STRUCTURE OF THE ESSAY

An essay on some aspect of a novel, play or short story is a piece of exposition that you must plan as carefully as you plan any other exposition. You must state clearly your thesis, decide what ideas you will discuss, the order in which you will discuss them, and then compose the topic sentences that you will use for each of your paragraphs.

The following is the usual overall structure:
1. statement of the thesis — one paragraph (usually one sentence);
2. a brief generalization of the novel, the play, the short story or the poem — one short paragraph of one or two sentences;
3. definition of any unfamiliar words used in the thesis — one short paragraph;
4. development of the thesis — several paragraphs;
5. restatement of the thesis — one paragraph (usually one sentence).

Before attempting to write essays on a particular play, you must understand its theme; recognize all the stages in the conflict that constitutes its plot; understand why the people involved in the conflict behave as they do; and be able to evaluate the effectiveness of the dramatic devices that the playwright has used to gain his desired effects.

INTERPRETING THE QUESTION AND COMPOSING THE THESIS

The most difficult part of such an essay assignment is the formulation of the thesis that you will discuss. First you must

215

interpret the question, which may be expressed in language or terms unfamiliar to you. Then you must compose your thesis. The development of this thesis is your essay.

To interpret the question correctly, follow these two directions:

a) underline the key words — the bare subject, the bare verb, the bare object or the bare complement;

b) bracket the modifiers that the person assigning the topic has used to limit your discussion.

Here are two examples:

1. a) *The Question*: Discuss the means (used by Shakespeare to reveal the nature of the main character in *Macbeth*).

   b) *The Definitions*:
      (i) *discuss* — formulate your own thesis;
      (ii) *means* — the methods. The examiner wishes the student to discuss the *methods* used by the dramatist to reveal character.
      (iii) *main character* — the protagonist of the play. The protagonist is the person in whose conflict the *author* is primarily interested.

   c) *The Interpretation*: The question asked means: Discuss the methods used by Shakespeare to reveal to the audience Macbeth's nature.

   d) *The Thesis*: Shakespeare uses several methods to reveal to the audience Macbeth's nature.

2. a) *The Question*: Evaluate three methods (used by the dramatist to reveal the character of Lady Macbeth).

   b) *The Definition*: Evaluate — *appraise the worth of*.

   c) *The Interpretation*: Appraise the worth of three methods used by Shakespeare to characterize Lady Macbeth.

   d) *The Thesis*: To characterize Lady Macbeth, Shakespeare makes skilful use of the following three methods: the soliloquy; contrast to her husband in her reaction to a somewhat similar situation; behaviour in a crisis.

WRITTEN EXERCISE
Interpreting a Question and Composing a Thesis

Below you will find six questions based on the Shakespearean play you have studied most recently. Interpret each question and then compose a thesis that answers the question asked.

DIRECTIONS

a) Copy the question into your note-book.

b) In the part of the question that tells you what you must discuss, underline the bare subject (if the question has one), the bare verb, the re object; and bracket the limitation.

c) Define any unusual words or terms used in the question.

d) Reword the question so that it is stated simply and specifically.

e) Compose a one-sentence thesis that will answer the question asked.

1. Evaluate the playwright's skill in revealing to the audience, in Act One, the nature of the protagonist.

2. Discuss the dramatist's use of the first soliloquy.

3. Shakespeare, in his tragedies, always included in Act Four a scene in which the mood was one of deep pathos. Show by what means he achieved pathos in Act Four of this play.

4. Evaluate the effectiveness of the climax in foreshadowing the protagonist's defeat.

5. By what means has Shakespeare aroused the sympathy of the audience for the protagonist?

6. Discuss Shakespeare's use of minor scenes or minor characters.

HOME WORK ASSIGNMENT
(Based on the Shakespearean play you have studied most recently)

Compose a thesis for each of the following questions:

1. Discuss the dramatist's use of the supernatural.

2. From Act Four, choose a scene that is important in plot development and explain how it contributes to the advancement of the plot.

3. Show that the playwright included in this play a scene, the atmosphere of which is in contrast with the prevailing atmosphere of the play. Explain the dramatic purpose of this contrast.

WRITING ESSAYS ON DRAMA

LESSON TWO

DEVELOPING THE THESIS BY TOPIC SENTENCES

After you have formulated your thesis, you are ready to compose the topic sentences that will develop it, and to decide what facts you will include in each paragraph.

COMPOSING THE TOPIC SENTENCES

In order to compose relevant topic sentences, first underline in your thesis the ideas you have undertaken to discuss. Then write the topic sentences that will develop them. The body of your essay will be composed of as many paragraphs as you have topic sentences. Here are two examples:

1. *The Thesis*: Shakespeare used the remarks of others, the soliloquy and <u>behaviour in a crisis</u> to reveal some aspects of Macbeth's nature.

   The Topic Sentences:

   a) Shakespeare used the remarks of others to reveal Macbeth's skill as a general and his personal bravery on the field of battle.

   b) Macbeth revealed his nature in a soliloquy made after he had left the banquet at which Duncan was his guest.

   c) Shakespeare used a crisis — Macbeth's hearing that Banquo had been killed but Fleance had escaped — to show the audience Macbeth's inability to control his emotions when he is under great strain.

2. *The Thesis*: Shakespeare revealed (i) <u>the nature of the protagonist</u> (ii) <u>by placing him in a position where he had to make an important choice.</u>

   The Topic Sentences:

   a) Shakespeare placed Macbeth in a situation where he was forced to make an important choice.

   b) This choice revealed Macbeth's nature.

CLASS DISCUSSION

Composing the Topic Sentences to Develop a Thesis

1. Below are two plans made by students to answer the same question on *Macbeth*. Which plan has topic sentences that develop the thesis? Give reasons for your opinion.

   Here you will find a record of the students' preliminary thinking:

   The Question: Discuss Shakespeare's use of dramatic irony in *Macbeth*.

   Definition: The *use* of dramatic irony means the purposes for which Shakespeare used dramatic irony.

   The Interpretation: Discuss the purposes for which Shakespeare used dramatic irony.

   The Thesis: In *Macbeth,* Shakespeare used dramatic irony for several dramatic purposes.

   Plan A

   The Topic Sentences:

   a) During the scene in which Duncan and Banquo arrive at Macbeth's castle, Shakespeare used dramatic irony to make the audience pity Duncan.

   b) After the murder of Duncan, Shakespeare used dramatic irony — the drunken porter's speech — to stress the wickedness of Macbeth and Lady Macbeth.

   c) Lady Macduff's conversation with Ross has dramatic irony. Shakespeare used the irony here to arouse our hatred of Macbeth and our pity for Lady Macduff and her son.

218

Plan B

The Topic Sentences:

    a) There is dramatic irony when Duncan and Banquo arrive at Macbeth's castle.

    b) Another place where dramatic irony occurs is in the drunken porter's speech.

    c) A third example of dramatic irony is the conversation between Ross and Macduff.

2. Below are two plans made by students to answer the same question. Which plan has topic sentences that develop the thesis?

The Question: By what means does Shakespeare create suspense in *Julius Caesar?*

Definition: "By what means" is the same as "by what methods".

The Interpretation: By what methods does Shakespeare create suspense in *Julius Caesar?*

The Thesis: Shakespeare used several methods to create suspense in *Julius Caesar.*

Plan A

The Topic Sentences:

    a) Shakespeare created suspense by means of Brutus's indecision when Cassius urged him to join the conspiracy.

    b) When the audience was anxiously awaiting the moment when Caesar would be assassinated, Shakespeare delayed this dramatic moment by introducing a scene in which Portia nervously questioned the young boy. This delay and vigil increased the suspense.

    c) Shakespeare created suspense by placing Antony in a difficult situation: before a mob that was shouting, "Long Live Brutus".

Plan B

The Topic Sentences:

    a) There is suspense when Cassius is trying to persuade Brutus to join the conspiracy.

    b) Suspense is created when Portia talks to Lucius while her husband is on his way to the Capitol to assassinate Caesar.

    c) When Antony addresses the Roman mob, suspense is created.

WRITTEN EXERCISE

Below you will find two theses that could be developed into essays. Place in the blank the name of the Shakespearean play you have most recently studied, and then compose topic sentences that would, if expanded, develop each thesis.

a) In Act One of.............................., Shakespeare used a variety of methods to reveal to the audience the character of the protagonist.

b) Shakespeare, in ...., used scenes involving minor characters to serve a number of dramatic purposes.

(Based on the 'Shakespearean play you have studied most recently)

Make a written plan for each of the questions that follow. Your plan should include:

a) the question;
b) definitions of any terms that need clarifying;
c) the interpretation of the question;
d) the thesis;
e) the topic sentences that would develop the thesis.

1. By what means did Shakespeare create suspense in the play?
2. Discuss the means used by the dramatist to reveal to the audience the character of one important person in the play.
3. Evaluate the dramatist's skill in arousing in Act One the audience's interest in the protagonist.

WRITING ESSAYS ON DRAMA

LESSON THREE

EXPANDING TOPIC SENTENCES

After interpreting the question, formulating the thesis and composing the topic sentences, you must decide how you will expand each topic sentence. Many students write poor essays because they do not expand all of the ideas implied in the topic sentence or they sometimes include irrelevant facts. A little planning, as shown below, will improve considerably the unity of your paragraphs.

The Topic Sentence: In the scene in which Duncan and Banquo approach Macbeth's castle, Shakespeare uses dramatic irony to arouse the audience's sympathy for Duncan.

Content of paragraph to develop this topic sentence:
a) an explanation of the dramatic irony in their conversation;
b) an explanation of why this irony arouses pity for Duncan.

Below you will find a thesis developed by four topic sentences. Decide what facts should be used to develop each topic sentence.

The Thesis: By placing Macbeth and Lady Macbeth in a somewhat similar situation to which they react differently, Shakespeare used the device of contrast to emphasize Macbeth's inability to control his feelings when he is under great emotional strain.

The Topic Sentences:

1. Macbeth and Lady Macbeth in the murder scene find themselves in a somewhat similar situation.
2. Macbeth, from the moment he returns from Duncan's chamber, is unable to control his mounting horror.
3. Lady Macbeth, however, exhibits throughout the scene an almost superhuman self-control.
4. This contrast in behaviour emphasizes Macbeth's inability to control his feelings when he is under great emotional strain.

WRITTEN EXERCISE
(Based on the Shakespearean play you have studied most recently)

Using one of the following topic sentences, write a unified paragraph. Discuss all of the ideas implied in the topic sentence, and do not include irrelevant facts.

1. In the soliloquy (*give occasion*), the protagonist reveals his mood and the reasons for it.
2. The protagonist (or the antagonist) reveals in (name a specific conversation or scene) two dominant traits in his (or her) character.
3. The dramatic irony in (name a specific incident) serves two important dramatic purposes.
4. The opening scene of the play gives, through a conversation that seems natural for the situation, information about past events.

WRITING ESSAYS ON DRAMA

PLANNING AND WRITING ESSAYS ON DRAMA

Below you will find two essays written by senior students in answer to this question: *'Shakespeare often used the device of contrast to emphasize some important characteristic of the protagonist.' Show that Shakespeare has stressed one of Macbeth's characteristics by placing him and his wife in a somewhat similar situation to which they react very differently.*

ANALYZING STUDENTS' ESSAYS

Use the questions that follow each essay to evaluate the student's skill in composing the correct thesis and in developing it. The paragraphs are numbered for convenience in discussion.

Essay I

1. The reactions of Macbeth and Lady Macbeth after the murder of Duncan stress the contrast in behaviour of these two people, who are in similar circumstances.

2. In order to show contrast in behaviour, it is necessary first to show that the people who are being examined are in similar circumstances. Macbeth, it was true, is doing the actual murder, but Lady Macbeth, had she been tried in a law court today, would also have been found guilty of murder. It was she who prodded Macbeth to his final decision to murder Duncan, and she gave Macbeth the outline of the action he was to take. She waited for him, heart beating, in the thick silence of the bewitching hour.

3. After having learned that Macbeth is a fearless soldier on the battle-front, we see that the behaviour which he exhibits after the murder is certainly not that of a confident, brave hero. Having done the deed, he is as if in a dream which has surprisingly taken the form of a nightmare. He has lost his power of action, and his conscience comes to the front. He therefore dwells on the amazing fact that he could not pronounce *amen,* until he is completely unnerved. As he gets more excited, he remembers the voice he thought he heard, which promised, with a gloomy outlook, that he should sleep no more. Completely overwrought by his bloody hands, and the terrifying, fresh memories of his awful deed, he refuses to put back the daggers, even though it is completely necessary. At length, like a sorrowful child, he shows his repentance and fear by the wish that Duncan could be awakened by the knocking at the door. His remark to that effect, shouted towards the door, shows his loss of presence of mind, for it could reveal the deed to the knockers.

4. Lady Macbeth's behaviour was quite unusual, also, as she was evidently not one of the fainting types so common in those years. At first, she was quite humanly afraid, as shown by her fear of the sound which turned out to be only an owl. But realizing that Macbeth had lost his presence of mind, she took charge. She considered it important to wake Macbeth from his reverie of fear, and consequently was very practical. She remonstrated to him throughout the scene for being so fearful, and tried to get him down from his cloud of fear to realize the importance of being practical and discreet. She tried to make him realize that he had heard no voice, by asking who had uttered the prophecy. She tried to shame him by appealing to his bravery while calling him a coward, and by her own act of returning the daggers.

5. The contrast in their behaviour is stressed all the more because it is between a man and a woman. It was she who should have been weak, and he strong. But since this normal pattern was reversed, Macbeth's behaviour was stressed, and made quite clear to the reader. Mary C.

Discussion Questions

1. In the first paragraph, this student states her thesis. Does it answer the question asked? Give reasons for your opinion.
2. By referring to the topic sentence in paragraph 4, show that the student has forgotten the idea she undertook to discuss, *contrast in behaviour*.
3. Has the student insight into the behaviour of Lady Macbeth, and that of her husband? When answering, refer directly to the text of the essay.
4. Does the concluding paragraph stress the question the student was asked to discuss? Give reasons for your opinion.
5. Explain clearly how you think this essay can be improved.

Essay II

1. Macbeth's lack of self-control when under great emotional strain is emphasized by the self-control of Lady Macbeth when they are both placed in a somewhat similar situation after the murder of Duncan.

2. Both Macbeth and Lady Macbeth are in a somewhat similar situation: they have undergone the tense and gruelling experience of planning the murder of another human being. Although only Macbeth actually perpetrated the crime, his wife had been the person who made him "bend up every corporal agent" to do the awful deed. They both, then, since they are in a somewhat similar situation, have occasion for a complete emotional breakdown after the murder.

3. From Macbeth's actions in this scene, we can clearly observe how the murder of Duncan has affected him. The sight of his bloody hands fills him with so much horror and guilt that he cannot bear to look at them. The fact that he found it impossible to return "Amen" to the groom's "God bless us" blinds him with a child-like cloud of fear that

223

obliterates his reason. Consumed with the anguish of remorse, he realizes that he can no longer find enough peace in his soul to enable him to sleep. Temporarily on the verge of insanity, he has even forgotten to leave the bloody daggers in the murder room in order to implicate the grooms, as was originally planned. Furthermore, after the realization of his mistake penetrates his foggy brain, he has not enough strength and determination to re-enter Duncan's chambers. When his wife returns, she finds him gazing in horror at his blood-stained hands:

> "Will all great Neptune's ocean wash this blood
> Clean from my hand?"

Suddenly she hears a loud knocking at the door, and tries her best to awaken her husband to their danger; but he, still in a daze of guilty remorse, shouts:

> "Wake Duncan with thy knocking! I would thou couldst!"

Lady Macbeth has to drag him from the room. The man who had been so fearful of the consequences — "We but teach bloody instructions to offer the poisoned chalice to our own lips" — now is so horrified at what he has done that the loud knocking at the door does not even suggest danger. When under this severe strain he is unable to control his emotions.

4. Lady Macbeth, on the other hand, behaves in a definite contrast to her husband. She has quenched her initial fears and assumed command of the situation. At first, she dons an air of bravado, and makes light of the ordeal. We perceive that her control and self-determination have triumphed over her womanly weaknesses. She pampers and soothes her hysterical husband by telling him not to be so upset, not to dwell on his dreadful deed, for his probing conscience will only further increase his horror. He hardly hears her. She scolds him and reproaches him for his cowardly behaviour. No effect. She then commands him to return the daggers; but realizing that he cannot control his horror, she scornfully replaces them herself. Her invincible will accounts for her ability to formulate practical plans in her extreme emergency. She realizes the precarious state of her husband, and as a last desperate chance she orders him to change into his nightgown, to wash his hands, and to act less preoccupied, for his face is too revealing. Lady Macbeth's iron-willed control saves them from destruction.

5. Thus, in this scene, Macbeth's inability to control himself when under great emotional strain stands out more clearly because of the effective contrast provided by the almost superhuman control of his wife, in a somewhat similar situation. Norma G.

Discussion Questions

1. Has this student composed a thesis that, when developed, will answer the question asked? Give reasons for your opinion.
2. Do the topic sentences of paragraph 3 and 4 develop the thesis? Refer to the student's text to substantiate your opinion.

3. Check the conclusion with the thesis, stated in the first paragraph. Is the student on-topic? Give reasons for your opinion.
4. In what ways is this answer better than the first one?
5. If the above essay-type answer had to be written in half an hour, it would have had to be shorter. Which two paragraphs could be combined and shortened? Supply the right topic sentence for such a paragraph.

HOME WORK ASSIGNMENT I

Planning and Writing an Essay-Type Answer

(Based on the Shakespearean play you have studied most recently)

1. Make a detailed plan for an essay-type answer of approximately 500 words on one of the following questions: Discuss Shakespeare's use of the supernatural (or dramatic irony or contrast) in this play.
2. Using the plan as your guide, write the essay.

Outline for the Detailed Plan of Essay

a) The question — state it
b) Definition of words needing clarification
c) The interpretation of the question
d) The thesis
e) The topic sentences that will develop the thesis

The Overall Structure of Your Essay

a) Statement of the thesis
b) Generalization of the play — one or two sentences only
c) Definition of any unfamiliar words used in your thesis
d) The development of the thesis — as many paragraphs as you have topic sentences
e) Conclusion — restatement of thesis

HOME WORK ASSIGNMENT II

(Based on the Shakespearean play you have studied most recently)

Write an essay-type answer to one of the following questions:

1. Describe the character of one leading person, and, by using definite references to the play, show by what means this person's character is revealed.

2. Select a scene or an incident of special importance in the plot. By reference to significant action and characterization, show how this scene or incident is related to the plot development of the play.

3. a) Name three important stages in the development of Shakespearean plot.
   b) Show briefly the connection between each of these three important stages and the career of the main character. Illustrate your answer with definite references to the action of the play.

4. Show how the nature of the protagonist is revealed in the following ways:
   a) by his attitude towards members of his own family or towards humble characters who are under his direct authority;
   b) by his speech and conduct during one period of critical emergency.
5. "Conflict is the essence of drama". Select and briefly describe two situations or incidents in which some form of conflict appears. In each case state the nature and the dramatic purpose of the conflict.
6. Select a full and well-rounded speech that has in a high degree both dramatic and poetic value, and (a) state concisely the ideas presented in it; (b) show its dramatic significance; (c) discuss its poetic merits.
7. Show how the nature of the protagonist contributed to his downfall.
8. Discuss the dramatic purposes for which Shakespeare has used any three minor characters in the play. Illustrate each dramatic purpose you discuss by reference to a specific incident.
9. Discuss Shakespeare's use of the protagonist's soliloquies. (Make specific references to two soliloquies.)
10. Define a Shakespearean tragic character. Illustrate your definition by referring to the career of the protagonist in the play you have most recently studied.
11. Read in *Shakespearean Tragedy* by A. C. Bradley the lectures on "The Substance of Shakespearean Tragedy" and the one(s) on the particular play you have been studying. Then write an essay of about five pages on the following topic: The characteristics of Shakespearean tragedy as revealed in (the play you have been studying).

APPENDIX

A. PUNCTUATION RULES

USES OF THE COMMA

1. A comma is used before the co-ordinating conjunction in a compound sentence that has no internal punctuation in any of its independent clauses.

   Examples:
   a) That fat man is eating his dinner, but the thin man is not eating.
   But:
   b) The tall man, sober and dignified, looks like a clergyman; but his companion looks like a pugilist.

2. A comma is used to set off from the rest of the sentence non-restrictive phrases and clauses. A non-restrictive phrase or clause is one that has not a limiting nor a designating function; it simply gives added information, which could be omitted without changing the meaning of the sentence.

   Examples:
   a) I never buy hats *that cost over ten dollars.* (Restrictive clause, *limiting* the noun *hats.* The sentence does not mean that I never buy hats, but that I never buy hats in the price-class described in the clause. The adjectival clause, then, is restrictive. Its omission would make untrue the meaning of the main statement.)
   b) Mary's hat, *which cost fifteen dollars,* is stunning. (This adjectival clause is non-restrictive. The clause does not limit: it gives added information. Its omission would not change the meaning of the main statement.)
   c) Jody, *leaping on his horse,* rode quickly out of the yard. (Non-restrictive participal phrase)
   d) The lad *eating his ice-cream so happily* is the best high-jumper in the school. (restrictive participial phrase that designates *which* boy)

3. A comma is used after an initial adverbial phrase or clause. If the phrase is short, the comma may be omitted.

   Examples:
   a) *When the party was over,* the committee stayed to tidy up. (Initial adverbial clause)
   b) *After the party,* the committee stayed to tidy up. (Initial adverbial phrase. Use of the comma is optional, because the phrase is short.)

4. Commas are used to separate the various members of a series of words, phrases or clauses that have no internal punctuation.

   Examples:
   a) The committee arranged for the hall, the orchestra, the decorations, and the refreshments. (The last comma, the one before the conjunction, may be omitted.)
   b) The burglar fled over the hill, across the field, and into the tangled streets of the old town. (The last comma may be omitted.)
   c) I know that the boy studied hard, that he had a good background, and that he never lied. (The last comma may be omitted.)

227

5. Commas are used to separate the month and the year, or the day and the year; the town, the province, state or county, and the country.
   Examples:
   a) The ill-fated plane left Halifax on January 16, 1956.
   b) During John's trip last summer, he visited Vancouver, B.C.
6. Use a comma or commas to separate direct discourse from the explanatory remarks (For use of quotation marks, see page 231.)
   Examples:
   a) "I shall be glad to go," Jim replied.
   b) "Will you call for me," Joan asked, "at eight o'clock?"
   c) "Yes, I shall," Jim answered. "How long will it take us to get there?" (Note the period used after *answered* because the following remark is a new sentence.)
7. Use a comma or commas to set off a word of direct address.
   Examples:
   a) Gerry, please close the window.
   b) May I make a suggestion, Mr. Chairman?
   c) My impression, David, is that you are not doing your best work.
8. A comma is used in a sentence to indicate the omission of a word that has already been used in the sentence and which is here understood.
   Example:
   Some schools have large gymnasia; others, small.
9. Use a comma or commas to set off an expression beginning with *not* and introducing a contrast.
   Example:
   The Student Council, not the Head Prefect, is responsible for that job.
10. A comma is used to separate *yes* and *no* from the rest of the sentence.
    Examples:
    a) Yes, I heard you!
    b) No, I will not tell.
11. A comma is used to separate a mild interjection from the rest of the sentence. A strong interjection is followed by an exclamation mark.
    Examples:
    a) Well, I must finish my work.
    b) Oh, I think he is honest.
12. Commas are used to set off parenthetic words or phrases from the rest of the sentence. A parenthetic *statement* is usually set off with dashes.
    Examples:
    a) Timmy is, to say the least, a dreadful nuisance when his mother is giving a party.
    b) I think, however, that he is usually a very good child.
13. A comma is used whenever its omission would confuse the reader on first reading.
    Examples:
    a) To win Gay must practise hard. (This sentence must be read twice before its meaning is clear.)
    b) To win, Gay must practise hard. (The comma prevents the reader from misunderstanding the sentence.)

14. A comma is used to indicate thousands, usually when the number has five or more digits.
    Example:
    We need 13,607 rivets.
15. Commas are used to set off a non-restrictive appositive.
    Examples:
    a) Mr. Jones, *the inspector*, called today to see the principal. (Non-restrictive.)
    b) I wish to see Miss Brown *the secretary*, not Miss Brown *the dietitian*. (Restrictive appositives.)
16. Use a comma or commas to set off a phrase placed out of its natural order.
    Example:
    The woods, dark and gloomy, stretched for miles.

Four principal uses of the semi-colon are:

1. A semi-colon is used in a compound sentence before the co-ordinating conjunction (*and, but, or, nor*) when one or more of the independent clauses contains a comma or commas.
    Example:
    John of Gaunt, stout-hearted and out-spoken, castigated the King for his scandalous behaviour; but the Duke of York, more timid by nature, reprimanded his sovereign gently.
2. A semi-colon is used to separate the principal clauses of a compound sentence in which the co-ordinating conjunction has been omitted. Such a sentence is structurally no longer one sentence, but two sentences containing ideas of equal importance. The semi-colon provides the necessary punctuation while preserving the impression of two closely related ideas. (The use of a comma in this sentence would reveal that the student was ignorant of sentence structure. Such an error is sometimes called *the comma fault* or *the comma splice*.)
    Examples:
    Right
    a) John went to the movies; his sister went home.
    b) John went to the movies; however, his sister went home.
    Wrong
    a) The sky darkened ominously, then a great gale blew up from the east.
    b) Those three boys did not study, therefore they failed.
3. A semi-colon is used to separate a series of clauses, some or all of which contain a comma or commas.
    Example:
    Macbeth was a man who coveted the throne; who was willing to do evil to obtain it; but who tried to batten down a conscience that, from the moment the witches uttered their electrifying prophecies, thrust tormenting images into his feverish mind.

4. A semi-colon is used before, and a comma after, such words and abbreviations as, *i.e., e.g., that is, for example, namely, viz.,* when they introduce a principal clause.

Example:
Read the three novels I mentioned yesterday; that is, read *Cry, the Beloved Country, Babbitt* and *The Forsyte Saga.*

If, however, one of the above-mentioned words or abbreviations does not introduce a principal clause, use a comma both before and after the word or the abbreviation.

Example:
Read the three novels I mentioned yesterday, that is, *Cry, The Beloved Country, Babbitt,* and *The Forsyte Saga.* (In this sentence *that is* introduces words in apposition to *three novels.* Hence the proper punctuation is a comma, not a semi-colon.)

USES OF THE COLON

Five principal uses of the colon:

1. A colon is used before a series or a list introduced formally.
   Example:
   Bring to the meeting the following equipment: glue, scissors, ruler, green paint.

2. A colon is used before a long quotation introduced formally.
   Example:
   A. C. Bradley in his discussion of the substance of Shakespearean tragedy has this to say of Hamlet: "Now, in Hamlet's moral sensibility there undoubtedly lay a danger. Any great shock that life might inflict would be felt with extreme intensity. Such a shock might even produce tragic results. And, in fact, *Hamlet* deserves the title of 'tragedy of moral idealism' quite as much as the title 'tragedy of reflection'."

3. A colon is used between two independent clauses when the second clause is used to clarify the meaning of the first.
   Example:
   Richard made several disastrous decisions: he decided to banish Henry Bolingbroke, to go to Ireland to fight the rebels, and to appoint old York regent of England.

4. A colon is used after the salutation in a business letter, although the comma is also frequently used in this place.
   Example:
   Dear Mr. Bowen:

5. A colon is used to separate:
   the hour and the minutes;
   the chapter and the verse of a Biblical reference;
   the volume and the page, usually in footnote only.
   Examples:
   a) Mr. Edward arrived at exactly 8:43 a.m.
   b) Read John III: 16, one of the most famous verses in the Bible.
   c) *The Life of John A. Macdonald,* Donald Creighton, 1:201.

THE USES OF THE DASH

1. Two dashes are used to separate a parenthetic remark that is a long or an abrupt interruption of the thought contained in a sentence.

   Example:
   The Tale of Two Cities — and what an absorbing story of the French Revolution it is — was required reading last year for all students taking modern history.

2. A dash is used to suggest hesitation in speaking or a definite shift in thought and construction.

   Examples:
   a) "Yes — but — well, listen to my side of it," pleaded James.
   b) "David borrowed money, gambled on the Stock Exchange, lost heavily — but let's talk of something more cheerful."

THE USES OF QUOTATION MARKS

1. In Canada, double quotation marks are used to enclose direct discourse.

   Examples:
   a) "Where did Diane meet him?" Anne asked curiously.
   b) "I think," answered Mary, "that she met him last summer in England."

2. Double quotation marks are used to enclose a quotation:

   Examples:
   a) According to Hamlet "Nothing is good or bad but thinking makes it so".
   b) The first two lines of the last stanza contain the theme of the poem:
      "Stone walls do not a prison make
      Nor iron bars a cage."
   c) John of Gaunt's bitter denunciation of Richard's behaviour,
      "Landlord of England art thou, not King!
      Thy state of law is bond-slave to the law."
      was cut short by the king's furiously angry retort.

   When you are quoting more than one line of poetry, isolate the quotation by starting it one line below the comment, and indent the lines. If, after the quotation, you continue your paragraph, be sure to indicate this by starting at the margin, as in example (c) above.

3. Double quotation marks are used to enclose the title of a short poem, a short story, an article or a chapter in a book. The title of a book, a magazine, a newspaper, or a long poem is italicized when printed; underlined when written by hand.

   Examples:
   a) In the short story "The Devil and Daniel Webster", Stephen Vincent Benét gives an amusing and memorable account of the devil's attempt to capture Daniel Webster's soul.
   b) Donald Creighton in his notable biography *John A. Macdonald* gives in the chapter entitled "Contract in Steel" a graphic account of the struggle to build the Canadian Pacific Railway.

4. Single quotation marks are used to enclose a quotation within a quotation.

   Example:
   "I agree with Shaw that 'a sneer does not become the human soul'," Joe said quietly.

231

Below are the rules governing the handling of numbers. Sometimes a number is written out; sometimes it is not.

1. A number of one or two digits is written in words; a number of three or more digits is written in figures.
   a) The city owns twenty-one snow plows.
   b) The farmers in the Valley exported this year 10,500 barrels of apples to England.

   However, any number that comes at the beginning of a sentence should be written out: Six hundred and five men and women are employed in that hat factory.

2. In the writing of dates, if the day follows the month, a figure is used. If the day precedes the month, or the month is omitted, a word is used.
   a) She arrived on January 9.
   b) The party occurred on the ninth of January.

3. In scientific or technical writing, numbers are usually written as figures; always when abbreviations are used.
   a) Each box contained 10 cu. ft.
   b) The books showed a net profit of 25 per cent.

4. The number of a page is written as a figure.
   Turn to page 6 of *Hamlet*.

5. The time of day, unless followed by a.m. or p.m., is written as a word.
   a) She left the house at seven o'clock every morning.
   b) The concert began at 8 p.m.

B. CORRECTION SYMBOLS

In order to help students identify and correct the errors they have made in their compositions, many teachers underline the faulty part and place in the margin a symbol. (See list below.)

Directions for Correcting Errors

It is a good idea for a student to make a correction sheet for every composition that has been criticized and returned. Use the directions given below.

   a) From your composition, copy the first sentence in which an underlined part occurs. Include the underlining; and, to the left, place the symbol used by the teacher. Then, following the suggestions you will find opposite the symbols given in the table, write immediately below the original sentence a revised version.
   b) For every punctuation error made, state in sentence form the rule you have violated.
   c) Repeat this procedure for every sentence in which underlining occurs.

Symbols	Meanings and Directions
abstract	Replace underlined abstract expression with a concrete word or detail.
amb. ref.	ambiguous reference, or pronoun reference error. The pronoun refers with equally good sense to either of *two* antecedents. Recast the sentence so that the pronoun refers to its proper antecedent.
coh.	Paragraph lacks coherence. Rewrite, arranging the ideas in logical order, and/or supplying the proper connectives where indicated.
choppy	too many short sentences. Combine related ideas into one good complex sentence with the main idea placed in the main clause.
colloq.	Colloquialism is inappropriately used. Correct.
comp. sent.	overuse of the compound sentence. Rewrite underlined passage, striving to get variety in sentence structure. An occasional complex sentence or a short simple sentence will break the monotony produced by overuse of the compound sentence.
climactic	Ideas in this sentence can be arranged in climactic order. Recast the sentence.
d.	diction. Inexact use of a word. Find the exact word to express what you mean.
dang. gr.	dangling gerund. Recast sentence, making the gerund modify the subject of the sentence.
dang. part.	dangling participle. Recast sentence, making the participle modify the subject of the sentence.
δ	Delete underlined part of sentence or paragraph.
dull	dull use of word. Select a more pictorial word *or* a more emotional one to stimulate your reader's imagination.
emp.	emphasis. This paragraph lacks emphasis. Rewrite paragraph, arranging ideas in ascending order of importance *or* keeping your best detail or example for the conclusion or composing an emphatic concluding sentence.
faulty agree.	lack of agreement between subject and verb. Correct.
faulty sub.	faulty subordination. Correct this sentence by putting the most important idea in the main clause. Subordinate the less important idea or ideas by placing in a subordinate clause or in a phrase.
fig.	Figure of speech is poor for some reason. Compose a more suitable one for this context.
gr.	grammatical error. Correct.
k	awkward sounding expression. Recast.
m.m.	misplaced modifier. Place the word or phrase or clause next to the word it modifies.

233

no ref.	pronoun reference error. The pronoun has *no* antecedent. Supply one.
orphan which	the "which" has no antecedent. Recast the sentence.
overlapp. cl. and/or ph.	Too many interdependent clauses and/or phrases make this a weak sentence. Eliminate the interdependent constructions.
parall.	faulty parallelism. Recast the sentence, putting the underlined parts in identical grammatical constructions.
pomp.	pompous sounding. Rewrite more simply and more sincerely.
position	Sentence lacks emphasis. Rearrange the parts of the sentence so that the ideas you wish to emphasize are placed at the beginning of the sentence and at the end of the sentence. Bury in the middle of the sentence the less important ideas.
pro. agree.	faulty pronoun agreement. The pronoun and its antecedent do not agree. Correct.
rhythm	Sentence lacks rhythm. Recast.
sent. unity	Sentence lacks unity. Recast.
slang	correct.
sp.	spelling error. Write a sentence using this word correctly spelled.
s s	run-on sentence or sentence fragment. Correct.
tense	wrong tense. Correct.
trite	hackneyed expression. Find a fresher, more original way of phrasing this idea.
unity	This paragraph lacks unity. Rewrite paragraph. Eliminate irrelevant ideas *or* supply a proper topic sentence.
variety	Paragraph has monotonous sentence structure. Improve the sentence structure by varying the length and type of sentence, and by using rhetorical devices.
w.	too wordy. Rewrite more concisely.
wrong ref.	pronoun reference error. The pronoun refers to the *wrong* antecedent. Recast the sentence, making the pronoun refer to the right antecedent.
∧	Word or phrase is omitted. Supply it.
¶	New paragraph is needed. Rewrite with proper indentation.
,/	Comma is required. Other punctuation errors are similarly indicated.

Acknowledgments

Thanks are due to the following for permission to use material from the works named:

Adprint Limited: *British Mountaineers* by F. S. Smythe, published 1942 by William Collins Sons & Co. Limited in the "Britain in Pictures" Series

Allen, George & Unwin Ltd.: Essays and Addresses by Gilbert Murray.

Appleton-Century-Crofts, Inc.: *Animal Life in Field and Garden* (copyright 1921 Century Co.) by Jean Henri Fabre

The *Atlantic Monthly*: "The Daily Theme Eye" by Walter Prichard Eaton; Editorial on "The Middle East" (January, 1957); "A Father to His Freshman Son" by Edward S. Martin; "The Rigger" by Henry Noyes Otis; "The Sea Above Us" by David C. Dejong; "Trees and Men" by H. E. Bates; "Wasted Years" by Elizabeth C. Forrest

Bedford College (The University of London): *Shakespearean Tragedy* by Professor A. C. Bradley

Blackwood, Wm. & Sons Ltd.: "American Sketches" by Charles Whibley

Brandt & Brandt: *The Forest* by Stewart Edward White

Cambridge University Press (Syndics of): *The Mysterious Universe* by Sir James Jeans

Cape, Jonathan, Limited: "The Dead", from *Dubliners* by James Joyce; *The House in Paris* by Elizabeth Bowen; Introduction to *Seven For a Secret* by Robert Lynd

Chatto & Windus Ltd.: *Disenchantment* by C. E. Montague; *A High Wind in Jamaica* by Richard Hughes

Craig, Mrs. Dorothea: *Blind Raftery* by Donn Byrne

Dent, J. M. & Sons, Ltd.: "The Heart of Darkness", "The Lagoon", "The Nigger of the Narcissus", "A Personal Record", "Tradition", "Typhoon", by Joseph Conrad; *Alpha of the Plough*, Vol. 2, by A. G. Gardiner; "I Tremble to Think" by Robert Lynd; "A Prospect of the Sea" by Dylan Thomas

Devin-Adair Company: *The Short Story* by Sean O'Faolain

The Dial Press: *Little Peter Vacuum* by Anthony Gibbs

Dodd, Mead & Company Incorporated: *Wild Geese* by Martha Ostenso

Doubleday & Company, Inc.: *Adventures in Contentment* by David Grayson; *The Fossil Book,* copyright 1958 by Carroll Lane Fenton and Mildred Adams Fenton. Reprinted by permission of Doubleday and Company, Inc.

Duell, Sloan & Pearce, Inc.: *The Edge of the Jungle* by William Beebee

Dutton, E. P. & Co., Inc.: *An Adventure with Genius* by Alleyne Ireland

Farrar, Straus and Cudahy, Inc.: *Lives Around Us,* copyright 1942 by Alan Devoe

The Forum: "Dowries for Daughters" by Le Clerc Phillips

The *Globe and Mail*: "No Need to Drown Yourself" by Bruce West; and "Stronger Than Any Bomb"

Harcourt, Brace and Company, Inc.: *Babbitt* by Sinclair Lewis, copyright, 1922, by Harcourt, Brace and Company, Inc., renewed, 1950, by Sinclair Lewis; *Wind, Sand and Stars,* copyright, 1939, by Antoine de Saint-Exupéry

Harper & Brothers: *Napoleon: The Last Phase* by Lord Rosebery; *Usage and Abusage* by Eric Partridge; *You can't Go Home Again* by Thomas Wolfe

Harper's Magazine: "Cheer Up, America" by William Allen White, from the February 1957 The Editor's "Easy Chair"

Harvard University Press: *Chaucer and His Poetry* by G. L. Kittredge

Heinemann, Wm., Limited: *A Sportsman's Sketches* by Ivan Turgenev, trans. C. Garnett

Hodder & Stoughton and the Tweedsmuir Trustees: *Augustus* and *Memory Hold-the-Door* by John Buchan

Holt, Rinehart and Winston, Inc.: *The Forest and the Fort* by Hervey Allen, copyright 1943 by Hervey Allen; *The Fraser* by Bruce Hutchison, copyright 1950 by Bruce Hutchison

Kirkconnell, Watson: *Twilight of Liberty*

Knopf, Alfred A., Inc.: "The Gentleman from San Francisco" by Ivan Bunin; "Paul's Case" by Willa Cather; "Ring the Bells of Heaven" by A. E. Coppard

Little, Brown & Company: *The Happy Profession* by Ellery Sedgwick

Longman's, Green & Company: *Terror at Daybreak* by Paul Horgan; *The Unknown Country* by Bruce Hutchison

The Macmillan Company of Canada Limited: *The Rise and Fall of New France* by George M. Wrong

Macmillan & Co. Ltd. (London), The Macmillan Company of Canada Limited and the Trustees of the Hardy Estate: *The Return of the Native* by Thomas Hardy

Macmillan & Co. Ltd. (London), The Macmillan Company of Canada and Mrs. Morgan: *Reflections in a Mirror* and *The River Line* by Charles Morgan

Macmillan & Co. Ltd. (London), The Macmillan Company of Canada and Mrs. George Bambridge: "Values in Life" by Rudyard Kipling

Macmillan & Co. Ltd. (London), and St. Martin's Press Inc. and The Macmillan Company of Canada Limited: *Robert Browning* by G. K. Chesterton

The Macmillan Company (New York): *The American Commonwealth* by James Bryce and *The Promise of American Life* by Herbert Croly

McClelland & Stewart Limited: *Blood, Sweat and Tears* and *The Unrelenting Struggle* by Sir Winston Churchill

Maclean's: Editorials of March 16 and June 8, 1957 by Ralph Allen

Maclehose, Robert & Co. Ltd.: *Browning As A Philosophical and Religious Teacher* by Henry Jones

The *Manchester Guardian*: Editorials of April 4 & 25, March 16 and August 8, 1957

Nelson, Thomas & Sons Limited (of Edinburgh and Toronto): *Recent Inventions* by Professor A. M. Low

Nelson, Thomas & Sons Limited (of Edinburgh and Toronto) and Mr. H. E. Bates and Laurence Pollinger Limited: *The Modern Short Story* by H. E. Bates

Odyssey Press, Inc.: *A Handbook to Literature* by William Flint Thrall and Addison Hibbard

The Ontario Department of Education: "The Modern Barber Shop" from Circular H. S. 4c, a Memorandum of the Ontario Department of Education

Oxford University Press (London), The Classical Association and Pall Mall Press: "The Classics and National Life" from *The Rainbow Bridge* by Sir Richard Livingstone

Oxford University Press (London and Toronto): *The Lady's Not For Burning* by Christopher Fry; *The Legacy of Greece* by Gilbert Murray; *Tom Cullen of Baltimore* by Judith Robinson; *English Idioms* by Logan Pearsall Smith; *A Study of History* (published on behalf of The Royal Institute of International Affairs) by Arnold Toynbee

Oxford University Press, Inc. (New York): *The Sea Around Us* by Rachel L. Carson

Pollinger, Laurence, Ltd. & William Heinemann Ltd.: *Mornings in Mexico* and *Sons and Lovers* by D. H. Lawrence

Press Publishing Company: Editorial, "Celia Cooney"

Princeton University Press: "Sport Versus Athletics" by Robert K. Root

Punch: "In Flanders Fields" by John McCrae

Putnam & Company Ltd.: *Lay Thoughts of A Dean* by The Very Reverend W. R. Inge

Queen's Quarterly and Sinclair Ross: "The Lamp at Noon" by Sinclair Ross

Random House, Inc.: "Barn Burning" by William Faulkner

Rupert Hart-Davis Limited: *Vanessa* by Hugh Walpole

The Ryerson Press: *The Victorian House* by Philip Child

Saturday Night: "Comment of the Day", September 26, 1959 by Arnold Edinborough

Secker, Martin & Warburg Ltd.: *Shooting An Elephant* by George Orwell; *Life and The Poet* by Stephen Spender

Sidgwick & Jackson Ltd.: *Letters from America* by Rupert Brooke

The Society of Authors: "Marriage A La Mode" by Katherine Mansfield

The Society of Authors & The Public Trustee: *The Philanderer* by Bernard Shaw

Scribner's, Charles, Sons: "Cross Country Snow" from *In Our Time* by Ernest Hemingway, copyright 1925 Charles Scribner's Sons; *Cry the Beloved Country* by Alan Paton, copyright 1948 Charles Scribner's Sons; *Cross Creek* by Marjorie Kinnan Rawlings, copyright 1942, "The Pardon" from *When the Whippoorwill*, copyright 1934 Charles Scribner's Sons, *The Yearling* by Marjorie Kinnan Rawlings, copyright 1939 Charles Scribner's Sons; *Companionable Books* and *Fisherman's Luck* by Henry Van Dyke; *Of Time and The River* by Thomas Wolfe, copyright 1935 Charles Scribner's Sons

Time, Inc.: "O'Neill Into Opera", Jan. 16, 1933

The Times Publishing Co. Ltd., All Rights Reserved (C): "The Critical Mind" and "English Prose"

Toronto General Trusts Corporation, Saskatoon: *Men of the Last Frontier* by Grey Owl

Vogt, William: *Road to Survival*, copyright 1948 by William Vogt

Watt, A. P. & Son, Macmillan & Co. (London) and Mrs. George Bambridge: "Love-O'-Women" (*A Choice of Kipling's Prose*) by Rudyard Kipling

Wilson, H. W., Company & Governor Adlai Stevenson: Speech from *Representative American Speeches*: 1951-1952

Wilson, Mrs. E. B.: Inaugural Address, March, 1913 and *The New Freedom* by Woodrow Wilson

World Publishing Company: *Sister Carrie* by Theodore Dreiser

Every effort has been made to trace the owners of the copyright material that appears in this book. The publishers offer their apologies for any unintentional errors or omissions in the acknowledgments and will gladly make any corrections in subsequent editions.

237

INDEX